Don Vito and the Mafia

LIVING WITH MY FATHER'S SECRETS

Massimo Ciancimino
with Francesco La Licata

Translated by N. S. Thompson

Quercus

First published in Great Britain in 2011 by Quercus

This paperback edition published in 2012 by
Quercus
55 Baker Street
Seventh Floor, South Block
London
W1U 8EW

A CIP catalogue record for this book is available
from the British Library

ISBN 978 0 85738 215 3

10 9 8 7 6 5 4 3 2 1

Text designed and typeset by Ellipsis Digital Ltd

Printed and bound in Great Britain by Clays Ltd, St Ives plc

MASSIMO CIANCIMINO was born in Palermo in 1963. At eighteen he became his father's aide. Since his arrest in June 2006 he has been collaborating with magistrates to help shed light on his father's secrets and forty years of links between the mafia and politics in Sicily.

FRANCESCO LA LICATA is a journalist who has written for *La Stampa* since 1980. He recently joined hands with the national anti-mafia prosecutor, Pietro Grasso, to write *Pizzini, veleni e cicoria: La mafia prima e dopo Provenzano* (Feltrinelli 2008).

For Vito Andrea and Carlotta,
my life's *raison d'être*
M. C.

Thanks, Maddalena
F. L. L.

For my son Marco,
G. C.

Contents

Introduction

I met Massimo Ciancimino at the beginning of 2008. He came to see me at *La Stampa*'s editorial offices in Rome and had an urgent wish to speak about his 'misfortunes', that is, about his difficulties with the judiciary. According to him, he had ended up in prison solely because he was the son of Don Vito, the Mafia mayor of Palermo. He was questioning a series of anomalies in his trial and feared repercussions in his relationship with his wife Carlotta. He also feared losing 'the only good thing in my life', his little son Vito Andrea, who at that time was not yet four.

Brushing aside my scepticism about the real motives for his collaboration and my reservations linked to his surname, he began to tell me about the reckless life he had led at his father's side. He came out with episodes that seemed to be taken from a Hollywood film script and asked if it all could be turned into a book, as he had intended to do with his late father. I cannot pretend that he didn't succeed in lighting a fire in my head. His story was a novel in itself: the Mafia, the secret services, corruption in politics, Sicily. And the reconstruction of an almost pathological relationship with his *padre-padrone* ('father-owner'), from whom the son could not free himself unless by means of self-destructive rebellion. Not bad as the plot for a good novel.

But there was a problem: Massimo was relating events that had happened in real life, he was speaking about real people and serious crimes. I explained to him that before thinking of a book, he would have to free himself of any burden in the correct setting before the magistrates. I honestly thought this would not come about. I was proved wrong: between the end of February and the beginning of April 2008 Ciancimino began collaborating with the Public Prosecutor's offices in Palermo and Caltanissetta.

And so was born the book you are now holding in your hands. The stories and the people it contains are the result of a 'live recording' confession, but also derive from the papers spread among three or four Prosecutor's offices and supported by the contribution of Massimo's brother Giovanni, whose precise and methodical memory of all the history preceding Massimo's involvement has been invaluable. Not everything is yet public and probably not everything will be supported by a judicial ruling. But one fact remains: the emotional force of a story that, freed from the bureaucratic fragmentation of the law, commands attention as dramatic proof of a piece of our recent history.

This book should therefore not be read only as a mere list of circumstances that Massimo Ciancimino swears to have happened because he was personally involved in them, or from having learnt them from his father Vito, but also as a large fresco of Italian and Sicilian life that, as is known, sometimes exceeds even the most negative stereotypes. It is with such a critical eye that the reader is invited to come to terms with what is told here.

F.L.L
Rome, 11 March 2010

Leading Players

Francesco Paolo Alamia
Sicilian entrepreneur very popular in the 1970s. He was a business associate of Vito Ciancimino. For a certain time he invested heavily in Milan.

Gaetano Badalamenti
Mafia boss of the Cinisi *mandamento* (Mafia district ruled by three 'families') just outside Palermo. With close links to the American Mafia, he held top positions in Cosa Nostra. He was found guilty of the murder in 1978 of Peppino Impastato, a young militant in the extreme left-wing party Democrazia Proletaria. He died in prison in the United States.

Banda della Magliana ('Magliana Gang')
A Roman criminal organization of the 1970s and '80s. Its activity has been described as a type of 'service industry' for very powerful interests: Mafia, Freemasonry, secret services, right-wing terrorism and finance (Calvi, Vatican Bank).

Salvatore Biondino

Mafioso of the San Lorenzo *mandamento* captured with Salvatore Riina on 15 January 1993 at a roundabout on Palermo's ring road. Biondino was driving the vehicle that was taking the boss to a Mafia meeting.

Stefano Bontade

Boss of the Palermo Mafia in the 1970s. Son of Don Paolino, a very influential boss in Sicilian politics, he opposed the Corleonese leadership and was among the first to fall in 1981 when the second Mafia war began.

Franco Bonura

Palermo building constructor, secret associate of Vito Ciancimino in the infamous business of cementing over the city (the so-called 'Sack of Palermo') in the 1960s and '70s. Later he was caught up in the 'Gotha' Antimafia operation and has been in prison since 2006.

Giovanni Brusca

Ex-Mafioso of San Giuseppe Jato *mandamento* in the Province of Palermo, now a protected witness collaborating with the justice system. A right-hand man of Totò Riina, but once he became a *'pentito'* (lit. 'penitent', a Mafioso who turns informant) he was among the first to speak of the so-called 'Deal' with ROS (see below) and the famous 'papello'.

Antonino and Salvatore Buscemi
Two brothers, important building speculators in Palermo, who were very close to the power base of Salvo Lima and Vito Ciancimino. Both condemned Mafiosi, they died of natural causes while serving heavy sentences, in Salvatore's case for murder.

Tommaso Buscetta
Famous *pentito* of the Palermo Mafia, he spoke about Cosa Nostra to Judge Giovanni Falcone and his testimony initiated the first Maxi Trial. An enemy of Riina and a representative of the Mafia's so-called 'moderate wing', he died of an illness in Miami.

Giuseppe (Pippo) Calò
The 'Mafia's Cashier', he moved to Rome during the 1970s to look after Cosa Nostra's financial interests. He is implicated in the Italian Republic's most tangled mysteries, and was sentenced for the 'black terrorist' (i.e. Neo-Fascist) attack on the Rapido 904 express train between Florence and Bologna (23 December 1984). He remains in prison.

Roberto Calvi
Known as 'God's banker' for his links with IOR ('Istituto per le Opere di Religione': Institute for Religious Works, aka the Vatican Bank) and the events implicating Cardinal Marcinkus, president of the Vatican Bank. He was found hanging from Blackfriars Bridge in London. Vito Ciancimino met him through the IOR.

Tommaso (Masino) Cannella

Mafia boss of the Madonie territories and linked with the Palermo administration of the 1970s and '80s. Participated in the division of the so-called 'contracts cake' on behalf of the Corleone Mafia.

Arturo Cassina

Businessman who for many years – since the end of the 1950s – owned the contract for Palermo's road maintenance. He wielded enormous power, aided by the influence he exercised through the Order of Knights of the Holy Sepulchre.

Antonino Cinà

Neurologist and Mafioso of the Corleone 'family' (Mafia clan). Massimo Ciancimino says he was the mediator of the 1992 'Deal' between the state and the Mafia and handed over the envelope containing the 'papello' with Totò Riina's requests. He has been in custody since 2006.

Carmelo Costanzo

One of those decorated with the 'Order of Merit for Labour' in Catania during the era of division of public contracts directed by Lima and Ciancimino.

Mario D'Acquisto

A Christian Democrat in the Andreotti camp, he was President of the Region of Sicily during the years of the 'Mafia killing spree' (1981–5), but has also held positions in the national government.

Giuseppe De Donno

An ROS officer who proposed that Vito Ciancimino help the Carabinieri find a contact with the Corleonese clan to bring an end to the Mafia's terrorist killing. For his part in the initiative he is under investigation by the Palermo Public Prosecutor's Office. Having been cleared in a first trial, he now faces charges in two new sets of proceedings linked to allegations surrounding 'the Deal'.

Marcello Dell'Utri

Senator and co-founder of Forza Italia, he was found guilty in the first degree of complicity in conspiracy with the Mafia. His appeal is under way.

Pietro Di Miceli

Business consultant and financial expert who was put on trial and acquitted for matters linked with presumed collusion with Mafia circles in the context of investigations leading to property seizures of Ciancimino's Canadian investments.

Liliana Ferraro

She inherited Giovanni Falcone's post in the Ministry of Justice and was told by Mori and De Donno that Vito Ciancimino's collaboration was being sought. Her testimony is crucial to current investigations into the two officials' actions.

Gaetano Fidanzati

Mafia boss at the highest level, held in great esteem in Palermo during the 'halcyon days', even in social circles. For a long while he was in charge of the business empire of the international drugs trade. He is serving a prison sentence.

Pietro Giammanco

Magistrate, head of the Palermo Public Prosecutor's Office when Giovanni Falcone was assassinated. In his diaries, the murdered judge named Giammanco as one of those responsible for his own isolated position. After the Capaci Massacre (the murder of Falcone, his wife and three policemen on 22 May 1992) he was removed from the Prosecutor's Office following protests from the deputy public prosecutors.

Giovanni Gioia

Christian Democrat in the Fanfani camp, he was among the leading players during the period of accord between the Mafia and the political system. The Antimafia Commission, created after the Ciaculli Massacre in 1963, wrote a highly critical report on that historical era.

Leonardo Greco

Mafia boss of Bagheria, owner of I.c.re (Industria chiodi e reti), which produced concrete reinforcing rods and whose offices functioned as the logistics base for meetings of the Cosa Nostra *cupola* (Mafia high command) overseeing the division of bribes and contracts.

Luciano Liggio

Godfather of the Corleone Mafia clan and Totò Riina's predecessor at the top of Cosa Nostra. After unsuccessful attempts to obtain release from his life sentence with the help of politicians and magistrates, he died in Nuoro prison in 1993.

Salvatore (Salvo) Lima

Chief of the Andreotti camp in Palermo. He was mayor of the city and an undersecretary in the national government. Suspected of conniving with the Mafia, but never successfully charged. His career came to a tragic end when he was assassinated in 1992 while serving as an MEP.

Giuseppe (Pino) Lipari

A surveyor for ANAS (National Roads Department) and faithful adviser to Mafia boss Bernardo Provenzano, for years he shielded his friend when he was in hiding, helping with his changes of address and his clandestine 'correspondence'. He served out a sentence for conspiring with the Mafia and was then released.

Nicola Mancino

Vice President of the CSM (Governing Body of Magistrates). As Minister of the Interior in 1992, he was believed by Massimo Ciancimino to be one of the politicians who knew about the deal between the state and the Mafia. He has always denied any involvement.

Calogero (Lillo) Mannino

A native of Agrigento, he was one of the most important politicians of the First Republic (1947–92). He ended up under investigation following the declarations of several collaborators with the justice system. After a trial lasting more than fifteen years, he was definitively acquitted.

Claudio Martelli

He was Minister of Justice during the terrorist period and the so-called 'Deal'. As with Liliana Ferraro, his testimony is crucial to investigations still being carried out.

Giovanni Mercadante

Physician, currently in prison. According to the charges, he was one of Provenzano's points of contact because of his family links with Masino Cannella, the boss's lieutenant. In the eyes of the judges he is an exponent of the so-called 'middle-class Mafia'. Though found guilty in the first instance he was found innocent on appeal, and his case is currently awaiting a decision by the Supreme Court.

Matteo Messina Denaro

Capomafia of the Trapani Province. On the run for almost twenty years, he is the last surviving member of a generation of godfathers killed or imprisoned. In his 'correspondence' with Provenzano, he writes more than once of Vito Ciancimino.

Mario Mori
Prefect and ex-Carabinieri General, ending his career as Director of the Civil Secret Service. With De Donno he is suspected of having made 'deals' with the Mafia, when he was with ROS, with Vito Ciancimino acting as go-between. At his first trial he was declared innocent under a special formula that referred to his behaviour as being motivated by reasons of state. He is currently awaiting re-trial on a substantially similar charge.

Michele Navarra
Boss of the Corleone clan in the 1940s and '50s, killed by the emerging Mafiosi (Liggio, Riina and Provenzano) in August 1958. It is said he ordered the death of a child eyewitness of the murder of trade unionist Placido Rizzotto.

Mario Niceta
One of Palermo's best-known and most prosperous tradesmen. According to Massimo Ciancimino, his offices were where meetings took place between Provenzano and Ciancimino.

Rosario Nicoletti
A Christian Democrat who was witness to the terrible period of Palermo killings and the overweening power of the Mafia over political life. He committed suicide in 1984, after having been impotently present at the tragic demise of provincial secretary Michele Reina and later Piersanti Mattarella, President of Sicily's Autonomous Region.

Salvatore Pappalardo

Cardinal of Palermo in 1982, he preached a hard-line sermon ('While they talk in Rome, Sagunto is wiped out') against the powers that be of the Sicilian political system during the funeral of General Dalla Chiesa. In reply, the Mafia boycotted his Easter Mass in Ucciardone Prison (Palermo).

Michel Pozza

Italo-Canadian lawyer, fixer and friend of Mafiosi. In Montreal he arranged for the property investments of Vito Ciancimino, later uncovered by the investigations of Giovanni Falcone. He was murdered in Canada in 1982.

Pietro Purpi

A member of the Palermo flying squad, later director of the second police district, who has come under much discussion, having been identified by many collaborators with the justice system as being close to the Mafia clan of Santa Maria di Gesù.

Sebastiano Purpura

A supporter of Andreotti who was identified in evidence as being involved with the head of the Palermo camp, Salvo Lima.

Virginio Rognoni

Christian Democrat, ex-Minister of Defence. According to the reconstruction of Massimo Ciancimino, he was the other politician who knew of the 'Deal' set in motion after the Capaci

Massacre. As with Nicola Mancino, he too has denied all suggestion of any kind of deal.

ROS (Raggrupamento operativo speciale)

'Special Operations Group', a branch of the Carabinieri created in 1990 with the task of fighting terrorism and organized crime. It succeeded in the capture of Totò Riina, but left a polemical and judicial question about the failure to find the boss's gang.

Attilio Ruffini

Christian Democrat, and several times minister, he appears to have had excellent relations with the prevailing political group of Lima and Ciancimino. According to Massimo, he was the one who informed Vito Ciancimino of the causes of the Ustica air disaster.

Nino and Ignazio Salvo

The two cousins from Salemi who ran Sicily's private tax collection and were both tried for being members of the Mafia. As generous financiers of Lima and Ciancimino's Christian Democrat party, for years they embodied the symbol of the untouchable. Ignazio was assassinated in 1992. Nino died of cancer in 1986.

Pietro Scaglione

Chief Prosecutor of the Republic in Palermo, he was murdered on 5 May 1971 with a large deployment of men and means.

Delegitimized and then 'rehabilitated', his end was explained
by Buscetta: 'Liggio wanted him dead.'

Giusto Sciacchitano
Magistrate, today working for the National Antimafia Prosecutor's office. For many years he was the Deputy Public Prosecutor in Palermo. He is currently the subject of two trials
being held separately in Catania and Caltanisetta.

Girolamo (Mimmo) Teresi
Mafia boss, brother-in-law of Stefano Bontade. A housing constructor during the period of the 'Sack of Palermo', he vanished
into thin air in 1981, victim of a *lupara bianca* (lit. 'white sawn-
off shotgun'), a Mafia killing where all traces of the body disappear, having fallen into a trap set by the Corleone clan.

Beniamino Tessitore
Magistrate who worked for the Tribunal for Preventative Measures (against terrorism).

Capitano Ultimo ('The Last Captain')
His name is Sergio De Caprio, a captain in the Carabinieri who
arrested Totò Riina. He was transferred to other duties well
away from the fight against the Mafia.

Romolo Vaselli, junior (7 February 1933 – January 2006)
Roman Count, entrepreneur and great friend of Vito
Ciancimino who guaranteed him for life the final say on

contracts for road maintenance in Palermo. When Don Vito moved to Rome, he saw Vaselli practically right up to the end of his days.

Francesco (Ciccio) Vassallo
Ex-haulier and extremely successful building speculator, following on the wave of easy licences from the City of Palermo in the 1960s and '70s. He built almost all of the new Palermo and was a frequent guest at gatherings in the Ciancimino house.

Luciano Violante
When he was President of the Antimafia Commission, Vito Ciancimino wanted to meet him privately and in 1992 sent Mori and De Donno to reconnoitre the situation. But he refused the offer and invited Vito to request a public audience.

Enzo Zanghì
Vito Ciancimino's cousin, he performed the offices of factotum and secretary for him. He also held the directorship of the city's water supply.

1

The Loss of Innocence

MASSIMO CIANCIMINO: It was summer and, like all the rich, happy and 'respectable' people of Palermo, we were on holiday in Baida in the old house of my grandparents Attilio and Adele in Via Falconara Baglia. My father, Vito Ciancimino, was a 'star' in political life - hated, feared and revered. He was attacked in the left-wing newspapers, yet he was also accepted on that side of the city, which was the largest, and was used to getting along with the powerful out of self-interest or love of the quiet life because, in short, it was from those in power that money and the good life could fall in spades. More went to the upper classes and less to the masses, as the poor were called.

My father didn't like to shave himself; he preferred the ritual of going to the barber, where he went almost every day. The 'salon' of Signor Lo Piccolo was in Via Sciuti in the heart of the new city that developed after the wave of expansion in the 1960s and '70s, a couple of steps from the top-floor flat where we lived, directly opposite our front door. One summer morning at the beginning of the 1980s I was sitting in Signor Lo Piccolo's waiting room while my father was having soap applied to his face.

At this point you should know that from my childhood onwards the tyranny of destiny had forced me into the role of official companion to my father. Of course, I would have preferred to be free to do the things young people like to do, but he had decided otherwise. I was, he said, too restless, too rebellious and incapable of using my freedom well. And so, in order to maintain a stranglehold on me, he kept me close to his side. Great fun for a lad who was not yet eighteen to be forced to have his hair cut the same day his father had his done.

Going with him to the barber was one of my duties and it's pointless to ask the sense in my having to be there simply to obey his stupid demands: 'Pass me my bag, or rather, take out the documents ... not those, dickhead! Give me my glasses, those with the patch, mind.' There was always a scene about his glasses. As the result of an apoplectic fit, he was blind in one eye and had to have glasses with one lens blacked out.

But I was used to all this. So, as you do when waiting your turn at the barber's, I was killing time flipping through the pages of an illustrated magazine, perhaps an issue of the weekly *Epoca*. At a certain point, a feature on the Sicilian Mafia's famous fugitives from justice caught my attention, all lieutenants of Luciano Liggio, at that time still thought to be head of the Corleone clan. There were old photographs of Totò Riina, but in particular I remember the magazine tried (by means of computer graphics) to reconstruct the face of one of the most talked-about Mafiosi and, at the same time, one of the least known – Bernardo Provenzano. Starting with the only known photo of the boss as a very young man – a square face under a quiff of blond hair – by means of the computer they had aged him and created the virtual image of a man now getting on in years: the oval shape was unmistakable, beard unshaven, close-cropped hair. It was a face I felt sure I recognized. Yes, of course I recognized him. It was a man I'd known for some time: Signor Lo Verde, the civil engineer my father had dealt with for years, who frequently came to our house, had dinner with my father, who even visited him at my grandparents' place in Baida. He was a family friend, a person my father – a Christian Democrat politician, city council assessor and once mayor – trusted as an adviser, a man with whom he could exchange views and even discuss his business in the administration of the city. Was it possible that this Lo Verde, the mild-mannered man who patted my cheeks and reminded me to do as my dad told me, was the terrible ferocious murderer they described in the news?

I chewed over my 'discovery' for some time and watched my father's self-absorbed face in the mirror as he followed the train of his own thoughts while Signor Lo Piccolo massaged it and I tried to imagine what his reaction would be when I asked him if my suspicions were right. As usual, I put it to him as we were going back to Baida in the car. In keeping with my provocative nature, I confronted him with the question: 'Have you seen those photos in *Epoca*? Tell me the truth, Dad, aren't they identical to Signor Lo Verde, your friend the engineer? Come on, it has to be him, hasn't it?'

He sat very still, as still as a sphinx, and kept silent without so much as looking at me. It was a long silence, perhaps the time necessary for him to find the right reply. He said neither yes nor no, but it was clear he was telling me my suspicions were right. He then felt it necessary to add a word in my ear, a warning to keep absolutely quiet, given the huge danger attached to the subject, because 'remember you aren't allowed to make a mistake, even I can't protect you in these matters' . He was evidently worried about my impetuous character. He thought I was a little too much of a braggart and quick-tongued, and perhaps he was right, and was worried that in some way – perhaps in an argument with another lad – I'd start bragging of my father's friendship with one of the heads of Cosa Nostra. But then this was how things went in Palermo: young Mafiosi at the bottom acting cool, hanging around the less important bosses, middle classes and Mafia mingling together at discos and parties, everyone sounding off about friendships you'd never normally discuss in order to get some attention and respect. So he was afraid I'd also go about bragging in some way or another: besides, if people were showing off about friendships with characters who were pretty down to earth, why shouldn't I cut them all to the ground by revealing that my father had a bombshell in the house and a fraternal connection with 'Don Binnu' Provenzano?

Thus, barricaded in his Bologna hideout, bodyguards standing by the door, Massimo Ciancimino tells the story of his 'loss of innocence'. He was still a lad when his enforced visit to

Signor Lo Piccolo's barbershop revealed a hidden world to him. Up to that morning, Massimo had seen his father in the same way as would any normal boy engaged in the traditional father–son conflict with a parent who was possessive, even violent, authoritarian, controversial and politically questionable. But also, on the whole, 'useful' for the privileges that his political system guaranteed to friends and family.

Massimo is now forty-seven and a father himself to a small boy he called Vito after his grandfather (Vito Andrea, to be precise), betraying – despite the trials, tribulations and misunderstandings – an attachment to his father and the consequences of a very Sicilian upbringing that, in the end, he now accepts. Almost thirty years have passed since that disturbing reading of *Epoca* turned his life upside down and led to his now becoming a valued witness of an era often described by the newspapers, but which in reality was far more pernicious than can be imagined and proven.

Since he discovered the true identity of *ingegnere* Lo Verde, Massimo has gradually come to be identified as the silent executor of his father's plans that were the result of the synchronization between politics and Mafia as exemplified by Ciancimino and Provenzano. From companion he became the 'postman' between the two men and the dangerous comings and goings have brought him to see for himself the unspoken links between Mafia and politics. Links personified by the property-developing bosses, the big contractors, corrupt bureaucrats, Cosa Nostra chiefs on the run coming to his father's house to discuss future public works, and dinners to celebrate illegal economic profits. Lima, the Salvo cousins, Cassina, Romolo Vaselli junior, Vassallo the developer, the 'brick twins' Bonura and Buscemi and the like, together with important Mafia chiefs sitting round the table dividing up the spoils. Yes, this was the 'Ciancimino system' and the happy face of Palermo in its heyday that stretched from a microcosm in the outskirts to touch Rome, and then further north in a spider's web that could catch the major institutions of the capital and poison the economic potentates of the hard-working North. Massimo Ciancimino's account reveals how instant fortunes blossom and make their way to Zurich, or even the United States and Canada. His brother Giovanni is also a valuable source of family memories.

But all this represents only the precursor to a story that is still unfinished, a troubled history that cuts across innumerable moments of national grief, the Mafia's violent opposition to state intervention and the 'Deal' to bring the violence to an end. Don Vito played a deadly game as mediator and messenger for Provenzano and Riina, a game also played out by Massimo as a witness and go-between in clandestine contacts between characters that seem to emanate from the imagination of a great thriller writer: undercover agents, the one time Signor Lo Verde appearing in the guise of 'moderate Mafia chief', the bloodthirsty Riina. And the mysterious 'Signor Franco', the hidden director of the play, a kind of grand old man who, after years of keeping a close watch and having something of a role in the 'Ciancimino system', follows the birth and evolution of the 'Deal' , careful not to upset its balance. All this is why Massimo Ciancimino's life had been turned upside down, still dogged by the shadow of Lo Verde, but with absolutely no support from an anonymous Signor Franco. His story is cut off from reality, as if it's not about him but someone else. There's no trace of any kind of sentimentality or emotion (if they ever existed) hidden under the irony that sometimes overcomes the need for caution. On the other hand, Giovanni's story is exact to the point of pedantry, but he too is careful not to give in to any detail that could be too risky.

Close Friends

MASSIMO: My father's relations with the Mafia revolved almost entirely around his friendship with Bernardo Provenzano. This doesn't mean he didn't mix with others in the circle; for instance, I remember a certain Don Pino Abbate who sent us tons of citrus fruit because he was convinced the miraculous properties of oranges and lemons would help in the prevention of a cholera epidemic that was announced but never came. He had many acquaintances, my father, but few friends. You could say that his contact with various exponents of Cosa Nostra was in some ways imposed on him by what you could call the environmental conditions that governed his political and administrative life. But with Bernardo Provenzano it was an altogether different case: they exchanged opinions and advice. In their 'operations' they worked with a successful division of labour. While my father looked after getting agreement among the politicians' diverse and often contentious expectations –

especially monetary ones, obviously – the other saw to the
territory, ensuring the Mafia's budget for the enterprise.
Naturally, here we're speaking of public contracts.

They were from the same town, my father and Provenzano,
both born in Corleone (although there was a difference of ten
years between them) and lived not far from each other. But
they were from different social classes: Provenzano the son of
poor peasants, my father of tradesmen who could educate
their children. My grandfather's name was Giovanni and he
emigrated to the United States, but had to return following
the illness and death of his elder brother back in Sicily.
To start with his family wasn't rolling in money, but the
break came when the Americans landed in 1943 and my grandfather – perhaps the only person in Corleone able to speak
and understand English – was offered the role of interpreter
for the Allied command. Was he only an interpreter?

Here a malicious thought arises about the motives that later
persuaded my father for years, right up to the notorious 'Deal',
to mix with strange characters such as the slippery and elusive
'Signor Franco'. Was he an establishment figure belonging to a
legitimate institution or something else? I'm well aware, for
instance, how incredible it must seem that in more than twenty
years of contact I was never able to discover his true identity.
And yet that's how it was. I couldn't ask my father questions
because he was very careful not to respond, and equally I couldn't
turn directly to a man who made a religion out of anonymity
and circumspection. I understood he couldn't reveal who he was
and I pretended it was nothing, as in any spy story. For this

reason I wasn't particularly surprised when I came across a note in all the documentation handed to the magistrates, where my father seems to state he had a part in Gladio, NATO's 'stay behind' operation to combat Communism after the Second World War.

It was my grandfather's relations with the Americans that allowed him to pick up the import–export business interrupted by the war. This was able to change my father's life as well, because the returns were so regular the profits could be used to fund serious enterprises, such as housing construction, roads, water supply, bridges and transport. So much for being a barber in Corleone, as the newspapers long insisted on calling him. This fairy tale grew from the mere fact that one of the premises he owned was rented out to a barber.

Bernardo Provenzano was younger than my father. He wasn't doing very well at school to the point where his parents turned to Vito Ciancimino, a surveying student at technical college, to give little Binnu a hand with his maths, the subject he was lagging behind in. So the link came into being and grew stronger over time.

I learned all this from my father directly following the discovery of Signor Lo Verde's true identity, because after this he started replying to a few questions, even if it was only in monosyllables. He was forever extremely cautious, until the time he completely opened up, or almost, during the period of his contact with the Carabinieri after the Capaci Massacre and the murder of his friend-and-enemy Salvo Lima. This was mainly when I was close to him in prison and, finally, when he was under house arrest. In all, his relationship with me changed over time and he decided to speak openly when writing 'all the truth in a book' – his truth, of course. That's how I came to learn about many things.

He talked about the lessons he gave to Binnu and told me with some amusement he was even allowed to give him a slap on the neck if he made a mistake. He told him off in his particular way, calling him a 'little bastard'. And he had a quip: 'I'm one of the few people alive who's called Provenzano a bastard.' I never heard him talk about these things to anyone else. There wasn't a hint, not even to his most trusted friends, if indeed he had any. His relationship with Provenzano was close but very discreet and exclusive, exactly in the style of his alter ego. He could boast that no Mafioso had ever met him together with 'the engineer', the title he sometimes gave Lo Verde.

I remember his regular visits to the houses in Via Sciuti in Baida and in Via Danae in Mondello. Lo Verde was short. He always arrived alone and on foot, a little hunched, at his usual slow pace and clutching a briefcase in his hands. He parked his car at some distance from the villa where we lived, because you never knew and couldn't be too careful. Once in Via Danae, he arrived with no escort, except Pino Lipari the accountant – the newspapers were full of articles about this man they considered one of the proven Corleone faithful – who was to attend the meeting. My father had put me on guard (he was forever finding ways to give instructions on his own form of strategic defence) ready to open the gate and let in the visitors and the car. But Provenzano preferred to park on the street, despite my father's doubts about the car's safety. Binnu cut him short: 'And who do you think would try to touch my car?' But when he came out, there was a rip in the Beetle Cabriolet's hood and an empty space where the stereo had been. Someone had swiped the car radio of the Cosa Nostra godfather right in front of our house. I can't forget my father's teasing little Mephistophelean smile with his quip about the Mafia's 'overwhelming power'. Lo Verde wasn't happy. So on a later visit he turned up with a car radio that, according to him, had been 'returned with many apologies'. My father couldn't resist and asked him sarcastically: 'Now tell the truth, how much did you pay for it?' Having seen Provenzano grow all the way to becoming godfather of the Corleonesi, he could get away with comments like that.

The two of them spent hours talking together. They were almost always alone, with no other ears to listen in. As I later learned, this was the natural caution of the Corleonesi that consisted above all else in not allowing anyone – because there was no one you could trust – to know what was going through their minds. But there were also relaxed moments over a good plate of Sicilian food or strolling up and down the bowling alley at our house in Mondello in the open air, an ideal place to talk without being overheard.

The Young Provenzano

Massimo's elder brother Giovanni is also a witness to the long friendship between their father and 'Don Binnu'. His story is particularly interesting because it relates the memory of the first meeting between Don Vito and another important *capomafia*, Stefano Bontade. A little gem of Mafia anthropology, Giovanni attempts to describe the scene in close detail, dialogue included.

GIOVANNI CIANCIMINO: In the mid-1960s we were on vacation in the spa town of Salsomaggiore, near Parma. There were several families from Palermo staying in the same hotel and judging from their cars they were certainly well heeled. One morning we were having breakfast in a large dining room and a man came up who gave the impression he was waiting to have a word with my father. He was about thirty, thin, tall and elegant.

When he saw my father was about to leave the table he introduced himself.

'Forgive me for disturbing you, I'm sure you don't know me, but on the other hand I do know you: Vito Ciancimino, the politician.'

With a facial expression that betrayed all his displeasure and irritation, my father cut him short with one of the usual arrogant replies of which he was a master.

'That's two things you've said that are absolutely correct: I'm Vito Ciancimino and I don't know you.'

The man, on the other hand, continued to speak politely, as if he hadn't caught my father's tone, saying that they had a friend in common, Don Pino Abbate. He went on:

'My name's Stefano Bontade, I'm in construction and also know your fellow townsmen. I'm not as friendly with them as I am with Abbate, but we have a good relationship.'

The reply was guarded.

'And who do you mean by my fellow townsmen?'

'Salvatore Riina and Bernardo Provenzano.'

My father was still on the defensive.

'Both of them were still young boys,' he said, 'being much my junior, when I left Corleone at the age of eighteen to study civil engineering in Palermo. Riina I've never met, but I have met Provenzano and can tell you how. One rainy winter afternoon I was at home studying. I looked out through the window and saw a boy who was finding it difficult to walk, perhaps because of a fall. He was soaking wet. I went out with an umbrella to help and offer him some shelter in the house. He told me he'd fallen while chasing after a dog. His speech was laboured, as if he'd never been to school, although he had the sharp look of someone who knows what he's about and was used to looking after himself whatever the circumstances. I asked him who he was and he said, "Provenzano, Bernardo. But they call me Binnu." I gave him a cup of hot milk and some bread, which he had with cherry jam. I took him home on my bicycle. The following day he appeared with a tub of ricotta. It was his way of thanking me. So there you are, my one and only encounter with Provenzano.'

After listening in silence, Stefano Bontade betrayed a little scepticism in his voice.

'And you've never met him in Palermo?'

'I've already told you, no. He's never looked me up and I've never looked him up.'

'I'm surprised by what you say, but there's no reason to disbelieve you because you have a reputation for not telling lies.

Nevertheless, allow me to give you a piece of advice: you can deal with Provenzano, but it's better to leave Riina alone. He's wilful, violent and it's difficult to change his mind. He and I have had more than one disagreement, but Provenzano's always brought us together.'

The meeting between my father and Bontade ended with the latter asking for an appointment with him in Palermo 'over a matter that concerns me greatly'. He explained that he'd prefer to meet my father at home in Baida 'because I don't like dealing with politicians' secretaries'. Bontade's suave approach was a success, because my father liked him, even if he was upset that, without his knowledge, on leaving the spa the man had also paid the Ciancimino family's bill. My father made a great scene, especially with the manager of the place, insisting he take a cheque for the bill and reimburse Bontade. 'And you'll never see me here again!' was his stormy goodbye.

Liggio the Bully

GIOVANNI: That summer Bontade often came to the house on Via Falconara Baglia in Baida. On the first occasion he apologized for the gaffe about the hotel bill in Salsomaggiore. Always extremely elegant, he arrived in a high-performance Alfa driven by a chauffeur. He and my father went to a small balcony where no one could disturb them and my father even locked the door to the room. I wondered why there was so much discretion in order to talk to a property developer. Others came to visit us, even the better-known such as Ciccio Vassallo, but they were happy to sit among company. I didn't know then that apart from being in construction, Bontade was also a Mafia boss.

One day he appeared without an appointment, accompanied by Don Pino Abbate and another tall, thin man with fair hair who dressed in a very refined manner by the name of Mimmo Teresi. I later understood he was Stefano Bontade's brother-in-law. My father wasn't at home and the three men had to wait some time. About two hours later he arrived with three city councillors from his political party but seeing the waiting group he immediately dismissed them. The meeting started with the ritual presentation of Teresi, whom my father had never met, the rest took place on the usual balcony.

There was an emergency: Bontade and his brother-in-law had a verbal agreement on the purchase of a plot of land where 'thirty villas could be built', and a deposit paid pending the deal's conclusion. Then all of a sudden the owner had changed his mind. He came to them in an arrogant manner, giving back the deposit plus 20 per cent interest saying, 'I want to build there myself.' Neither Bontade nor Teresi believed this was the real reason for the change of heart. 'Just imagine,' Teresi put in, 'that cocky little sod coming on to us like God Almighty. The fact is, we've found out, the land's wanted by Luciano Liggio and his fellow townsmen Riina and Provenzano.'

My father asked them what he had to do with the matter. According to them he should speak to Liggio to persuade him to give up the land. But he categorically refused, given his past poor relations with the head of the Corleonesi.

To be more convincing, given he was speaking with 'respected men' who'd never betray a secret, he told them the story of his cousin Pietro Maiuri, killed in Corleone during the feud between Liggio and Michele Navarra. 'They killed him,' my father told them, 'despite Liggio's assurance at a secret meeting in the centre of Palermo that, as far as he was concerned, my cousin could live until he was a hundred. I assured him Pietro would move to Palermo and Liggio agreed: everything was fine; Corleone was no longer a place for him. He saluted me with a kiss on the cheeks. That's why I'll never again speak to Luciano Liggio, whatever the reason.'

A Father with Power

MASSIMO: And yet Baida in my memory was an oasis of happiness. In the house of my dearly loved grandparents, Attilio and Adele, who brought me and my brothers up, filling the space of absent parents, I passed the best days of my life. It was where we spent the summer holidays. As soon as school finished we moved there and stayed until the beginning of October. We lived in complete freedom, almost in a state of nature, playing simple games on the street. All we needed was a piece of wood and a car tyre to set rolling and chase after. We ate out on the beautiful large terrace overlooking the Palermo coast and had a cistern, an irrigation tank that often became a swimming pool.

The sea was a long way off, but not impossible to reach. We

went every Saturday and Sunday and preparations often began as early as the Wednesday. A carefully drawn up menu would include baked pasta, hard-boiled eggs, cutlets and omelette. The day of the trip was a real celebration. I remember the red Fiat 128 driven by my mother Epifania. The front seat went to Giovanni as the eldest, the rest of us piled in the back with my little sister Luciana in our arms. The choice of music always caused a scene. Giovanni had a really barbaric taste for sad, melancholic styles: Battisti, I Giganti, Lauzi and other tear-jerkers. Roberto and I went for more popular rhythms labelled 'Tascio', which today we'd call 'national-popular'. Our gems were the groups I Cugini di Campagna, Franco IV e Franco I and early Celentano. Standing out over everyone was my brother Sergio, the one we always disowned, who tortured us with the mournful songs of Demis Roussos, a strange overweight guru always dressed in kaftans.

Our destination was the beach at Mondello Valdesi where each summer, from time immemorial, the Società Italo-Belga of *ingegnere* Castellucci had the concession of the entire Mondello coast and ran a bathing establishment, complete with VIP area.

Our beach hut was in the heart of this 'reserved area', complete with a little terrace and private parking space at the Hotel Palace. In this domain of powerful politicians naturally no one paid for anything.

I saw my father rarely during the periods in Baida. My memories of him aren't happy. I was only small, but beginning to understand that he was very singular, both for his crude, self-absorbed and domineering ways and for the role he played and the way others saw him. His marriage to my mother wasn't the most peaceful because he allowed himself plenty of distractions. He liked women and, given his character, whatever he wanted he tended to take, which could include a beautiful woman.

I remember the first time I began to realize the weight he carried in the city. My mother was obsessed by the danger from cars speeding past outside the house where we children played. They argued about the problem and my mother accused him of not caring about his children. It was a continuous torment that only ended when he couldn't ignore her objections any longer because an accident happened right in front of the house. My mother demanded the fixed presence of traffic police to fine drivers who wouldn't observe the speed limit. But my father did more: he arranged for a meeting in Baida with the head of the traffic police, the relevant city councillors and Conte Cassina, whom I already knew because he often came to our house. We boys knew him for his magnificent cars and an unmistakable goatee like Pirandello's. But why was the Count there with traffic police and city councillors? I came to understand shortly after. Cassina was the owner of the firm that was regularly awarded the road maintenance contract, in short, one of the habitual participants in the Ciancimino system. [This accusation was made by Massimo Ciancimino in the course of testimony he gave to the courts.]

The day after the Baida crisis summit, Cassina's workmen and traffic police invaded the area. In the record time of two days, they constructed a series of traffic-calming humps fifty metres apart to slow things down. But without any warning signs put up, these 'bumps' – as they were known to Baida's residents – caused a series of accidents that forced the councillors, traffic police and mayor to create suitable signposts for something that until then had been unheard of.

There's one more Baida episode I can't forget. A stray dog had bitten a number of children and one afternoon my father found it in our garden. With the utmost simplicity he took his revolver and with the assistance of two imperturbable traffic policemen shot it dead in front of us children. A special detail, like the death of my grandfather Giovanni whom I remember only for his crude manners, which he must have passed on to his son. But, as I said, Baida was where I first began to see my father's 'odd moments', which in time would be explained by his activities and dangerous relationships. Baida was where I first remember the visits of *ingegnere* Lo Verde and Signor Franco in that climate of suspicion that fed my curiosity.

2

Palermo – The High Life

During the 1960s and '70s a power bloc practically dominated the entire city of Palermo, including the institutions placed in charge of controlling and combating criminal activity. The police and the Carabinieri floundered midway between Mafia wars and rare investigations into poor administration and corruption. Investigations into economic crime, which was the responsibility of the Excise Police, simply did not happen. The law courts were an immovable mausoleum, unsuited (and perhaps resistant) to collecting pathological symptoms of an infected society.

These were the years when the very existence of the Mafia was questioned. Whoever uttered the name was declared to be 'running down Sicily'. In inaugural speeches at opening ceremonies for the judicial year, the Public Prosecutors talked euphemistically in order to avoid mentioning those three syllables. Celebrated anthropologists of the past went out of their way to certify that as a criminal organization the Mafia was a figment of the imagination on the part of Communists and fanatics and that, if anything, one could speak of a 'way of life' and 'way of thinking' that was fairly widespread. Could you put the traditions of a whole community on trial? Over time it came to the point of impunity for the power base of politicians and Mafia. This was the case even in the face of fortunate as much as 'accidental' circumstances that could have ripped open the Mafia veil. How much would Palermo have changed if, in 1972, the magistracy had listened to Leonardo Vitale, a young Mafioso who had undergone a profound religious crisis? He wanted to confess and signed a written memoir. But in those days it was impossible to think of betraying the code of silence: only someone ill or mad would think of it. He ended up in an asylum for the criminally insane, then prison and finally exile. He was the only one to pay. And he had explained Cosa Nostra in detail: the men, the chiefs, the organization and the link with politics. He had already named people like Riina, Provenzano and the mayor from Corleone, Vito Ciancimino. Everything was thrown to the wind: in order to open up the question of the Corleonesi again it would be necessary to wait for Giovanni Falcone, almost fifteen years later.

But perhaps it was not only a matter of cultural backwardness, an innocent short-sightedness. Perhaps the cancer that was eating away at civil society was also at work inside the old Establishment. It was a fact that the city was based on the existence of a 'scandalous' power bloc that was capable of neutralizing any attempt at control by the legal authorities. And the law, slow and cocooned, was careful not to disturb the delicate equilibrium that governed an accepted and shared system.

Vito Ciancimino was the central driving force of this power bloc. City assessor for public works in the City of Palermo from 1959 to 1964, he even became the city's mayor in 1970, albeit for a few weeks, until forced to resign over the clamour his nomination caused, and a campaign from the newspaper *L'Ora* that hammered away at him. Speaking to his sons years later, he attributed the responsibility of that humiliating defeat to the pressure exercised by Riina and his associates: 'They forced me to become mayor out of some delusion of omnipotence, to be able to boast of having a man from Corleone in the seat of first citizen. But I knew I couldn't manage it.'

Even at that time he was totally discredited: the scandal of the three thousand licences handed out in a single night to front men who were concealing the identity of a few property developer friends, the protests over the destruction of the Art Nouveau villas along the Viale della Libertà, the 'gold mines' entrusted to private individuals: refuse collection (Romolo Vaselli junior) and road maintenance (Cassina), and then water and gas supply run literally from inside the family. Yet for years he continued to maintain and nurture this system founded on corruption and criminal activity.

Don Vito's fortunes would be tied to his cultivation of criminal activity and corruption, along with those of the other leading player of Sicilian political life, Salvo Lima. Together with Giovanni Gioia, the Christian Democrat provincial secretary, several times MP and minister in the national government, it was they who promoted the Fanfani line in Sicily and inaugurated the so called 'membership card strategy', transforming the Sicilian

Christian Democrats into the party of business and able to keep
a firm hold on the local reins of power. These would be the years
of cementing over the city in the so-called 'Sack of Palermo':
building speculation across the lands of the Conca d'Oro valley
that quickly changed from the colour of oranges to the grey of
cement. They are the years when the city's profile was defined by
its being hostage to the Mafia and a political life strongly influenced by criminal activity.

City administrators and politicians on the one hand, and
Cosa Nostra chiefs on the other, were on the same wavelength.

'In local politics our two chief points of reference were Salvo
Lima and Giovanni Gioia, the Christian Democrat secretary,'
Tommaso Buscetta said. 'I knew Lima and met him many times
in the town hall, when he was mayor of Palermo and also at his
home . . . A true friendship couldn't develop between us . . . The
way I saw Lima was on the basis of his official role: he was the
mayor of my city. He saw me as an important *capomafia*. Our
relations were similar to those between two institutions and
so had a certain official flavour. It didn't surprise me therefore
when, some time around 1961 or 1962, preparing to go to the
United States as member of a City of Palermo delegation, Lima
told me that he wanted to meet some influential Mafiosi over
there. We both agreed that it would be necessary to observe a
certain protocol. I then wrote him a formal letter of introduction addressed to Joe Bonnano and Charles Gambino, Mafia
chiefs of New York. On his return from the journey I went to
see him in the little villa in Mondello where he lived in the
summer and received his thanks for the warm welcome he had

received from the American men of honour . . . Lima was aware of my passion for opera and sent me gratis a block of tickets for the entire Palermo season. He was a serious, intelligent man who minded his words. He spoke very little, like a true off-spring of men of honour, and kept his promises.'

In effect Salvo Lima's career was more of a straight line than that of his friend and rival Ciancimino: he was deputy mayor from '56 to '58 under Fanfani's time as national Christian Democrat secretary, then mayor from '59 to '63 and yet again from '65 to '68 when he switched camp to join with Andreotti, bringing with him all the baggage of friends and alliances, including those with the Mafia, accumulated over the years. Don Vito followed him into the camp of the 'divine Julius' (as Giulio Andreotti was known) eight years later in 1976, after a meeting in the Chigi Palace: he entered as a dissident and came out of the Prime Minister's office sporting Andreotti's colours. In his proverbial and prolix diaries he noted, 'the meeting came about through Andreotti's camp in Sicily'. At the meeting Ciancimino disagreed with the line of the national secretary Zaccagnini on the matter of 'national solidarity' with the Communists, making his dissent clear in a letter. Andreotti mediated in person in the presence of his Palermo supporters – Lima, D'Acquisto and Matta – and was victorious.

But the slow process of the law would only deliver the film of the handshake between politicians and criminals after a long delay. It would have to wait until the 1980s: Ciancimino in prison, the disastrous fall of the cousins Nino and Ignazio Salvo (for twenty years the tax collectors famous as the *padroni* of

Palermo) and Salvo Lima splashed across the front page as 'the big stick' of the system in the employ of Cosa Nostra, then gunned down like a vulgar boss; the names of the city's entrepreneurial class forever associated with investigations into Mafia corruption; and the mechanisms that allowed a few 'friends', always the same ones, to milk the cow of the public coffers and private property development. It was a picture we all knew was real, but difficult to protest about because of the protection the system enjoyed. This was protection from institutions at a high level, as it seems to emerge today from the mysterious figure of Signor Franco (or Carlo), evoked by Massimo Ciancimino, the treacherous operator and absolute boss of that grey area, the no man's land between the illegal and the machinery set against it. Lastly the protection over the dangerous territory of the Sicilian Mafia of Lo Verde/Provenzano and the Corleone team.

In the recent history of the fight against the Mafia there are ample traces of the existence of the 'Ciancimino system'. To hear it delivered first hand by inside witnesses, such as his sons Massimo and Giovanni, is a confirmation of the past and a warning to the present that perhaps it is still not immune to the cancer.

The Swamp

MASSIMO: In the 1960s and '70s the Mafia enjoyed a very large social consensus that ranged from theoretical neutrality to out-and-out competition to be seen as the friends of the bosses. The cream of the professional classes didn't hide the fact they felt pleased if they could be useful to the heads of Cosa Nostra, and the politicians saw an inexhaustible reservoir of votes in this social consensus. Then among the youth the proximity of the 'padroni of Palermo' was even more appealing. We looked enviously at the boys our age who swaggered about in stupendous cars and motorbikes and spent astronomical sums in the evening. The desire to emulate them overcame any moral hesitation.

I clearly remember one of these offspring: he was Guglielmo, the son of Gaetano Fidanzati, known as Tanino, a very famous Palermo boss. Guglielmo lived in Arenella on a street noted for the city's best ice-cream cones, made by Il Mago dei Gelati. Below his apartment there was always a procession of young men from the so-called Palermo élite going there to ask a favour, to do with taking some action to recoup a stolen moped or car. Guglielmo never disappointed and afterwards celebrated his reputation in the discothèques where – at night – the two worlds mixed and got along together perfectly happily, side by side. Typical were the scenes where the sons of the 'drug king' Masino Spadaro would show off around the sofas of the Speak Easy, then Palermo's most fashionable disco, or the son of property speculator Rosario Spatola. They did nothing else but replay in miniature an agenda learned from their parents, making themselves out to be peacemakers, showing nuisances the door, and putting down fights which the owners certainly didn't want, all so they could gain some respect from them. And for the trouble they often didn't have to pay for the costly shows put on with their high-class champagne and whisky.

Dividing up the Cake

MASSIMO: The adults mingled together at social clubs and parties. I even went to the Country Club and the high-society Lauria club. But then I was part of the well-to-do middle class: parties and dinners at the homes of the Tasca family or Giorgio Inglese, noble and respected people. Or the homes of successful businessmen: Cassina, Maniglia, and the Salvo cousins who owned a transatlantic yacht. There were excursions on Benny D'Agostino's yacht where you could meet well-known professionals and politicians: I looked at them and saw them again in a different light as they made another kind of handshake – a less elegant one, for sure – when they were discussing and handing out money and contracts with hard-bitten Mafia bosses. There was Prof. Sebastiano Bosio, a leading angiologist with a chair at the University of Palermo, who came to a terrible end. My brothers and I were friends with his daughters and were horrified when they killed him with a revolver in the centre of the new part of the city, in front of the Bar Cuba in Villa Sperlinga. It was November 1981 and the Mafia war had already begun its endless killing spree. We were dumbfounded at such unjustifiable violence. Why had they shot Bosio? What on earth could a heart specialist have had to do with the reasons for the bloodbath?

At the time there were no answers. Some people explained hurriedly that the professor had perhaps treated one of the Mafiosi on the losing side who was wounded in an ambush. Others said the opposite in that he'd perhaps refused to treat someone. But there was nothing certain and in fact the crime was never fully explained.

Several weeks before the case was to be closed Silvia, one of Bosio's daughters, suggested to the judges to 'ask the Ciancimino family who might know something about my father's death'. She told them that one evening she'd been in the Brasil, a disco I ran in Monte Pellegrino, and met my father there. They fell into conversation about the unfortunate business of her father. Silvia said my father let her know that he knew something of the background to the case, but nothing more because it was better not to speak about certain things. This is why she now wants to know if the rest of the family knows anything.

She may be on the right lines. My father hinted at something in 2000 when we were working on his book. I can't remember exactly, but I recall him having said that in some way or another it involved the Mafioso Giacomo Giuseppe Gambino and Bosio (to whom he'd been specially recommended) being rude to him. But I don't believe this was the real motive. My father also mentioned some disagreement with the director of public health (at that time Giuseppe Lima, brother of the more famous Salvo) and professional jealousies arising during the period when appointments and consultancies had to be made. Bosio wasn't an easy character to get on with and was continually threatening to go to the magistracy.

Who knows whose interests the poor professor found himself tangled up in?

My father had little respect for Palermo's well-off middle class, given that he knew its every intimate vice. He got along with it, as he went along with the invasive tactics of the Mafia, conscious as he was that in order to function properly his 'system' couldn't do without one of its vital components of business, politics and Mafia.

The cake they had to divide was a considerable one. At one single meeting, I remember, they established a long list of public works to be handed out. It was the beginning of the 1980s and my father was the established main channel for this stream of business he managed with Bernardo Provenzano, the man who was by now his alter ego.

So one morning my father dismissed the chauffeur and told me to get the car ready because we had to go. When he spoke like this it meant that we were about to take part in one of the secretive meetings.

They were so secretive that they often required the help of what we called a 'trailblazer', or decoy. This role was more often than not carried out by a boss called Nino Madonia, who went ahead of us in his red Peugeot 205. To shake off any potential tail he went into a building site or works yard and came out by another gate, thanks to the remote controls that friends would lend him.

Let me digress on this ritual of constantly changing direction which my father treated as a deadly serious business. First you had to take out the car, a grey metallic Alfa GT, park it in the apartment block's inner courtyard and wait for his arrival. Then you had to get out and help him with his bag full of numerous spectacles – those for reading, those for distance, those with the patch for the affected eye – his working papers, and the usual supply of music cassettes, the sadistic torture of which he visited upon whoever happened to be travelling with him. My place was then to sit beside him because he insisted on taking the wheel himself, despite the problem with his eye, which put in danger petrol station signs or anything on the roadside that wasn't in his direct line of vision. Then off we went in second gear because 'first is only for steep slopes and lining the pockets of petrol station owners and mechanics'.

And so it was that morning, but with an unforeseen hitch. The destination was Bagheria where the new offices of I.c.re were located, owned by Leonardo Greco, whom we called Nardo. Unfortunately four kilometres away, smoke began to appear from the Alfa's bonnet. Now it would have been logical to stop and check what the problem was, but he was against this because – aware of the delicacy of the meeting we were about to have – he was afraid of 'attracting attention'. This was a scarcely credible motive, given we were certainly more visible with all the smoke spewing out. But it was useless trying to reason with him. While we were travelling along the stretch that led to I.c.re, I thought how easy it would have been to surprise the whole cream of Cosa Nostra in conclave. Like the Wise Men who followed the star, all you had to do was follow the trail of smoke we left.

And they really were all there waiting for us in those offices:

Provenzano who, when he was looking after and handing out
the money, was known as 'the Accountant', and his trusted side-
kick, Pino Lipari, together with Totò Riina, Masino Cannella,
Mafioso and self-styled impresario of the Madonia areas, Nitto
Santapaola, head of the Catania Mafia, Ciccio Virga, head of the
Trapani Mafia, Benedetto Spera, our host Leonardo Greco and
Masino Scaduto, whom I already knew from previous meetings
in the house of architect Sam Scardina, who was the main man
of the Salvo cousins. Among the last to arrive was Nino Salvo
and his son-in-law Tani Sangiorgi, the doctor now serving a life
sentence for his part in the homicide of Ignazio Salvo, his father-
in-law's cousin. Finally, the last to arrive in a Golf, driven for him
by a youngster, was Salvatore Greco, known as 'the Senator',
brother of Don Michele who was at that time head of the Mafia
Commission. Without getting out of the car, nor taking the cigar
from his mouth, he spoke with Nardo and made an appointment for dinner at a restaurant in Porticello, Francu 'u Piscaturi.

The subjects for discussion at that meeting, as told by my
father afterwards, were various and fundamentally about the
decisions on the contracts put out to tender for important public
works, which finally came for approval on Palermo city council's
political agenda. I can't remember all of them, but they ranged
from development of the coastal stretch between Palermo and
Termini Imerese, to doubling the size of Palermo's ring road;
from the construction of a conference centre and the so-called
'Palazzo di vetro' ('glass office block'), to elevated roads, the management of refuse and modernizing Sicily's harbours. A package
of several hundred thousand million lire in the old money.

On the agenda that day was also the discussion of the umpteenth rift which had opened up between my father and Riina. As I've said, there was no love lost between the two, but they were condemned to work together. What was the problem? It centred on Conte Cassina and his sudden closeness to the Corleonesi. As it had become consolidated over time, the political agreement was based on the expectation that contracts would be given to some large and friendly business concern, chosen because it possessed all the necessary requirements detailed in the public notice, with the agreement that it would sub-contract the work to local concerns controlled by the 'system', which couldn't compete in the tender process because they didn't fulfil the requirements. Cassina, it appeared, had 'stepped out of line': ignoring the above procedure he'd acquired a Milanese business, Farsura S.p.a., in order to compete directly for several large contracts.

Inevitably, after the discussions and protests, everything ended up round a table for a meal. In Bagheria, the places proposed for dinner came down to three: Francu 'u Piscaturi, La Muciara di Nello El Greco and Don Ciccio, a trattoria with home cooking then directly attached to the level crossing that marked the entry of the main 113 road into town.

That day we went to Francu in Porticello. As on every occasion, the premises were monopolized by our group. Already inside were Salvatore Greco and two other people I didn't know. At a sign from the Senator, the owner pulled the roller shutters down and no more customers were allowed in. But some people did gain entrance. Indeed, there was almost a procession of supplicants. As in *The Godfather*, each one had a personal request, someone demanding 'justice' over some lack of respect they'd suffered, another wanting exemption from military service for their son, someone else wanting easy terms to buy building materials . . . And Nardo, the local boss, sent for people, smoothed things over, asked people to make sacrifices and, in short, had the right word for everyone.

That wasn't the only meeting in Bagheria. Many years later I learned that I.c.re. functioned not only as a centre for making business decisions, but also as a Mafia court that handed out death sentences. This secondary function was reserved only for 'men of honour', but it still makes my hair stand on end thinking of a place that, over the years, the *pentiti* have described as the 'Auschwitz of Cosa Nostra'. At the time I was eighteen and didn't really understand what was going on in this ambiguous world I found so fascinating because of the feeling of power it gave out. It was a world that gave you security and made you feel strong and respected: it was enough to be seen with these people to get consideration and privileges. It was a per-verted mechanism, and one which weakened the moral defences of so many respectable professionals and entrepreneurs who today keep well away and even criticize.

The Wrong Airport

Nothing escaped the ravenous attention of the 'Ciancimino system': everything was perfectly planned and studied in order to fulfil the aspirations and interests of friends and 'friends of friends'. The meetings in 'I.c.re style' were the rule: the only one – according to Massimo and Giovanni Ciancimino – that guaranteed the peaceful development of business. The politicians decided on priorities, which they called 'lines of development' in relation to the 'necessities' that emerged from the contacts among the various components of the power group.

MASSIMO: My father made a definitive entry into the world of the entrepreneur. Immediately after the Allied landings my grandfather Giovanni – whom we've already met – succeeded in obtaining the management of a transport company, in partnership with Rosario Maniglia, progenitor of an important family of entrepreneurs, using lorries from the American command. In 1950, however, he transferred assets to my father so that he could request and obtain a State Railways concession for rail transport right to the door, a revolutionary concept in those days. It meant using new technology that allowed the entire wagon, and the heavy goods it contained, to be loaded onto special bogies that could run on metalled roads. It was similar to what later became containerization. It couldn't have been easy to be awarded a concession that had tempted numerous enterprises from the North to put in a tender. A fundamental help must have come to my father from his first political godfather in the shape of Bernardo Mattarella, a Christian Democrat like himself, and his point of reference on the wider national front at that time.

From there he spread his wings and eventually was able to

'break into' – as the saying goes – road works, housing construction with Buscemi and Bonura, for whom he was the secret
financier, managing a pharmaceutical warehouse in Palermo
and also a filling station put in the name of his mother-in-law,
my grandmother Adele.

So there was the 'system' that produced the good life. And
for this reason it knew no stopping. A shining example,
between the 1960s and '70s, is the business of the closure of
the old airport of Boccadifalco and the construction of the
new one at Punta Raisa. As assessor, my father was aware (as
were all the technical experts) that the correct choice would
have been an area in the direction of Termini Imerese. This
was suggested by the morphology of the land, which was very
level, and its geographical position, closer to the provinces of
Enna and Caltanissetta that had to rely upon Catania.

But these arguments were not enough to allow logic to prevail because, on the other side of the scales, were the interests
of two powerful bosses like Gaetano Badalamenti and Totò
Riina. The first was interested, over and above the increased
value of the land there, in having an airport at the centre of
the international drugs trade. The second was motivated by
the guaranteed building expansion in the direction of the airport, together with its relative services, from the motorway to
all the other infrastructure, that would put an astronomical
price on the areas of land that were already in his hands. To
judge from the kilometres of cement that later invaded the
territory, from Via Lazio right up to the airport itself, the
calculation wasn't wrong.

The Conference Centre

MASSIMO: With the building of this work, which – with its pretentious Italian name, Palazzo dei Congressi – was never realized, came the risk of a bloody confrontation. It was 1981. Once again, the rift between my father and Totò Riina became obvious, with the latter – perhaps looking forward to more recent times – thinking a Mafioso could prevail over any political understanding. My father, as ever with Provenzano's support, made great efforts to maintain a balance. There were many hopefuls in the field, and all of them well placed: there was Salvo Lima, the Christian Democrats' representative in Sicily, and at his side a variegated world that ranged from the Salvo cousins to Maniglia and a whole plethora of wheeler-dealers and entrepreneurs who expected rich pickings from the development. As if this were not enough, the people in Catania had also shown an interest, both from the construction industry and the Mafia, in the persons of Carmelo Costanzo and the boss Nitto Santapaola, who was present at the I.c.re meeting in Bagheria.

According to the strict shares for all of the 'system', the contract for the conference centre should have gone – as my father maintained – to a company from Palermo. On the other hand, Totò Riina was working behind the scenes to have the contract awarded to Carmelo Costanzo of Catania, who was sponsored by Nitto Santapaola, a great friend of the Corleone clan. The development remained in the balance for some time, during which everyone tried to move things along in their own way.

Riina was so determined to come out on top that he even came in person to the house in Via Sciuti. Not worried for a second, my father received him as he did everyone else, stretched out comfortably on the bed in his pyjamas.

Riina, however, was dressed up to the nines: blue over-coat, special briefcase for important business and a gift package in his hands. He was in the company of Pino Lipari, the A.N.A.S. ('National Road Maintenance') accountant who worked full time with the Corleone bosses, and forced him-self to project a good mood. But Dad wasn't happy about the visit, which he felt was an imposition. He didn't hide his annoyance and began with a sarcastic eulogy on the 'beauty' of the gold Rolex presented by the godfather. Obviously Riina didn't catch my father's mocking smile, nor the condescending air with which he took the gift, without even taking it out of the box.

Riina opened the discussion, addressing my father politely in the Italian way with the title of *Ingegnere* (civil engineer), although he'd never completed his studies.

'*Caro ingegnere*, I'm here to see you because I'm convinced that the most suitable solution is the one I've previously out-lined.'

My father barely let him finish.

'I'm sorry, dear Totò, but there's no point in continuing this discussion. It's already been agreed to everyone's satisfaction that the contract goes to Palermo.'

'Well, I didn't expect such a negative response, I have to con-fess. For the moment, however, I won't insist. I'll take my leave, but I have to say it's my firm belief that this business should go according to the way I think.'

The farewells were frosty. Riina wasn't used to being crossed and would have been beside himself. Confirmation of this comes from Pino Lipari in his account of what happened as the two went down in the lift afterwards: 'He grabbed me by the collar and, with his eyes coming out on stalks, said, "If I'm crazy enough to tell you to take me to Ciancimino again, and you actually do, I swear I'll wring your neck!"'

This was while my father found that inside the package of gifts was a gold ingot, which he quickly shunted off to Franco Bonura who, besides construction, also had an interest in a silverware business and could therefore melt it down and work it into something. I have to say that the incident aroused some concern that things could slip way out of control. For this reason it was decided not to make a choice, and to this day Palermo still doesn't have its Palazzo dei Congressi.

I should say that gifts were a long-established custom, all except with Provenzano, where the relationship went beyond the usual formalities. The above occasion wasn't the only time Riina paid us a visit, even if he was in hiding, and each time he came bearing a gift. I remember a silver lamp offered in the presence of Don Pino Abbate who was with him. And I also recall a gold watch, another Rolex, offered by Gioacchino Pennino, a doctor and Christian Democrat.

The story of the 'Palazzo di Vetro', on the other hand, was at the centre of a complex division of spoils. This modern glass structure to be slotted into the Art Nouveau buildings on Via

Libertà was a symbol of Maniglia's megalomania, a delusion of grandeur that would cause his downfall and ruin, bringing an end – after the splendours of his Roman offices – to the huge investments, private aeroplanes and similar wasteful spending.

But an amount of assets that large couldn't be allowed to float away. For this reason the failure of Maniglia's company was managed, as they say, 'in the family'. The still unfinished building was bought in the middle of the 1980s for L14.5 thousand million – in accordance with a decision taken in a meeting presided over by my father – by Gei-Sicilia (Gruppo Costanzo) in competition with the Sicilcassa pension fund. The Gei group then sold it on to Sicilcassa for L26 thousand million; the Sicilcassa bank therefore paid L26 thousand million because it couldn't acquire at L14 thousand million. The later inquiry by Giovanni Falcone focused particularly on the fact that the Costanzo group was a privileged client of Sicilcassa and, therefore, there should have been some competition between the participants at the auction. But instead the Sicilcassa bank had given Gei the finance of L15 thousand million in order to complete the building.

The Ciancimino 'System'

There was a vast amount of money in the hands of a small group of people. A restricted group of a few chosen friends. Practically nothing escaped notice from its command post, not only in Palermo but also in the rest of Sicily and, as we'll see, beyond to the island's continental offshoots. Its members were entrepreneurs and developers with two faces: part businessmen, part Mafiosi in that they were members of Cosa Nostra. Nino and Ignazio Salvo, Mafiosi from the Salemi 'family', important collectors of the tax concession and financial backers of the Christian Democrat camp in Sicily, were friends of Salvo Lima and represented the most prominent part of this tangled web. It's enough to recall their management, in the form of a decades-long monopoly, of Sicily's tax collection which gave them a premium that was three times what it was in the rest of Italy. And then there was the business side, the industrial transformation of agricultural production, wine, citrus fruits, irrigation, public works. The Salvo cousins ruled over a great dynasty: a luxury yacht with Monets and Van Goghs on the walls, grand parties, friends in high places, their 'personal assessor' elected to the regional administration to look after the interests of their group. They still tell stories in Palermo about the reception given at the Hotel La Zagarella on the occasion of Nino's daughter's wedding: a fountain that sparkled with Veuve Clicquot and lobsters fished out live from a huge display tank.

MASSIMO: But the real family group was something else, they were the 'Bo.Bu. Twins', so named because my father had the habit of giving nicknames to all and sundry. Pino Lipari, for example, was 'the Lieutenant' because 'he believed he was a general, but he would never make it past lieutenant'. 'Iolanda', on the other hand, was Dr Nino Cinà, the physician who, during the so-called 'Deal' between the state and the Mafia in 1992 and '93 (about which more will be said), was the spokesman for Totò Riina. His nickname derived from where he lived: Via Principessa Iolanda in Mondello. The 'twins' were Franco Bonura and Antonino Buscemi, two property developers very much on the inside of Cosa Nostra. Salvatore Buscemi, brother of Nino, was later arrested after a double homicide with the smoking pistol still in his hands. They were in charge of the Boccadifalco and Passo di Rigano *mandamento* as far as Uditore, an area in which they had built a great deal. But at the time we had no knowledge of this, they were just friends who came to visit the house. There were unforgettable lunches on Sundays at a restaurant named La Scuderia, often with the special participation of Signor Lo Verde, before and after the revelation of his true identity. All this while he took second spot on the most-wanted lists. In first place was Totò Riina, who was also able to come and go as if he were a free man. But, in Palermo, everything was possible in those days.

Buscemi was a tall stout man with a flashy style yet few words. The shorter Bonura, who had fair hair, was always hidden behind dark glasses but was jovial, the life and soul of the party, and got on even better with my father than with his partner. They always came to our house together, hence the nickname 'twins'. I wonder if my father ever knew his sons in turn had pinned a nickname to him: 'Baffo' ('The Moustache').

GIOVANNI: The most famous of my father's friends in property construction was Francesco Vassallo, or Ciccio. He was a man in middle age, fairly robust, with a flamboyant dress sense, which was inevitable for a man who, before he frequented high society in the post-war years, had trodden Sicily's beaten paths in his horse and cart. To see him you would take him for an old manual labourer, and yet he was the most important man in Palermo construction. He was a dead ringer for Dave the Dude in Frank Capra's *Pocketful of Miracles* (1961) and like him he spat on his shoes in order to polish them on the back of his trouser leg, or else he breathed on the ruby on his finger so as to make it shine after the ritual of rubbing it up and down his jacket. My father used to say that, although Ciccio had little formal education, he possessed an exceptional entre-preneurial intelligence and capability. He had quicker wits than the 'civil engineers whose chicken brains were only capable of presumption'. These words betrayed all his dislike of civil engi-neers, whom he hated out of jealousy, seeing that he hadn't been able to complete his own degree.

Romolo Vaselli junior, a descendant of Roman aristocracy, came to our house regularly and was one of the pillars of the so-called 'Ciancimino group'. For years he was in charge of the firm that dealt with Palermo's rubbish. He was truly in the confidence of my father, who could ask anything of him. Once he begged him to 'do something' for Gaspare, a man with a family to support who had attempted suicide in a stone quarry because he found himself out of work. One of my uncles, the legendary Mimì, had taken Gaspare's story to heart and asked Dad if he could help the man. All it took was a phone call to Conte Romolo Vaselli junior and a day later Gaspare had a job that paid more than the one he had before. Needless to say how attached and grateful to my father Gaspare was.

And then there was Conte Cassina, a refined gentleman from another age. He was one of the few people who were spared having to wait to see my father. Dad certainly considered him as the most influential businessman in the city, probably for his belonging to the Order of Knights of the Holy Sepulchre, the powerful religious institution very close to the Bishopric of Monreale (Palermo). In all those years I never heard my father once raise his voice to him, as he regularly did with everyone else, especially when he was being crossed.

I also have a clear recollection of the 'Twins'. One day they came to the house with a huge bottle of champagne and an enormous silver bowl overflowing with Sicilian confectionery. On that occasion they were all especially happy, so I presumed they had something to celebrate together. I wasn't wrong. They were toasting my father's entry into the construction firm Lu.Ra.No. – obviously a hidden role, given the political one he held on the eve of his election as mayor. From the moment of that toast, the 'Twins' became regular visitors to the house. They often went out with my father who, on those occasions, did without his driver.

Investments in Milan and the Relationship with Calvi

MASSIMO: Many years later, when relations with Baffo were more open, I learned about the background to Bonura and

Buscemi's Lu.Ra.No. construction company. My father told me the story. In 1970 he'd invested L150 million in several property developments of the firm. After six or seven years, the return was enormous: about L1,500 million and several apartments in Palermo in the Via Don Orione area. It had been estimated that the mezzanines of these buildings would all go to a large private health centre. A hidden partner in this initiative was to have been Bernardo Provenzano. I don't know how or why, but in the end this didn't happen. The allegations are that by means of, and on directions from, Buscemi the L1,500 million profits were deposited in the Banca Rasini and Banca del Gottardo so they could then be invested in the firms Edilnord and Immobiliare San Martino, involved in the construction of the huge Milano 2 residential project. It meant purchasing numerous apartments under construction and then selling them on at an increased price. This type of economic agreement was finalized in Rome, in the offices of Immobiliare San Martino in Via San Nicola da Tolentino. [The Palermo Prosecutor is currently investigating these allegations.]

In this business deal there was no Mafia influence at all: it was a normal entrepreneurial investment in Northern Italy. When we were close together again and wanted to establish his recollections in a book, my father told me that − parallel to his own dealings − Stefano Bontade and Mimmo Teresi had also invested just over L3,000 million in Milano 2. According to what he told me, the go-between was Marcello Dell'Utri. [This later formed part of Ciancimino's testimony to the Palermo Prosecutor's office.]

Almost at the same time, my father invested about L300 million in Inim Immobiliare. This company came in to being in Via Ariosto in Palermo in the same premises that housed his electoral committee. The 300 million were the proceeds of a kickback my father had never used and left with the entrepreneur Francesco Paolo Alamia until he could use the sum as capital in the Inim company. At this moment my father became a partner, albeit not officially, with the owners of the company, Alberto Rapisarda, the brothers Alberto and Marcello Dell'Utri and obviously Alamia himself. [This would also form part of Ciancimino's testimony to the Palermo Prosecutor's office. Those accused also included Dell'Utri and Alamia. As yet there has been no verdict.]

Following an initial period of success, Inim was facing failure after a series of speculation errors on Alamia's part. The bankruptcy was followed by a judicial investigation for fraud that concluded a couple of years later with a general acquittal. My father never publicly mentioned his official involvement in Inim and justified his presence there only as a consultant.

It was a period of 'great contacts' outside of Sicily as well. A part of the proceeds from the Milano 2 investments, for example, came to my father through Roberto Calvi, the man notorious as 'God's banker' who was found hanging under Blackfriars Bridge in London. My father knew Calvi. He had been introduced to him, through goodness knows what channels, by one of the Buscemi brothers. It was the banker who saw to collecting around L3,000 million, part of the profits from 'Sicilian' investments in Milan, and consigning them to my father in Lausanne, where he had an account and a safe deposit box at the Union de Banques Suisses. Some investors, however, demanded the money in diamonds, an operation undertaken with the innocent help of the largest diamond expert of the time, Leos Gluths, who was a top man in his field.

My father's association with Calvi wasn't occasional. I know that they met quite often and always received or handed over conspicuous sums of money in cash. This kind of financial compensation took place mainly inside the Vatican's bank, the IOR.

At the IOR my father had access to safety deposit boxes. In one he kept the money he took in Rome, accrued from bribes to politicians and Cosa Nostra members. This money, which wasn't his, was a kind of resource to hand out – indeed he kept it in a communal chest he called 'the big pot'. Here he held the 6 per cent kickbacks from large contracts, 4 per cent of which was destined for financing the politics, the remaining 2 per cent going regularly to Cosa Nostra for 'fixing'. A handsome sum that ended up with Signor Lo Verde, the other collector of bribes, who redistributed it inside the Mafia.

The politicians were the terminus of the system my father called 'fair shares'. Each political party received a percentage proportionate to its electoral weight. Obviously the lion's share went to the Christian Democrats, with an electoral share of over 40 per cent. Then the smaller parties, each with its own share. As I told the prosecutor I remember L50 million going to Giacomino Murana, a Social Democrat, but more on Ciancimino's side than all the others. No money went to the

Communists, my father said, but they were provided for by assigning work to left-wing companies.

In the other safety deposit box twinned with 'the big pot' went my father's personal reserves that he then took steps to make invisible by means of transfers in Italy and abroad. On more than one occasion, I accompanied him myself to guard the bag filled with money he was taking to the Vatican pharmacy. One or more clerics were waiting for him inside, who then led him into the interior of the IOR. The same clerics had procured him one of his safety deposit boxes; Conte Romolo Vaselli junior had put the other at his disposal. Why the IOR? He told me that its advantage lay in the impossibility of any control on the part of the Italian judicial authorities, who had no power in the face of the extraterritorial protection of the Vatican State.

3

Head Office

In 1965 the Antimafia Commission, presided over by a Christian Democrat Senator, Donato Pafundi, finished its report and sent it to Parliament. It remained unpublished until June 1971 when its results finally became known. Amazingly they showed that

the housing sector and the purchase of land for housing construction, together with the decisive contribution of administrative irregularity observed in town planning departments and in the granting of building licences, have constituted a highly propitious field for the furthering of illicit activities and the exercise of power by pressure groups outside the law seen with notable regularity in the form of parasitic mediation and the practice of favouritism ... In the development of housing construction, individuals of obscure origin have surfaced in the space of a few years that have become rapidly wealthy in ways that are suspicious at the very least. Not least among the irregular practices, in particular in the field of

building licences, is that they have gone to the benefit of
individuals known from police reports and later criminal or
judicial events as belonging to the Mafia.

This is not the screenplay from Francesco Rosi's masterpiece *Le
mani sulla città* (*Hands over the City*, 1963), but simply the reality
of Palermo in those years. A reality that the popular imagination has stamped in its memory with the acronym Va.Li.Gio.,
the initials of the directors of a company that long dominated
housing construction. According to the ex-president of the
Provincial Inspectorate Commission, Ferdinando Umberto Di
Blasi, giving evidence to the Antimafia Commission in 1964, the
names were that of Vassallo, the property speculator often seen
at the Ciancimino home, followed by those of Lima and Gioia.
Here is what Carlo Alberto Dalla Chiesa had to say about Ciccio
Vassallo in 1971: 'The person concerned is not simply a humble
and anonymous haulier with horse and cart who has risen to
greater economic and social position thanks to his intelligence
and astuteness alone, when we take into account that his family
of origin, without being able to define it as in the Mafia mould,
has always lived closely in touch with a milieu dominated by
the Mafia to the point of supporting it and having close ties of
kinship with a dangerous Mafia family.'

The Antimafia Commission's picture, of which Dalla
Chiesa's report forms a part, makes the following conclusion:
'Several of the main players in the most sensational criminal
activities in the Palermo area appear in the transfers of own-
ership of building land and are indicated in several reports

as individuals able to exert a considerable influence on the city's administrative organs.' The roundabout manner of expression cannot hide the reality that Palermo was completely in the Mafia's grip. And in that reality Don Vito Ciancimino comes to have a high profile, as we can infer from a sketch outlined again by Carlo Alberto Dalla Chiesa in 1971 when he commanded Palermo's Legion of Carabinieri. He wrote:

His lively temperament, enterprising and unscrupulous, led him almost instinctively to side with that which in Palermo was then considered an all-out protest against the important Christian Democrats of the regional and national parliaments; a protest with a vast radius and labelled as very close to the Fanfani camp that brought overwhelmingly into the limelight the famous political duo Giovanni Gioia and Salvo Lima. At this point it is difficult to establish whether the 'new political line' followed the 'new Mafia line' or vice versa, but what is certain is that the phenomenon has been noted almost contemporaneously on both the Mafia and the political stage and certainly not in terms of an opposition. (Cf. Salvo Palazzolo, *I pezzi mancanti: Viaggio nei misteri della mafia*. Roma-Bari: Laterza, 2010.)

Dalla Chiesa's words carried weight and were not alone, given that as early as 1963 the system's leading players were in the sights of the Commission of Inquiry headed by the Prefect Tommaso Bevivino, sent to Palermo to investigate the insatiable appetites revealed by the discovery of irregularities that favoured not only runaway property speculation, but also the private contracts for road maintenance, refuse collection and tax collection given respectively to the firms of Cassina, Romolo Vaselli junior and Trezza. We have already met the names of some of these contractors; Romolo Vaselli junior in particular never ceased to have close ties to Don Vito, right up to being imprisoned with him during the investigations into tenders in 1990. About the contract awarded to Romolo Vaselli junior, Prefect Bevivino said, 'A private company was given a service that in reality would not cost L16,000 million over ten years, as specified in the contract, but L30,000 million.' While to Cassina went the gift of renewal for a further nine years, and to Trezza an unprecedented premium for the collection of tax on consumer goods: 'For every hundred lire taken, he kept fifty.'

The picture of those years is hard to believe. It strains credibility to see the vast jigsaw puzzle of politics and business, with its branches in different cities in Italy and abroad, having its cellular origin in Palermo inside a small community and inside the power system of a few men with no particular intellectual gifts but who were decidedly astute and avaricious. This gallery of rogues, sometimes mediocre but forming strong links in a chain, united the apparently distant realties of politics and crime, the professionals and the corrupt. The ritual presentation of affiliates of Cosa Nostra took place with this formula: 'We are one and the same thing.' And it was just the same in Palermo's melting pot, except that no one – especially in decent society – wanted to see the subtle thread that linked good and evil, cops and robbers. How many times could you see people feigning despair over the arrest of a Mafia boss who only a few hours before had been the subject of praise and reverence: 'He was always an excellent man, so gracious and kind! Whoever would have thought he belonged to the Mafia . . .' All lies and hypocrisy: everyone knew who was in charge, everyone knew whether an electoral candidate was part of the 'system' or not.

MASSIMO: Important decisions were made at meetings held at the house in Baida as well as those in Mondello and Palermo. Both main players and simple messengers came and went with statements of position and requests from the *éminences grises* unable to move about freely because they were in hiding. And yet as significant players their voices had to be heard. There was a time in Palermo when it was enough to say 'Via Sciuti' to refer to the head and heart of the city's economic powerhouse. There was a continual coming and going from that top floor. We've met the 'noble' side of it, the wealthy ones, and also the less presentable, the foremost names being Provenzano, Riina, Abbate and associates. To these I could add the names of people like Dr Antonino Cinà, a neurologist with close links to the Corleone Mafia, as shown in the business of the 'Deal', which I'll talk about later.

Liggio at Sirmione

MASSIMO: My father knew Cinà from way back. They met in the 1970s when he was ambassador on a very special mission coming directly from Luciano Liggio. Preceded by a letter of presentation/recommendation from one of the Salvo cousins, he brought my father the entire documentation of the trial that cost Don Luciano his life sentence. Without really hiding the fact, the request was to sound out the magistracy to see if it would be possible to obtain a retrial. The Salvo duo knew that my father was close friends with the high-ranking magistrate Salvatore Palazzolo, who was then President of the Higher Tribunal on Public Water Supply. My father tried to escape from this unprecedented proposal, aware of the trouble he would find himself in, not to mention his magistrate friend. In fact – he told me – in the first instance Palazzolo even refused to accept the files. Only after his friend's insistence did he examine them, then a few days later gave a decisively negative opinion.

The life sentence was Liggio's abiding obsession. It demoted him to half the role of *capo* because he was forced into a life on the run. In fact, even before Cinà's appearance, he'd approached my father directly in a rather unusual way. All the family was on holiday on Lake Garda with some close friends in a hotel in Sirmione, 'Il Giardino', one of the usual havens that Baffo chose. One morning the whole group was buzzing with activity and orders were given to the proprietor to prepare 'a good room' for an unidentified but very important guest. I even remember a row – not that they weren't frequent – between my parents over the choice of room, which my father considered inadequate. Later that morning the awaited guest arrived to talk to Dad in private. No one ever heard anything about him again. I was about seven years old and took little notice of the matter. It was Dad who later confided to me that the man was Luciano Liggio, then in hiding in Milan, and he'd come to talk about his trial. It was on that occasion that Cinà was named as the person who would let him have the relevant documents. However, there were many other attempts to 'adjust' Liggio's life sentence. My father also tried speaking to the Prosecutor Pietro Scaglione, who was another good friend. But the result was the same: only an action that was more than embarrassing could have put the sentence back under discussion.

The relationship with Cinà, however, continued and intensified. I saw the neurologist both at our house in Via Sciuti and at the villa in Via Danae in Mondello. On one occasion he asked my father, the one-time assessor of public works, to arrange to have a public mains supply put in and a road completed in the area between Palermo and Altofonte. My father suspected it was a matter of aiding a fugitive, making it easier for them to hide out there. The suspicion was reinforced by Cinà himself, who reassured him: 'If you need any help from your Corleone people, come directly to me.' Who knows if that request for help had to do with the villa in Borgo Molara, situated in the Altofonte-Monreale district, where – as we've come to know from the *pentiti* – Riina was hiding at the end of the 1970s?

Masino Cannella, a businessman from the Madonie area who represented the wishes of Riina and the Corleonesi, was another person I knew well from meeting him in Via Sciuti. My father called him 'The Cigar' because he had one permanently in his mouth, except when he had to put it out before entering our house because Dad couldn't abide the smell. I often saw him when he came to visit and we talked about luxury cars and watches and I found him very likeable. The last time I saw him was at the wedding of Dottore Mercadante's daughter. Cannella had a company that made posts for electric cables and had a wide range of business thanks to Mafia protection. He often came to the house. Even though he was one of the smaller fish, by that I mean less spoken of in the newspapers, Masino carried a certain weight in the sharing out of contracts.

Vito Ciancimino was born and brought up in Corleone and therefore knew directly the entire group of Mafiosi that for decades did away with people to the sound of sawn-off shotgun and .38 revolver, first in the town, then later in the Palermo it had conquered. Liggio, Riina and Provenzano were the three who earned the eloquent nickname of 'Father, Son and Holy Ghost'. We've seen how relations with Riina were far from idyllic and we know that Vito's understanding was only with Provenzano. In the course of the story we'll have the opportunity of returning to this close link. The one man he seriously feared and despised for his pathological approach to the use of violence was Luciano Liggio. On many occasions, Ciancimino avoided having anything to do with him directly, being mindful of the past in Corleone. The following narrative reconstruction by Giovanni sheds some light on this.

*

GIOVANNI: It was one of the times I went with him to Lausanne in Switzerland for his regular medical check-up. We were taking a walk after the traditional supper, which he often thought would be his last on earth. So it was understandable for him to indulge in a few youthful memories. He told me that he'd had a risky moment in his life when he was eighteen.

'Because of illness?' I asked.

'No, it was a moment that had nothing to do with illness.'

And he began to tell his tale.

'It was at a very important dance with the cream of Corleone's youth. We were in the villa of a wealthy Corleonese celebrating his eighteen-year-old daughter's debut into society. The guests were in formal dress; there were flowers, decorations, bright lights, waiters in white gloves, and the orchestra and singer all in dinner jackets. The only thing I'd seen like it was at the cinema. At a certain point, in the middle of the party, a young man more or less our own age came to the door. He was dressed simply but showed great self-assurance. The waiter at the door politely stopped him and asked to see his invitation. The response was arrogant: "I don't need an invitation, I go where I want." And with a push he made his way into the drawing room.

'Not even when the owner of the house stepped in to suggest he leave could the desired result be achieved. Instead, the gatecrasher piled on the insults with a mocking grin: "I already told the waiter that I go where I want without the need of invitations and haven't the slightest intention of leaving a good party like this, full of young women. In fact, seeing as you're the hostess, go and get me something to eat because I find I'm hungry." And he took hold of my young friend by the arm.

'At this point I stepped forward before it could go any further, and delivered him a punch in the face. The young man hit the floor, blood trickling from his lips, but couldn't react because of everyone pressing round him. He could only mouth off threats, screaming like someone possessed: "I know who you are and where you live, I'll make you pay for this, I will." I gave him as good as I got, and he went off threatening practically all the guests.

'That young man was Luciano Liggio. I knew him by sight, having seen him wandering near the bar around the town centre. But I remembered him particularly from a strange occurrence that had happened some time before. We were on the bus coming back to Corleone from Palermo. The road was narrow and winding and the driver couldn't make way for a Carabinieri squad car that wanted to overtake us. At this point Liggio, who'd been right at the back of the bus, ran down the entire length of the aisle to the driver who was having difficulty with the road. He demanded the driver make every effort to stop the Carabinieri overtaking and began yelling like a madman, "Get them off the road and make them crash." As if that wasn't enough, he tried to take the wheel from his hands, causing the bus to swerve around dangerously. So the driver stopped the bus, letting the Carabinieri finally overtake him, and furious for the risk we'd run, stood up with all his might and pointed with his finger to the door, making Liggio get off, despite the fact that we were about ten kilometres from Corleone.'

We were walking along the boulevard in Lausanne that he called the 'Avenue of Remembrance' and I was totally captivated by this recollection. It seemed natural to ask him, 'But how come a guy like that gave up any vendetta against you for the offence at the party?'

'I told your grandfather Giovanni what happened,' came the reply. 'He took charge of the matter and went to speak to his friend the doctor, Michele Navarra, who was able to keep a rein on the young tearaway. That settled the matter.'

The Doctor Betrayed

MASSIMO: I remember Cannella as well because of an episode I witnessed at first hand. My father was brought in to play a role in 'adjusting' a family drama that exploded in the house of Gisella Mercadante, who was my steady girlfriend when I was twenty. She was the first great love of my life and I remember her with great affection. Her father Giovanni was a radiologist who was quite well known about the town, and he was Masino Cannella's cousin. He wasn't keen on my presence in his daughter's life. There was always trouble with him, especially as she was very young. However, in the end, I think his problem with me was the fact he didn't like my name. We were about to enter the stormiest period of my father's life leading up to his arrest in 1984, and the newspapers were beginning to come down hard on the name of Ciancimino.

It was also the time of a big health care scam. This was investigated at the trial of radiologist Prof. Mercadante, which revealed allegations of a rich seam favoured by Cosa Nostra and Provenzano in particular. Mercadante was found guilty but later cleared on appeal'. D'Amico's appearance created some disagreement between Lipari and Cannella. The rift was made worse by an unpleasant personal situation that came into being between Prof. Mercadante and D'Amico. It appeared that Mercadante's wife Bice was drawn to young D'Amico's attention and this developed into a love affair between the two, which then turned into an 'affair of state'.

Masino Cannella made it a matter of honour and demanded reparation for the behaviour of Lipari's nephew, which, among other things, he called 'unprofessional' for mixing business with his private life. This would have been nothing dramatic in normal life, but in Palermo nothing was normal, especially if the main players in the drama happened to be friends and relatives of Mafia bosses. And so Cannella went to the high court to 'get satisfaction', which means that he turned to Binnu Provenzano.

It was decided to entrust the practical side of the mediation to my father, given that he was a friend of both Cannella and Lipari. Provenzano offered him advice: 'Try to calm these characters down. You know them well and what arguments might convince them not to go to the last resort.' I was an eye-witness to preparations for the ritual of 'making peace' between the parties. I'd been my father's factotum for some time and he carefully explained what I had to do.

The contending parties had to be brought together, but weren't to meet before each had been heard separately. The

'Sanhedrin' was set up in the Mondello villa and I had the job
of receiving and ushering in the two sides. They arrived punc-
tually, each one at a different time, and I put them in separate
rooms. When the first went in, I stayed with the other to keep
them company. Then it was a matter of showing the first group
out and ushering the second in without letting them meet. A
follow-up meeting the next day saw the 'offender' presented,
Enzo D'Amico. But this meant that an agreement had already
been reached to the litigants' mutual satisfaction. D'Amico
would have to scatter ashes on his head, but not a hair of it
would be harmed. The 'penalty' – which in the code of honour
could even have gone to capital punishment – was commuted
to a period of three years' exile in Brazil. It was a sentence he
didn't even serve in full because a later 'remission' reduced it
to little over a year.

Massimo Ciancimino's story, documented and witnessed personally, is one of the numerous versions circulating on the
Mercadante affair. Someone else has spoken of the downright
nerve of Provenzano who – as was his custom – didn't want
to stick his neck out with either Cannella or Lipari, and tried
to bring about peace by invoking Mafia ideology which he
dressed up hypocritically in the terms of maintaining family
unity. But it was a bloodless solution that was justified by the
fact that Mercadante had 'forgiven' his wife and the family had
been reunited. In this justification lies all the pantomime of
Mafia morality: if the husband hadn't shown 'weakness' in
choosing family unity, then aggravating circumstances would

have come in to play for D'Amico and it would have been the maximum penalty.

The Mutual Benefit Society

According to the work of art historian Nino Basile, 'Palermo felicissima' was the Arab–Norman city of the eleventh and twelfth centuries where the arts and intellectual life flourished and where, later, Frederick I, known as 'Stupor mundi', reigned. It was a city that never suffered drought because it was the centre of great hydraulic engineering studies. But in its own way the Palermo of Ciancimino and Salvo Lima was a 'very happy' one, where all its profiteers, large and small, could grow fat without expending too much effort. Nor even for the water for drinking and washing, which only ran twice a week.

But no one, apart from the usual malcontents (trade unionists and Communists), protested very much. Everything ran smoothly. Even during the Mafia wars, when the streets turned red with blood, no one was seriously alarmed. The rich carried on with life as if they lived on another planet, the whiff of corpses and corruption coming nowhere near them. As for the poor, they gathered up what crumbs they could and managed to survive. It was as if, at any moment, a huge machine labelled 'mutual benefits' was put into gear to dispense salvation. There was no limit to the help you could ask from 'Providence': a non-existent disability, treatment in hospital when there were no more beds, a false certificate, a subsidy for works never carried out. And among respectable circles the protection of the mutual benefit society came in to act at higher levels, as told in the following chilling episode.

MASSIMO: I've already mentioned when I first became aware of my father's omnipotence when I was a boy. But those stories in Baida were nothing compared to the trouble we lived through in the following years.

One story that sticks in my mind is the one he told me about the help given to one of his friends in respectable circles, a professor at Palermo University. The professor had met some 'bad luck': he'd killed a thief who was mugging him. It happened in a dark car park in the evening. He was about to open the car door when an armed robber confronted him. He was armed himself and happened to shoot and kill the man. It then occurred to him that he could be charged and arrested for excessive use of self-defence. This was a terrifying prospect because in prison he might come across some criminal who wanted to avenge his dead 'colleague'. So he calls my father who – as always – wasn't slow when it came to helping a friend, even if it meant personal risk. And so he calls a friend of his, the police commissioner of the time (I don't remember his name), who comes up with a solution: the professor should get rid of the weapon, then come in to see him at the police station and sign a declaration (obviously backdated) of the theft or loss of the pistol. Lastly he should move the car a long way away from the body of the assailant. What other organic cooperation between influential friends could so brilliantly resolve a problem that would appear insurmountable to ordinary mortals? After several days the investigation into the homicide was deemed the settling of a score between rival gangs and shelved.

That commissioner wasn't the only friend my father had among the police. For a while he regularly saw the head of the second police district, a deputy commissioner named Pietro Purpi. The police station was in Via Libertà on the corner with Via Giusti near my grandparents' home, so in an excellent position for my father to come and go without attracting too much attention. He used to enter by a gate into the station garden and gain access directly to the deputy commissioner's office without having to go past the duty officer. I don't know what business they had together, he and Purpi, but I do know, however, that the Via Libertà office was chosen more than once for secret meetings with Signor Franco, who was seen by Purpi as a sort of high-ranking colleague who was meeting my father regularly, even when there wasn't a glimmer of the business of 'the Deal'.

And so functioned the solidarity of the caste, even for everyday matters that could easily be dealt with via normal channels. But this they didn't do: privilege was a kind of status symbol for them. My driving licence, for example, is a case in point. I was already driving happily before my eighteenth birthday. My father knew of this and was always on at me about it, also thanks to my dear brothers snitching about how I used to take my mother's car without her knowing. 'If they ever arrest you,' screamed Baffo, 'I'll see you rot in gaol, before I lift a finger to help you!' On my eighteenth birthday, however, he got to work to get me a licence right away. He called me in one day to issue one of his usual orders: 'Go right now to Vehicle Licensing. I've called them and they're expecting you. And please, don't be a dickhead, and try to get there on time.' In the Vehicle Licence office they were very obliging and the very same day I had my licence. I passed it round to all my friends and each one of them asked me how I could have taken the exams in theory and practice both in the same day.

Although he could be ill-tempered, Baffo was also capable of coming to the help of people he didn't know personally. What mattered was the introduction. One time he promised a young man a job as a workman on the city road works on Provenzano's recommendation, I believe. In order to be taken on you had to undergo a kind of practical test in front of a committee designated by the local authorities, on which sat my cousin, Enzo Zanghì.

The day of the test my father phoned Zanghì to make sure he'd be present at this examination because the recommended party 'had to pass at any cost'. Who knows how many times Enzo, one of my father's favourite victims, had received similar requests? Anyway, it was obvious he'd have given ample assurances the thing would go through. On the morning, however, my father had a call from Zanghì: 'Vito, listen to me, have you actually met this man you're recommending? You see, the thing is, Vito, he's only got one arm. Do you follow? How can a man with one arm put in a pole?' 'So?' came my father's sharp exasperated reply. ' It means you put the pole in, instead

of this poor guy! And Enzo, my friend, would I have called
you if this were a normal case? If it were, all you needed were
his particulars!'

He Was My Father

MASSIMO: By now you'll have gathered my father was no
saint. Even in the family his temperament meant he was a
violent, arrogant bully. My mother knows something of this,
as do we children. But above all it was me who, from childhood, challenged him, regularly disobeying all his orders and
regularly suffering the heavy consequences. I was the rebel and
gave him more cause for concern than all the other four put
together. Giovanni, Sergio and Roberto followed Baffo's law,
even if they enjoyed my acts of bravado on the quiet, and so
they concentrated on their studies and consequently all have
good degrees and have found a path in life. It was my sister
Luciana and I who dropped out after taking the secondary
school leaving certificate.

GIOVANNI: All the children went to kindergarten and the
Sacred Heart primary school, a prestigious institution run by
nuns. Except that in his third year Massimo managed to get
himself expelled. It was a wonderful school with huge grounds
to play in, and at the centre stood a large enclosure with a
majestic peacock.

As it was getting towards carnival that year, Massimo had

been given a Red Indian costume, but not the one he wanted. He was after a headdress with more feathers, as befitting a great warrior. Grandad Attilio tried to help out, but couldn't find one. Massimo seemed resigned, but really he was greedily eyeing up the marvellous multicoloured plumes of the peacock behind the wire.

The problem was how to get some without being seen. The most suitable time was during morning mass. So one day he slipped out of the chapel (helped by his size, even then being small for his age) and attacked the peacock's compound. He just climbed the fence and went in. When he came back into chapel with his innocent little face, he had a dozen precious feathers hidden in his pocket.

He was only found out because he was throwing himself around with a ball during break time and lost the booty, which fell to the ground. He tried to make excuses, but they were too improbable to be believed. The mother superior was implacable: he completes the year and doesn't come back.

As punishment he went to no carnival parties that year and the costume he had just acquired was confiscated. An inglorious end for an Indian chief.

Another memorable episode in the history of Massimo's scrapes was when he was twelve. One day the manager of the Standa department store on Via Sciuti phoned the house to say that a boy had been caught with several pieces of stationery that weren't paid for, and who claimed he was the son of Vito Ciancimino. 'I'm on my way,' said my father. Before setting off he called Standa's head office in Milan so that a word could precede his visit. I went with him and when we arrived the branch manager was all sweetness and light, now 'aware that there'd been some misunderstanding'. He even politely wanted to consider the ill-gotten gains as a 'free personal offer' . This seemed too much even for my father, who paid up and took the angelic-looking Massimo by the arm in a manner that left no doubt what would happen to him back at home.

MASSIMO: But school wasn't my father's main concern. He was extremely worried that with my character, one day or another, I'd end up in deep trouble. It's true that I wasn't a simple soul. I forged my father's name in his chequebook to buy the motorbike he'd never get me. You see, even when I became his personal secretary and general factotum, managing the delicate relations in his world, he still lived in fear that I'd create some irreparable damage. He knew that a mistake in those circles would carry grave consequences. Today, now that he's no more, I have to say that I did step out of line more than once, but fortunately was never discovered.

I was thirteen when I experienced at first hand just how violent his punishments could be. I was in my second year at the Gonzaga secondary school and succeeded in having to resit my exams for the year. We were in the Mondello house in Via Danae for the holidays and I still remember the string of harsh slaps he gave me in the face. But even more clearly I remember what happened next: Baffo ordered my brother Giovanni to go and buy a chain nineteen metres long and two strong locks. He gave me two turns around each leg; the sixteen metres left were enough to cover the exact distance that separated me from the bathroom. This was my imprisonment. I'll never forget the humiliation, the sense of shame and mortification when I heard my brothers' friends talking about the state I was in. And my rage when, as revenge, I showed the instrument of my torture to the outside world and accused my father to the few passers-by.

This wasn't the first time he deprived me of my liberty as punishment: something that made me literally go out of my head. I still have the musty smell in my nose and remember the stink of sweaty shoes I had to breathe when, as a punishment for low school grades (especially in Italian), he locked me in the lumber-room which the domestic staff used as a changing room. Sometimes I was in there for a whole week, only allowed out to eat by myself at the table and to go to bed to sleep. As a kind of fitting retribution, given I was lacking in Italian, he locked me in with Edmondo De Amicis's children's novel *Cuore*, which naturally I've detested ever since.

We were always at loggerheads. He liked to keep a low profile, prudent and never ostentatious, while I liked the high life. I loved watches, so much so that for a time I was the agent for Rolex, a brand name that earned me that nickname in Palermo. I loved beautiful cars and motorbikes and couldn't understand my father's reasons for denying himself and all of us life's little luxuries when he had the economic wherewithal. For this reason I was fully classified under the heading he gave to almost all the human race, written off by him as a collection of 'dickheads'. And obviously no one was more deserving of the moniker than me. Indeed, in his eyes I was the rising star in

the whole 'dickhead' firmament. On the other hand, as we knew,
I was always only number four on the list. Four rings of the
bell and in dashed Massimo. This was a custom all the boys
had to observe: Giovanni, the eldest, one ring, and so on following the order of birth. As a girl, Luciana was exempted. The
domestic staff had to give one long ring. So even in the door-
bell league I was bottom. On the other hand, I was always the
smallest, which earned me the nickname of 'Shorty', which I've
had ever since. But I came up with a reason for this to the
point of being able to joke about it, saying I was made from
the leftovers and was therefore the smallest.

My father was the classic Italian *padre-padrone* ('father-
owner'), aware of his authority and always ready to exercise it.
But he was head of a family that was barely united, only held
together by the presence of the grandparents on my mother's
side, Attilio and Adele, who provided emotional support for
us grandchildren. I've always considered it a non-family. My
mother was too weak to stand up to the all-powerful pater-
familias, even in the face of his manifest unfaithfulness. They
were different times and their generation still lived under the
myth of the family unit, united at all costs. Separation and
divorce were still the object of scandal.

While I saw him as Moloch, I really did try to love and
understand him, especially when I was a boy, and to fathom
the reason behind many of his incomprehensible actions. But
I can swear on oath that, despite all my efforts, I was never
able to do so. The saddest thing is that even today I have no
nostalgia for a single day we spent together. I don't recall a

spontaneous hug or a kind word, and given the lack of these, I even took weird comfort from his 'dickhead' tag. Nevertheless he was my father and I had to defend him to the outside world, managing to hide the bitterness of a son who felt he was never loved.

The feeling of rage when he died was sadder than you can ever imagine: it was not being able to offset the pain with a single moment of true joy that we'd shared together. There was nothing to fill up the years of emptiness. And to think that we were always physically close, first when I was running about after him through Palermo and its suburbs, on duty keeping up with Lo Verde and company, and then when he was in exile. Then the discussions in prison, the help he needed while under house arrest, right up until his death. A life of being in touch without ever really being together. I don't remember anniversaries, birthdays or Christmas celebrations. Did we have a tree, a Nativity scene or decorations? At most there was the Christmas Eve ritual when, with the usual custom of the bell, he called each one of us into his room to hand over a present. Even this was performed without any great affection: one of the first times I remember he simply put a ten-thousand-lira note in my hand. But perhaps it was better like that; given that the rare times he was present for dinner it always ended in the same way, with my mother in tears and him cursing.

Sometimes I even took consolation in seeing how his coarseness wasn't only directed towards us. I remember his relations with his mother Pietrina, whom he saw only on high days and holidays. Even with her he showed practically no emotion and betrayed all his arrogance and egoism by rubbing it in when he gave her money, which embarrassed her dreadfully. I've always wondered about the reason for such an attitude. Perhaps the answer lies in the death of his elder brother Vincenzo. They both came down with diphtheria, a deadly illness in those days. The two brothers were separated and perhaps this saved my father. Vincenzo, on the other hand, didn't survive. My grandmother Pietrina was especially attached to her eldest son and the pain made her lose her mind. My father heard her cursing the heavens: 'My God, if you had to punish me, why was it him you had to take?'

It's possible even he wasn't a happy man. Who knows; in his own way he probably did love us and just couldn't find the right way to show it, being all-consumed with his passion for power.

GIOVANNI: It's true, Baffo couldn't communicate his feelings. He was a prisoner in his own shell. You could count on the fingers of one hand the times he allowed himself to play the role of loving father. I experienced one of these occasions and it was to do with the death of the little puppy Lampo, my childhood playmate. With some fundamental help from my granddad Attilio, who was a good man, and also grandma Adele, I'd managed to get him to accept the pet, despite a mania for hygiene that meant he was against all contact with animals.

When Lampo became seriously ill, it was necessary to put him down, so we took him to the vet. I'm grateful to my father for choosing to stay with me because I was a little boy and the end of Lampo was a real tragedy for me. For once Baffo set aside his political commitments to offer paternal support. While the vet prepared the lethal injection, my father tenderly stroked my head, a rare thing for a man who never expressed his emotion with any gesture. 'I know this is going to be very painful for you,' he whispered. 'I'd be lying if I said it won't happen to you again in life, possibly even worse. But these are the times when the real men stand out, knowing how to bear pain with dignity. Remember, Giovanni, keep the pain inside; don't expose it to the eyes of others. When I was your age I lost a brother, but no one ever saw me crying. I did that in the privacy of my bedroom. Now try hard, please.'

And yet there was one time when people saw the granite-faced Baffo in tears. People who were at his side for years have told me the story. It comes from when a domestic accident was nearly the end of me, again when I was still a child. My father didn't know the full extent of the trauma I'd suffered, so when he arrived at the hospital he wasn't expecting to see me lying in a coma. Those present feared one of his violent outbursts, but instead he put his hands over his face and burst into tears.

4

The Idiosyncrasies of Don Vito

On the surface, Vito Ciancimino seemed as hard as a rock. But the truth is that even he had his existential problems, well hidden below that look of 'a man who has to ask for nothing'. It seems that his true weak points were his fear of death and his horror of illness. Naturally, it follows that, at least until he couldn't manage without it, he refused to travel by aeroplane. The idea of flying disturbed him, he said, and he was afraid of having a heart attack while he was far from help at high altitude. It was a fear that sprang from the fate of one of his friends.

In short, Don Vito was a hypochondriac, as well as super-stitious, and ever ready to ward off the 'unhappy event'. If a conversation turned towards incurable illnesses or sudden deaths, he would think nothing of spouting off the most extreme oaths or making superstitious signs against them. Perhaps his knife-edge existence had accustomed him to living with the knowledge of life's transience.

*

GIOVANNI: My father was a hypochondriac like few others in this world. He felt he was exhibiting all kinds of symptoms, all totally imagined: irreversible heart conditions, imminent cerebral strokes and tumours in an advanced stage. For these he underwent check-ups every six months in Switzerland, naturally, with the only doctor he really trusted, Prof. Raul De Preux. I used to go with him and each time the journey there was an excruciating experience. Often we'd get to the hotel and he'd stretch himself out on the bed in a state of total prostration. According to him, he was sure the next day the professor would say he only had a few months to live, perhaps only a few weeks at that. For dinner we'd always go to the same restaurant in a precise, unchanging ritual to ward off evil: the same menu of clear broth and a small piece of low-fat cheese, certain as he was that his system couldn't tolerate anything else. Conversation at the table was of one thing only: his passing away and, in consequence, what I'd have to do to take care of my brothers, Massimo in particular, 'because he's the one that worries me the most'. I tried to contradict what he said and asked him: 'What illness do you think you have?' He never replied but made a gesture with his hands that said, 'There's no hope, nothing more that can be done.' The restaurant owner also played his part in this psychodrama, drawn into the leaden atmosphere that clouded our table.

Facing the Swiss physician the next day in the grip of his pessimism he lost all his arrogance and self-assurance. But after a thorough examination would come the usual result: 'Signor Ciancimino, you're as fit as a fiddle. I'll see you again in six months' time.' These were the words that would work a miracle, able to dissolve melancholy and loss of appetite in an instant. Immediately the next stop would be the restaurant to make up for all that he had renounced the previous evening. You can imagine how different the return journey to Palermo was.

That doctor was his lifesaver, his guru, the answer to all his ills. Without him he would have felt lost and defenceless. It's easy to understand, therefore, the tragedy he felt when one day my mother went into his bedroom, where he habitually lived when he was at home, and told him: 'Vito, there's some shocking news. Professor De Preux died a few days ago. A friend told me. It was a sudden heart attack.'

I was present at these words and saw my father turn pale as a ghost. Beads of sweat came out on his forehead, while he slid further down into the bed until he was looking like a corpse. I also stood stock-still, dumbstruck, not knowing what to say. The only person who seemed unconcerned was my mother: 'But why are you taking on so? You can always find another doctor, Switzerland's full of specialists. I don't think it would be difficult to put yourself in the hands of someone just as skilled as he was.'

Irritated by my mother's dismissive treatment of the event, Baffo burst into a towering rage and cried out that there was no physician who could ever substitute for the professor. He asked us to leave his room and see the door was closed because he wasn't feeling well and wanted to be left alone.

For the whole of the following week he cancelled the major

part of his political commitments, doing the bare minimum of work, remaining shut in his bedroom for almost the whole time in a state of deep depression. At the same time the search began for his new miracle worker. The list was long, but in the end it seemed to come down to a doctor in Lugano. Still feeling uneasy, my father prepared himself for the new pilgrimage, resigned to one thing only and that was life's cruelty. Then, a short while before the departure, he received a visit from his friend Pino Mirisola, who also had a few problems with his health that had led him to have an appointment with Prof. De Preux, of whom he'd heard a great deal. The check-up had taken place in Lausanne two days before.

As soon as my father heard this, his eyes popped out of his head and, incredulous, he had Mirisola repeat the news several times. Pino confirmed everything, adding that he had the pleasure of passing on the best wishes of the professor who, as a matter of fact, was wondering why he hadn't booked himself in for his regular appointment. All this was said without hiding his amazement over my father's reaction, and he repeated: 'Yes, exactly that Swiss professor, the one you told me about. Why are you getting so agitated?'

Like a man possessed, my father grabbed the telephone and in three seconds had an appointment booked with De Preux. But that wasn't the end of it. There was the reckoning to be had with my mother. He waited until she returned home, then had her come to his room where a serious interrogation took place.

'I want you to tell me which friend of yours told you the news of De Preux's death.'

'Why, is it so important? Don't torment yourself any more, these things happen, that's all.'

'True, but the thing hasn't happened at all. De Preux happens to be alive and well.'

'That's impossible. This friend of mine couldn't make a mistake about anything so serious.'

'Oh, of course, then I just happen to have made an appointment with a ghost, have I? Now I want you to tell me the name of this friend of yours because I never want her to come to my house again.'

'I'm not telling you, because you're bound to get steamed up and give her a piece of your mind.'

'Well, I think you invented the whole thing just to take revenge on me for I don't know what.'

Shouting like someone not right in the head, he booted her out of the room, but my mother fled the house and stayed with a cousin for a few days. That was the first big row between my parents and it created a permanent rift in their relationship. Even after they'd made it up, he'd bring it up again whenever they had a row: 'You're the one who said Raul De Preux was dead so you could take it out on me in revenge.'

GIOVANNI: We've already seen how bad my father's character was. He was ill-tempered, argumentative and a chauvinist: in short, he embodied all the worst of the authoritarian patriarch. But my mother's also quite a character with her flights of fancy and absent-mindedness that alienate her from reality. She's a devout Catholic, deeply convinced that there's another life after

this and what we live in with this body is only a brief parenthesis. Baffo didn't think this way and, although he was an activist
in the Catholic party par excellence, his relationship with religion was limited to official ceremonies – baptisms, weddings,
confirmations – which are daily bread for politicians. Inside
himself, though, he remained a non-believer.

But my mother Epifania, who used the name Silvia, wasn't
limited to orthodox belief then. She believed in the existence
of people with special powers who were able to communicate
with the dead and through them could tell the living which
direction to take. In short, she believed in parapsychology and
all its branches. She would visit these elect souls at least once
a week. Everyone in the family knew this and we all made fun
of her for her esoteric beliefs, which of course provoked some
sharp responses.

Everything would have remained relatively normal if she
hadn't also been the wife of Vito Ciancimino and if the devil
hadn't also had something of a hand in it. The fact is this
superstition of hers ended up as part of the investigations.

It so happened that during the summer of 1984 my mother
bought a new red personal phone book. When she gradually
came to fill it in with her old numbers, I thought it would be
a great laugh to include the names of a few famous historical
magicians and wizards, such as Simon Magus, Merlin, Nostra-
damus and even the present Othelma, followed by numbers I
completely made up.

She never ever noticed the extra numbers and I forgot about
them myself, distracted by the clouds that were beginning to

gather over our home as events unfolded leading to my father's arrest. Then the police officers in charge of the fingertip search of the house seized my mother's red phone book.

For months the newspapers printed the most unbelievable versions of my father's vicissitudes. But the article that left me speechless was the one in *L'Espresso* that spoke of a mysterious personal phone book with a red cover that contained names written in code with numbers in cipher that probably referred to bank accounts abroad.

Asked about this phone book, my father resorted to his right to silence – he knew nothing about the numbers I'd added as a joke. At the time I hadn't the courage to say what I'd done. But then I spoke to my father's lawyer, Prof. Orazio Campo, who advised me to see Judge Falcone as soon as possible and clear the matter up, given that an army of investigators considered that address book one of the most incriminating items taken from the house. Fortunately the judge believed me and nothing more was heard of it except in the article in *L'Espresso*.

Uncle Mimi's Little Bags

GIOVANNI: Furthermore, superstition wasn't only the common ground between my parents but also among their wider circle of friends. For my father it was the cure for all his ills. He was quite capable of showing complete indifference for the unhappy, the unfortunate, or as we'd say today, those who 'bear the evil eye', that is, misfortune. At the same time he believed every fairy story about people gifted with supernatural powers, holy or charlatan, who could tell the future. At bottom, he needed reassurance.

We had a relative, a real character, who answered perfectly to the needs of my father's obsessions. This was my uncle Mimì, our neighbour in Baida. He was well off and as well as being recognized as a skilled water diviner, he enjoyed the reputation of a healer and clairvoyant. I can remember the queue of people waiting outside his house to have him lay his hands on them for every kind of malady. Although my father never believed in anything, he thought very highly of my uncle. When we were in Baida during the summer, he came back from his political meetings and went to see him every evening. They'd speak for hours, because Uncle Mimì's words were like a soothing balm of reassurance. This was because this particular miracle worker predicted he'd 'precede him by some time into the life beyond' so therefore he 'could be calm'. Incredible as it may seem, such a certainty buoyed my father up in his depression. Whenever he thought he was ill or when his judicial tribulations began, he always consoled himself with 'Uncle Mimì's promise': 'You'll live a long life, but when your time comes I'll come to get you while you're asleep and you won't feel a thing.'

If any difficulty did happen in politics or business, my father was led to believe that it was a misfortune visited upon him by someone with the evil eye. And that was when he needed to refill his talisman-lucky charm. This operation consisted of opening a tiny little bag that he always carried with him, pouring out the contents, which were cooking salt mixed with a type of flour, and filling the bag again with the same, but fresh ingredients. Perhaps he thought the old ones had lost their power. In order to work, this apparently banal exercise could be undertaken by only one person in the world: Uncle Mimì. The operation had to follow a precise ritual: the little bag was emptied and its contents spread over the garden to the accompaniment of prayers and novenas; then he laid his hands on my father's, which held the little bag. Only then could the person, 'miraculously cured', put it back in their pocket, sure of its future beneficial effects. Obviously Baffo was never parted from his precious talisman; indeed, more than once, he had one made for his most trusted friends.

So Many Good Friends

Then we come to his trusted friends. There were those who visited the Ciancimino house 'for work' or business, that is, out of professional necessity, and then there were the close friends, those with whom the control-freak politician shared his free time and days of rest. From Massimo and Giovanni we have been able to gather a picture of the Ciancimino map of power: the generals being Cassina, the Salvo cousins, Vassallo and then the Mafiosi, Provenzano, Riina and Bontade. Of these only Bernardo Provenzano, as we know from Don Vito, held a fixed position in his hierarchy of friends.

But then there were the others: the loyal ground troops who

were also, in a certain sense, the victims of Ciancimino's touch-iness and overbearing nature. A gallery of people 'faithful' to their protective deity who moved in the circles most familiar to Don Vito: the houses in Via Sciuti, in Baida, in Mondello. They were the people Massimo calls 'puppets in the hands of the puppet master'.

MASSIMO: In essence, my father was the head of a clan. His relatives and friends were the means that allowed him to obtain almost total control over everything he was connected with. He worked at home precisely because it was where he felt most secure and in full control, far away from prying ears and eyes. Secrecy was the most potent weapon in the power structure he built. On the other hand, it was impossible to think of Lo Verde, one of the Mafia bosses always on the run, coming down to an office or the town hall for a meeting. As one of his most trusted friends, Lo Verde had access to the most secure houses in Baida and Mondello, especially when it turned out to be particularly difficult to organize the usual appointments in those places made available by the friendly network that represented a well-heeled Palermo above all suspicion. But with Baffo there was one line of communication he always kept open. By his bedside were four telephones, like a business manager's desk. He always knew which telephone was ringing and never once lifted the wrong receiver. At night, seeing that he needed silence to the point where he used earplugs, he disconnected three of the four phones, leaving only the one plugged in. This was a highly confidential number, which was used at the Mondello villa as well, and I can still remember it: 454279. (A prefix wasn't necessary then.) There were only two telephone points in the whole house, one in his bedroom, the other in the drawing room so he could use the phone during meetings. This number was known only to a very few privileged people, the only ones who could reach him at any time of day: first and foremost was Signor Lo Verde, then Salvo Lima, his political friend-and-enemy, and also Giovanni Gioia, the minister, then Attilio Ruffini, another minister, and the Hon. Franz Gorgone and obviously Enzo Zanghì and Signor Franco, who was always there behind the scenes.

One of my father's most valued collaborators was his secretary Enzo Zanghì, who was a second cousin. Under his protector's umbrella he was politically active, obviously for the Christian Democrat line. He was the main channel for all daily business: if you wanted an appointment with Assessor Ciancimino, you had to go through him.

In Via Sciuti there was the tradition of the Wednesday meeting. One by one the faithful Enzo summoned the various members of the society and welcomed them as they arrived. That house was set up as if it were, let's say, a ministry. I can still remember the sadness of the meeting room that had been decorated to order by Aldo Rappelli, the architect: a glass table seating twenty was placed in the centre and, at the far end, an enormous sofa running along the wall was able to seat another fifteen. That was the drawing room for politics; the other one – the good one – my mother would never have given over to that mob of city and provincial councillors and goodness knows who else.

These meetings would go on for ever; they could start at five in the afternoon and last until midnight, often with heated discussion. When the meeting proper was finished, those who counted most lingered on to chat with my father until the small hours. Naturally, one was Zanghì, who at one time was appointed head of the city's water supply, but also Totuccio Castro, one of the loyal ground troops who had held important positions on Palermo's city councils, Councillor Totò Midolo, the Hon. Franz Gorgone and Gino Pennino, the doctor. This last would be much talked about in the 1990s when he was placed under arrest and persuaded to collaborate with the magistrates. [Testimony regarding this can be found in both the Palermo trial documents, as well as the records of the National Anti-Mafia Commission.]

And lastly there was the poker group, completely dominated by my father's whims. He even decided people's vacation plans, both the length of time and the place. I never knew if people were happy to spend their holidays in Salsomaggiore or Sirmione. On the other hand, Baffo's every decision was final. Even that of bringing his lover and her husband on holiday with him or his ban on smoking, which only happened after he'd had to give up himself. So there were friends at the gaming table, but also welcome guests at the dinner table for a meal at La Scuderia, which we have already mentioned: Uncle Aldo, Piazza the construction developer, Dottore Galbo the physician, *Ingegnere* Biondo, head of the city's engineering division, and Pino Lisotta, a relative of ours who lived in the same building in Via Sciuti.

He came to a terrible end, this relative of ours. He was born in Corleone, a Christian Democrat like my father, and was also elected a town councillor. He was a doctor with the local health service and, at a certain point while my father was at the top, was appointed director of Corleone's Ospedale dei Bianchi. I remember that he was always afraid that he might unwittingly commit some illegal act. In the years following Dad's arrest by Giovanni Falcone, this fear would become an obsession.

In order to understand exactly how dogged he felt by this fear of ending up like his cousin, there's an example in the occasion when, in quite a rage, he sent back a present – a silver bowl – sent him by the builder who had renovated the Corleone hospital. This was a gesture the builder couldn't understand, as it was absolutely unheard of in the ambit of his working relationships. Indeed, he misunderstood it so much so that he saw its return as a demand for something more precious. So the builder had an enormous one delivered that cost a good deal more. Pino went ballistic and, equally without ceremony, sent that gift back as well. It was then that the man really began to worry and asked my father to enlighten him. Dad let out a roar of laughter, knowing his cousin and his fears all too well. However, the episode served to discourage once and for all any act of generosity or offer of favours in Pino's regard.

The day of the arrest, Baffo was taken ill and Pino was called to help him out. But when we saw him, we could see that he felt worse than my father, so much so that we had to convince him to forget about it and get himself home. But from then on, like the drop of water that carves out rock, the horror of ending up in gaol and losing everything began to eat into him. He rallied a little when he was appointed director of Palermo's most important health centre, but it didn't last long because first the death of his wife and then retirement spiralled him into depression again. He went back to living in fear, and suddenly lost weight so he looked physically ill: he would wake up in the night after imaginary rings of the entry-phone thinking the police had come to arrest him, and during the day would keep away from the house because he was afraid of officers arriving at the door. And yet he never received any judicial summons, even in Palermo's hotbed of confusion. He was a rare honest thing in the panorama of the city's health service administration.

For us boys Pino Lisotta was more than a cousin, he was a second father: we could count on his help for anything. During the time of the second Mafia war and its killing spree and the death of Salvo Lima, the ex-mayor in Andreotti's camp and Christian Democrat MEP, Pino picked up the anxiety of Nando Liggio, a university lecturer and eyewitness to the killing who became obsessed with coming to the same end as Lima. The same terror was also transmitted to him by Sebastiano Purpura, Lima's right-hand man, who was frightened of the consequences of knowing his boss's secrets, but primarily of becoming a dangerous witness himself and therefore a target as well.

Lisotta couldn't stand all this stress, as he was convinced that in a short time the lid would be lifted on all the corruption of that period. Then after my father was arrested a second time, this became a certainty for him. He was found hanging in his bedroom: he had used the cord of the roller blind to kill himself. But as far as the public knew, Pino died of a heart attack, which was recorded on his death certificate. In order to hide the marks left by the cord, they 'dressed him up' in a rollneck sweater. We all mourned him, especially us boys.

But there was another method of receiving guests in Via Sciuti 85R. We have already had an image of it in the unusual scene of a Cosa Nostra boss standing at the foot of the bed where my father received all his visitors. This bedroom truly was his office with papers and newspapers spread over the covers and the floor, together with pens, pencils and an ashtray brimming with dog ends, including those of whoever had been sitting in the armchair facing the bed.

A good office that is secure and trustworthy must also possess a safe or have very good hiding places. My father kept his cash in a metal box set in the lower part of the wall of his dressing room hidden behind three false sockets that could be lifted out with a light pressure of the hand. The key to the box was camouflaged by many other keys together in a bowl on the bedside table in the bedroom.

Then there was the hiding place for his papers and his bankbooks in particular. A metal box wasn't very trustworthy because a metal detector could discover it. So my father turned to a Signor Pellerito, a carpenter he had been put on to by his friends Bonura and Buscemi. An exceptional cabinetmaker, this man had invented a magnificent system and had already tried it out in the homes of many *capimafia*, including Totò Riina.

Pellerito built a long and narrow wooden drawer designed to take the papers and bankbooks under false names, which he hid in a part of the kitchen wall. When my father wanted to transfer illicit sums, he called up this carpenter, who came at 1.00 p.m., which is when the caretaker's lodge closed. The man then went silently and professionally to work in the kitchen and removed six tiles known only to him and the owner of the house. At 2.30 p.m. my father would go to the bank where he had made an appointment with the manager. He made his deposits; the bank updated the books, which were quickly put back in their place by Signor Pellerito, who was so scrupulous that he camouflaged the operation by discolouring the fresh grout with one of my mother's shoes. This practice was repeated every two to three months; each time my mother and we children were politely asked to eat in the drawing room.

Living Dangerously

A system of politics and business like the one created by Vito Ciancimino naturally couldn't be sustained solely by the 'good manners' of the celebrated kiss on the cheek of Mafia iconography, or the word of honour or the much-trumpeted supremacy of politics. It was a much more complicated system than that. Indeed the peaceful coexistence between the two powers – Mafia and politics – rested fundamentally on the guarantees offered by single individuals in continuous dialogue that assured a smooth pathway to wealth and economic security with no excessive moments of crisis. According to the story of his sons, which has also been handed to the magistrates, it was all possible because their father was above all the guarantor not only of a policy of 'equal shares' but also of the calming and providential presence of a Lo Verde/Provenzano and the ineffable Signor Franco's wise suggestions towards maintaining a stable status quo.

But if politics was ready to accept an unnatural dialogue with the Mafia it is also possible that in any extreme situation – perhaps any disturbance at all – then a problem of communication could arise with the two sides speaking two different languages. The criminal side ended with recourse to the only language it knew, namely that of violence and bullying. And despite all his precautions and the protection he enjoyed, even Don Vito found himself having to deal with the rough side of Cosa Nostra's communications.

GIOVANNI: I was still a young boy of fifteen when I could really experience for myself the fact that my father – who was mayor at that time – had a job that was anything but tranquil.

As happened every Sunday morning after the ritual visit to my grandfather's grave in the Capuchin Cemetery, we were in the car driving to the usual bar for the usual chocolate ice cream. The road was narrow but nevertheless a high-performance car was able to come screeching past and overtake us. From the car door emerged a hand holding a police 'Stop' sign, while another dark car came up close behind to the back bumper. It seemed like a normal traffic control. A man wearing a brown suede bomber jacket came up and my father opened the conversation.

'Here are my papers, everything's in order.'

'We're not interested in them, we're not the law. We stopped you because there's someone who wants to speak to you urgently.'

'Perhaps you don't know who I am. I happen to be the mayor and if a certain gentleman wishes to speak to me, you can tell him to make an appointment with my secretary and perhaps I'll be able to see him. Now would you please tell your friends to move their cars, because I've no more time to waste.'

'We know very well who you are. Now please don't create any problems for me. We received the order to take you to this person and, believe me, there's no way any disobedience will be tolerated.'

'Your problems are no concern of mine. You can tell whoever's sent you that I've no intention of speaking with him, especially after an introduction of this kind . . .'

All this time there were some very unreassuring faces coming up around the car. One ugly brute was about to make a move on us, but the one who seemed to be in charge kept him back.

'Mr Mayor, do please come along with us. Don't force us to use uncongenial methods, we're all armed. Now I'm the quiet sort, but then I'm only speaking for myself. My friends here, well, they can get upset.'

My father, who knew these weren't empty words, tried to get them to release me, but only managed to get our middleman to drive me in our car, while he agreed to go with the

others. The journey took a little over half an hour along dirt
roads through a village out in the open country. The house to
which we'd been invited was part of a farm, two storeys high,
and very anonymous, in a farmyard full of implements.

My father went upstairs, while I was taken through to the
ground-floor kitchen and left with soft drinks and ice cream.
I was alone for nearly an hour, until I couldn't resist the temptation to slip out. This was something I shouldn't have tried.
I found myself face to face with a massive dog, a pedigree
Molossian [a type of mastiff] breed that was ready to go for
me. While I broke out in a cold sweat of fear, I made a mental
calculation of my chances of successfully reaching the kitchen
door without getting bitten. I began a desperate run chased
by the baying brute that ended up biting my index finger just
as I was slamming the door on its muzzle. The finger was
bleeding a lot and I was feeling faint from the pain. I was able
to staunch the bleeding with large amounts of sugar, as I'd
seen used in kitchen accidents at home. But the waiting wasn't
over. Although my finger wasn't bleeding any more, I couldn't
get out because of the dog, and so with time to kill I began
to go through the kitchen drawers. To my great surprise, in
one I found a complete set of surgical knives, all clean and
set in the right order. In another were two brand-new gleaming
pistols: one an automatic, the other a revolver. I picked up the
revolver and, pointing it at the light fitting, was about to squeeze
the trigger when the man in the suede jacket came in and,
with his usual phlegm, told me to hand over the weapon immediately as it was 'loaded'. 'And remember,' he said, 'when there's

a pistol in your hand, you have to be ready to shoot, or you'll risk coming to a bad end.' But he saw to the injured finger as skilfully as a doctor.

I joined my father, who was already at the wheel of our car. He was looking gloomy. I'd never seen him with such a black expression, not even on the day his father died. On the way home I tried to get him to tell me who'd organized a meeting in that way. He was silent, and then he looked for a place to stop and speak to me while looking me in the eye.

'Now listen to me carefully. You're no longer a child. And promise me you'll never speak a word to anyone – I mean anyone, relatives included – about what happened today. So no more questions, just forget about the whole thing. When I'm no more, then you can please yourself.'

About a year later, at some festivity open to non-members at an old traditionalist sailing club on the Mondello waterfront, I saw the man in the suede jacket again. I recognized him immediately and went up to greet him and remind him of the occasion we first met.

'Don't you remember? You put a dressing on my injured finger that the dog had bitten. Look, you can still see the scar.'

'I'm sorry, I don't think I know you. Perhaps you're mistaking me for someone else.'

He said goodbye and went off to mingle with the other guests.

I told my father about seeing the man and he was perhaps even more perturbed than the time before.

'I hope you pretended you'd never set eyes on him.'

'No, it was the opposite, Papà. It was he who pretended not to know me.'

'Son, you're an idiot. You should never have done that. I told you to wipe the episode clean from your mind and you start a conversation with the man, saying that you recognize him? Those are dangerous people who'll stop at nothing, as you've seen for yourself. I'm telling you for the last time to forget all about the matter.'

I never came to know who arranged to take us to that house, nor the nature of the talk with my father. I imagine it had to do with some special favour that went beyond the normal problematical bounds of politics.

However that wasn't the only time that there was serious friction within the community. The latter half of the 1970s offered several other difficult moments and was the stage of a dangerous proximity with that world of – let's say – business, inhabited by questionable property developers, men who swindled the public purse and Mafia constructors, such as Stefano Bontade, Mimmo Teresi and Don Pino Abbate.

Around 1976, just before the middle of August, there was a top-secret meeting in our house in Via Danae in Mondello that was longer and more explosive than usual. The subject of this animated assembly was the construction of a huge residential area on the outskirts of Palermo with housing, schools, shops and sports facilities. Despite my father's mediation, they couldn't agree on the division of the contracts cake and a first attempt at reconciling their differences at the home of Don Tano Badalamenti, boss of the Cinisi, had proved useless.

The meeting ended in the early hours after a great deal of shouting. A little later I heard a sharp squeal of braking tyres outside the house and a very noisy departure. At the entry gate the following morning, our housemaid Pina found a package and an envelope containing a card that she brought into the kitchen. My mother took one look at the letter and knew it wasn't the shopping she ordered. On the card the following was written in capital letters: 'This is a gift for Sig. Ciancimino. Before throwing it away, look at it carefully and reflect.' Distracted as she always was, my mother told the maid to open it and away she went. It was Pina's cry that called her back into the kitchen. Inside the package was the decapitated head of a young goat, still fresh with blood. To make the message even more macabre they'd put out its eyes, leaving sharp pieces of wood a little smaller than the one stuck in the poor animal's mouth. Pina started to scream, while my mother had to lie down on the sofa and regain her senses with a glass of sugar water. I wasn't feeling very well myself, being really upset at the gory sight. They asked me to call my father, but – remembering the scene he made the last time we'd woken him to take a call from the Hon. Mario D'Acquisto – I thought twice about it. That decapitated head wasn't going anywhere, I thought. But the racket was such that Baffo woke up anyway, ready – as always – to give us hell. He didn't even notice the 'gift' in full view on the kitchen table. When my mother pointed to it he didn't seem very upset. He read the card and calmed us down with his 'I'll see to it.' After which he shut himself up in his room and was on the phone for a long time.

The same day he asked me to come with him to a meeting. He drove, but as usual wanted someone with him because of his fear of suddenly falling ill. While we were crawling along the motorway at a funeral pace, I asked him to explain the meaning of the gift package. His reply was evasive.

'You have to understand that being in Sicilian politics, especially in Palermo, is one of the most difficult things in this world. Apart from other politicians, you have to deal with developers impatient to realize their plans and those on the other side who are even more dangerous and more demanding. Everything was ready to bring about a huge residential development and it looked as if we had an agreement, when suddenly an outside interest sent everything to pieces.'

'What do you mean by "those on the other side"?'

'There's no reason for you to know because we're talking about people who only create problems and with whom it is difficult to discuss things. That goat's head gives you a clear idea of what they're like.'

We linked up with a car outside Cinisi that took us to a villa by the sea. An elegant man in a dark jacket and tie met us and greeted my father respectfully in the third person, kissing him on both cheeks. He kissed me as well, introducing himself as Gaetano Badalamenti. He mentioned some mutual American acquaintances I'd met recently on a dangerous mission in New York, as usual on my father's orders, of which we'll speak later.

There was a lavish spread on the table with many people dressed all the same for a special occasion who all began to speak with my father. I have to say I felt as if I was on a set of

The Godfather. The atmosphere wasn't very relaxed, everyone engaged in talking rather than eating. The climax came when Badalamenti, who never desisted from his honeyed but menacing manner, came up to his VIP guest with a bottle and corkscrew in his hands.

'I want you to drink,' he said, 'one of the best red wines in my cellar. It's a bottle that's waited years to be opened and today the moment's come. As with a man, when the hour comes no one can escape his destiny.' As he spoke these words with a serious face and with slow studied gestures pulled the cork out of the bottle, everyone in the room fell silent.

'It's a very fine wine and this glass is for you.' He held the first glass up to the light to show its clarity, then offered it to my father who, although he was teetotal, had no choice but take the wine and appreciate the taste. What followed was a disaster: to the boss's evident disappointment, no argument could reconcile the different quarrelling sides. And so when two guests, who were far from happy with the way the discussion was going, decided to cut short the debate, the host pointed to the door and didn't see them out. The meeting had practically broken up when Badalamenti asked my father to stay behind for a few more minutes. He left the house looking as if he'd had terrible news. I don't know how the matter ended, but I do know of a small coda that was unsettling.

Several days later, there was an envelope with no stamp in our post box addressed to Signor Vito Ciancimino, but that was in some way something to do with me.

I was summoned to his room and naturally found him in

bed, listening to tunes from his younger days. There was no dialogue, only a soliloquy.

'I'm sure that your mother, who can never keep her mouth shut, has told you about the letter we received. Its authors are the same people who sent us the goat's head. Among its many ravings, the letter also contains vague hints about my eldest son, which would be you. At the moment I haven't yet had time to discover if we're dealing with people who are really dangerous or only with bigmouths who're simply trying to intimidate me. Let's give them the benefit of the doubt, however, and I'm going to ask you to keep your evenings out to the bare minimum. I've nothing else to say, you're free to go if you wish.'

I had a lot of questions, but his look didn't invite them. Was he frightened? I don't know, but it was symptomatic that, immediately afterwards, he brought forward one of my American trips.

5

America, the Vatican and the Mysteries of Modern Italy

In contrast to the other big names in the party – from Lima to Gunnella to Purpura, who denied the existence of any dangerous relationships – Vito Ciancimino was the only one to justify his questionable dealings with the Mafia by recourse to metaphor. 'If you're born in the jungle,' he used to say, 'then you have to learn to survive in the jungle. If not, what do you do, shut your door and never go out any more?' Don Vito believed that environmental conditions were part of the game and there was no getting around them: there wasn't any kind of direct opposition to the Mafia – 'that's like the lion in the jungle' – that would have had any chance of success. And so it was a matter of continuing with the sly winks and compromises, which in any case was the choice shared by the majority of the people who were used, as ever, to making a virtue of necessity in the name of 'the quiet life'.

It is evident, however, that a similar politics of delimited sovereignty hung like a sword of Damocles over the heads of the administrators and strategists of alliances in the parties. In his notes Vito Ciancimino himself repeats obsessively a series of arguments that tries to explain the logic, if there is one to be discerned, of this unscrupulous approach to politics. He did nothing but underline the 'difficult' nature of the business at every opportunity: 'You have to satisfy everyone, and also be accountable to those people you'd happily rather tell to get lost.' And then there was the Mafia. Certainly there was Lo Verde/Provenzano, with whom he found himself in harmony in the job of perpetual middleman in taking the Christian Democrat party line. But there were others on the offensive that were greedy and insatiable. These were the thugs, the ones with no brains and no education who were capable of a sense-less violence that was even counter-productive given the judi-cial difficulties it regularly created. These were the men whom Don Vito defined as 'those on the other side', as he explained when his son Giovanni came to be threatened.

Ciancimino's capacity to divide his loyalties was hard to believe: half of him was adviser and associate of 'the other side', the other half of him was critical of their decisions especially when, annoyed at the obtuseness of 'those dickheads', he had to put up with them. Given his arrogance, Totò Riina came to be one of those most frequently charged with this epithet.

But the business was 'difficult' for other reasons as well. There was the danger of criminal investigations: you couldn't trust the ordinary cops, and the Carabinieri were even worse. Matters were different with the judiciary and we shall shortly see why. Then there was a whole world – a world of different stripes – that troubled the perfect consensus machine: the dirt-poor disappointed by empty promises, the trade unionists claiming their workers' rights, the opposition parties and their newspapers. The afternoon newspaper *L'Ora* caused a great deal of trouble. Every day there was some headline against them, some exposé, a new criticism; its continual banging on about the Mafia and its collusion with politics had already instigated the setting up of a special parliamentary commission whose curiosity was potentially harmful. The 'long arm of the Communists' was how the friends of the 'system' labelled the newspaper's penniless journalists, without even the merest suspicion that only half of its editorial staff were card-carrying members of the Italian Communist Party (PCI).

The red peril of the Communists was Don Vito's other real obsession and that of many of his happy gang of supporters who were fearful not so much of losing their good name as of the advance of the 'Cossacks' who were ready to deprive them of their accumulated wealth. This fear was also fed by the more or less hidden persuaders like 'Signor Franco' that Ciancimino was already associated with in the 1970s, making capital out of his analyses and suggestions that were always angled – as Don Vito later told his son Massimo – towards the maintenance of political and business stability, which were the greatest guarantee against the Communist threat.

Over the years those suggestions would bring Ciancimino and Sicilian politics to the centre of the large jigsaw puzzle created by hidden forces that have repeatedly put the country's democratic colours at risk. It is surprising to track the one-time mayor's movements as, even with the Gladio shadow falling on him, he's continually on the move and comes into contact with the main players of the mysteries of modern Italy, from Calvi and Gelli to the Mafia paymaster Pippo Calò: a cocktail of money, Mafia, corruption and political conspiracies – above all of which the case of Aldo Moro stands out – and all justified by the necessities of American anticommunist policy.

During one of the case hearings in 1991, Vito explains to the magistrates the motives that led him to make investments in Canada.

'Everything came about,' he says, 'from the successes the Communist Party had in the local elections in Italy in 1975. This caused apprehension in the whole business world because of fears that if this success were repeated on a larger scale in the following year's national elections, then there could have been a complete changing of the guard. For this reason there was an exodus of around L35 billion that placed the government in such difficulty that it had to issue the famous law in 1976 on the export of capital, which has now been rescinded. The idea of acquiring property abroad was born at that time in order to safeguard people's wealth. One of the countries pointed out to us in which to make investments was Canada. And there we went.'

GIOVANNI: In Palermo, even before the swing towards property, they began to have dealings abroad through the banks. Switzerland seemed like a sort of paradise because it was beyond the Italian authorities' reach. In effect, the secrecy associated with the credit institutions there – at that moment truly unbreachable – was the most concrete guarantee that neither the Italian tax authorities nor the excise police could have any chance of gaining access to any Swiss accounts opened by Sicilians.

There was a moment in my adolescence when, following the accident that left me in a coma, I had to go for treatment to a special clinic in Lugano. It was probably 1970. My father took the job of taking me there on the train. As usual we stopped over for two days in Rome, then in Milan. Here my father had countless meetings with people I didn't know. On the day before we left for Lugano, one of them gave him a black leather briefcase and a small key. From that moment on and for the whole journey my father was extremely anxious and wouldn't be separated from that piece of luggage. He ended up eating in the hotel room so as not to lose sight of it.

He couldn't even relax on the train, and when we arrived at the frontier, waiting to be checked by customs, he hid the briefcase between the seat cushion and compartment wall, covering it with his overcoat. The customs officials came on and one extremely fussy one asked us to open our baggage. My father kept up the seraphic demeanour he adopted and explained the reason for the journey was the problem I had with my health, which was confirmed by the medical papers the officials had meanwhile found. The inspection was thus brought to a close and they went away after giving me a consoling pat on the head.

Once over the border, my father's expression changed. He

was beaming and, with the briefcase always at his side, said to me: 'Today's a great day, treasure it in your memory. I want to celebrate straightaway in a good restaurant and I'll make an exception to the rule and order a slice of chocolate cake.'

At the station in Lugano we were met by a tall bony gentleman dressed all in black. After the promised lunch, the three of us went into an austere building on which were the words 'Union de Banques Suisses'. The man in black asked us if I was also coming in and my father said yes: 'He's coming in with us, he's still a boy but I think it's right for him to start to understand the business of life.' Then, turning to me, he whispered in my ear: 'I'm putting my trust in you, so everything you see and hear has to remain a secret between the two of us. You mustn't say a word even to your mother.'

We were welcomed by an obsequious director who had us sit around a table where my father opened the briefcase, saying with great aplomb: 'This is the sum of one million Swiss francs.' The money went into the safe deposit box and Dad was given a receipt and an instruction: 'Please remember this account number because for us it's essential, the deposit's completely anonymous.' We exited from a side door onto a back street. As we were leaving, we were given other precautions to observe: 'Next time come to this door, don't give your name over the entry phone, only the account number. And it's better not to use the main entrance; it has happened that the Italian police have photographed clients and you're a public figure who wouldn't escape notice.' This was the first current account my father opened abroad.

The American Adventure

The link with Brooklyn and its American cousins, the 'Broccolini' (Brooklyners) of Cosa Nostra, helped many Sicilians open a road towards a better life. Everyone used the relatives they had there. Honest workers knocked on the doors of friends and acquaintances who had landed in New York and already settled in through their own efforts, others sought support among the 'fellow countrymen' who in essence had exported the questionable system of favours and friendships from the clans and the words they put in for them. The story of investing in property in America that Giovanni tells is an entertaining episode, a sharply drawn sketch of a mentality, a culture, a world that perhaps has not entirely disappeared: the welcome in the Italo-American community, the guaranteed willingness of people not personally known but motivated by the links of belonging. The man behind it all was Michel Corrado Pozza, the lawyer and 'fixer' – part friend, part gangster, whom Vito had met in Milan when the lawyer was investing on behalf of businesses in the North – who supervised the entire operation.

GIOVANNI: In the years that followed, the advent of Communism and the end of private property became rooted in his mind as a fixed obsession. He talked about it all the time and with everyone: there was hell to pay if you contradicted him and he went especially berserk if it was his own party members who attempted it. Included in this hypothesis of the future was the flight of the whole family to the United States, and thus he began the plan for property investment in Montreal in Canada, on the advice of several friends in Milan.

The operation appeared complicated because it had to be done without his setting foot there. At that time he would never ever take an aeroplane. And so I had to go in his place.

I was a little over twenty when I took the flight to Montreal. Michel Pozza had already pointed out two properties to purchase: a shopping centre and a residential complex. A notary friend had already been brought in to register the deeds and the money already transferred from the Union de Banques Suisses to a current account opened by Pozza in my name at Montreal's Canadian Bank of Commerce.

The transaction was celebrated with a stylish dinner at the home of Pozza and the girlfriend who was about to become his third wife. Michel was different from the way my father had described him. He was neither overweight nor in poor health and bald, but quite the opposite: he was slim with an enormous quiff of hair. The 'miracle', as Pozza defined it, was the work of Liz, the beautiful fiancée with whom he was dreaming of a happy old age. But the plan would remain only a dream because Pozza wasn't able to reach old age, killed by someone in that dangerous world, the same one that I encountered on my very first evening there during a dinner held in my honour. There were more than thirty people, fellow lawyers of Pozza, property developers and even two federal judges. Michel introduced me to a huge obese man at the head of the table whose name was Sam and who, as I later learned, was financially the most powerful man in the city. I held out my hand, but Sam said, 'You only offer your hand to strangers,' then he rose from his seat and kissed me on both cheeks.

The mission had an unusual extra. My father had given me a cine camera to make a film of his new properties and show it to him and the family. But as the machine Baffo had given me wasn't up to it, I had to turn to the latest American technology. I returned to Italy with a decent video recording in which I was immortalized against the background of the shopping centre just purchased, while I was singing its praises. The performance was shown in the evening in the presence of the entire nuclear family marshalled into the living room.

On the same trip I stopped over in New York where my father had rented a small apartment. Here too I made contact with a series of notable characters, one of whom was his good friend Frank Ferro. According to what Sam had told me in Montreal Frank was the son-in-law of the 'good soul Charles Gambino', head of the New York 'families'. In fact one evening I had the opportunity to see the strength of this when I came up against a few problems in a New York discotheque. I was at a table with a friend and two girls when three threatening and volatile types invited us to vacate the premises, but only after having left our two girlfriends with them. I don't know how, but I managed to phone Frank, who said, 'Don't worry, don't do a thing, just hang on. I'll see to the rest.' There then passed several minutes that I'll never forget. Then two characters came in, one small with a large stomach, the other slim with a thin moustache. In any eventual exchange of blows they would probably have come off worse than us. But it didn't come to that. The shorter one approached without even a glance at the other three.

'Frank told me that there's some problem. Perhaps you don't like the music or maybe the whisky's not too good? I can't think there'd be any problem from the presence of these three idiots here.'

In my mind I had already resigned myself to the idea that my life would come to an end in a New York disco, thousands of miles from home. And in fact the ugliest of the volatile types leaned over more threateningly than ever.

But the short man stopped him.

'Now don't get overexcited, come over here with me. I'll spell out the fact that you're an idiot and then it's up to you.'

They went to one side and he whispered something in the guy's ear. Whatever it was it transformed the wolf into a lamb.

'I beg your pardon, but I had no idea you might be a friend of Frank's. If you won't take offence, I'd like to buy you a drink.'

But my guardian angel with the belly answered for me.

'We don't want to have a drink with you guys. Because of you I was woken up in the middle of the night while I was having a beautiful dream. Now beat it, the three of you.'

The other angel, the thin one with the moustache, who had been silent up to that point, went up to the head of the rough nuts and took him by his ear.

'Didn't you hear my friend?' he said. 'Now get lost and remember this date because it's been your lucky day.'

Calvi, the Vatican Bank and Lucio Gelli

MASSIMO: The decision to get funds out of the country was neither by chance nor off the cuff. My father told me that it was a matter of a strategy worked out in theoretical terms. The Canadian business, for example, was born in the wake of experiences that had already happened to other friends. Montreal hosted the 1976 Olympics and a huge building expansion was taking place together with excellent opportunities to take out bank loans on very easy terms. My father got news of this in Rome at a meeting with Caltagirone and Nino Salvo.

Besides, the search for a better means of hiding money was his abiding obsession. As we know, there were homemade hiding places and bankbooks hidden in the walls of the house. There were bankers ready to allow him to make deposits and withdrawals without leaving any record of the transactions. The first qualitative leap forward in hiding illicit funds came when he succeeded in joining the mechanism – up to a certain point reserved only for a few privileged individuals – that allowed him to make use of the huge cover of the IOR (Institute for Religious Works), the Vatican's bank which has already featured in several parts of this narrative.

It was the property developer Count Romolo Vaselli junior who introduced my father into these secret chambers and put a first safe deposit box at his disposal. The Count told him he had first heard about the IOR from a well-known and influential Roman politician, who said he had several boxes he used for cash and documents. [Massimo Ciancimino would make these accusations as part of an investigation into the origins of Berlusconi's assets at the Court of Palermo.] These particulars had been confirmed for my father by Salvo Lima, who it appears had been introduced to the Vatican earlier than he was. When later we began to work on his memoirs, my father told me he met Lima many times inside the IOR. Payments and transfers of cash took place there and the account of the so-called 'large pot' was very busy. I've never actually been inside the bank myself. I used to go with him and saw that he would go into the chemist's under the pretext of buying some Tonopan, an analgesic for my mother, while I stayed outside and waited for him.

He also met Roberto Calvi many times, either at the IOR or the Nord Italia bank. I witnessed one of these encounters in June or July 1980. As usual, I'd been drafted to accompany him on one of his six-monthly visits to Prof. De Preux's practice in Lausanne where he had a safety deposit box and a bank account with the UBS. The trip therefore perhaps had a double function for him: he could check up on the state of his health and on his finances at the same time. The five or six times I went with him, the journey never changed once: we left Palermo on the panoramic Peloritano train with Rome the first stop and a night at the Hotel Mediterraneo on Via Cavour; after which we took the first class Settebello express to Milan where we stayed at the Hotel Duomo.

It was here the 1980 meeting took place. I met Roberto Calvi at the hotel entrance and, having no idea who he was, made him welcome until my father came down. They talked for over an hour, giving me the impression from the way they greeted each other that they had already met before. I was sitting some distance away, but kept in sight and was ready to respond to any possible requests. After a couple of days we continued on our journey to Lausanne, De Preux and the UBS. And in that city my father would meet an intermediary.

At other times, my father later told me, he and Calvi met inside the Vatican Bank, as ever over the business of money. Indeed, he specified, it was during one of these appointments that Calvi gave him considerable sums siphoned from state-owned industries. It was a matter of funds to be divided up between my father and other politicians. My father left the cash in the Roman deposit box – he wasn't happy travelling with lots of money – with the intention of distributing the cut to each 'colleague' using money from his accounts in Palermo. The same system was used for the kickbacks around the famous Enimont scandal, the mother of all such scandals, at the end of the 1980s. Inside the IOR my father received around L800 million, which was then distributed by the hand of Salvo Lima to Sicily's politicians.

I saw Calvi again, but this time on the television when he was found dead in London. It was the year of the World Cup in 1982 and I was confined to bed in the Via Danae villa in Mondello.

A motorcycle accident had resulted in a broken femur and other fractured bones, so that I was watching the football without being all that fond of the sport and saw the banker's photograph. The meeting at the Hotel Duomo two years earlier came to mind. When I mentioned the news, my father didn't seem particularly surprised and let the matter drop. Only several years later, when we were sketching out the plan of his memoirs, did he tell me that Roberto Calvi had been killed because he'd made risky investments with money that was not his, illicit money that belonged to Cosa Nostra.

My father also encountered Licio Gelli at the beginning of the 1990s, before his second arrest that occurred in December 1992. The first meeting happened at a conference organized to found an alliance that would unite the separatist movements of North and South. The assembly took place in Rome in a hotel on the Via Aurelia, close to one of the private clinics where he'd once been treated. The second took place in Cortina in the summer of 1991 in a hotel or Alpine chalet. I remember the year well because, apart from myself, my father was in the company of my sister Luciana, who was then expecting her daughter Adele, and a friend of hers, Roberta Alongi. Among those who counted in Palermo, the Alongi clothes shop owned by her family was an obligatory stopping point. Its window was always well set out with the latest designs in full view for Palermo society on Via Ruggero Settimo, the place for luxury items of all kinds: diamonds and fine cashmere, Rolex and Vacheron. Giovanni Alongi had been an excellent salesman at Battaglia Esquire Fashion, Palermo's other cathedral of style, then spread his wings and set up in competition ten doors away. It was a great success because for almost all the clients able to afford cashmere he was able to supply sweaters by the dozen, one in each colour, according to the season.

I think that for the Cortina meeting between my father and
Gelli investigations have already been carried out that confirm
the presence of the Ciancimino group at the Hotel Savoia and
of Gelli in a convent. The two men met in a discreet little room
in the well known restaurant Il Caminetto.

Pippo Calò and the Moro Affair

Don Pippo Calò was the Corleonesi's man in Rome. He left
Palermo during the first Mafia war that culminated in the Via
Lazio massacre in 1969 and the kidnapping and silencing of the
L'Ora journalist Mauro De Mauro in the following year. He
then disappeared, swallowed up by the black holes of the
capital that in those years was in the grip of the thousand
tentacles that the Mafia, Camorra and maverick secret services
were able to flex at will. These are the 1970s when Luciano Liggio
and Calò, who had become cashier of the 'families', financed
Cosa Nostra with the proceeds of kidnapping, reinvesting the
money in property development and the widespread traffic in
drugs. Furthermore, until the middle of the 1980s, these are the
years of the secret synergy between the Mafia and the Magliana
gang, as has emerged from a series of investigations that has
the gang in the role of service agency for the security appa-
ratus. A conspiracy runs through several of the most disturbing
episodes of these years: from the terrorist attacks using TNT in
the manner of the Camorra (Rome, January 1983, Vincenzo
Casilla, Raffaele Cutolo's right-hand man in the capital), to the

Mafia collusion in the 'black' terrorist conspiracies of the extreme right (the attack on the Rapido 904 train of December 1984 for which Pippo Calò was given a life sentence), to the 'film noir' of the disappearance of Emanuela Orlandi (June 1983) and the strange proximity of the Magliana's evil thugs with the upper echelons of the Vatican.

MASSIMO: My father knew Pippo Calò very well. Their relations were naturally nearly all of a financial nature. I know this because he told me so directly when we were thinking of writing his book of memoirs. There's a precise moment when I recall having seen them together in Rome.

It was 1984 and dark clouds were looming over my father: Judge Giovanni Falcone's investigations were in full swing and the *pentito* Tommaso Buscetta had already pointed my father out as a politician 'in the hands of the Corleonesi'. So that, with the usual medical check-up in Lausanne with Prof. De Preux coming round, that summer we decided on a longer trip. We stayed nearly a month in a place between Lausanne and St Vincent, for the most part in the Hotel Billia, which was directly linked to the Casino by means of a tunnel.

That long stay was neither a prearranged holiday nor a sudden whim. Baffo would never have stayed away from Palermo for so long without a good reason. The fact is that it had been suggested he stay away because judicial proceedings that looked to be serious were in the offing. As ever his friend Signor Franco, who appeared to be well informed about the innermost secrets of the courts of justice, had warned him about the possibility of being hit by a warrant for his arrest, the withdrawal of his passport or the seizure of his property.

During the course of the journey, the usual stopover at the Hotel Mediterraneo in Rome took place, which was at the end of July. I remember that in the Via Veneto my father met a man outside Capuano the jewellers. He came out from the shop, greeted him and together they set off walking in the direction of Porta Pinciana. They were in close conversation for over an hour. A good deal later, my father revealed that the man was Pippo Calò and that he had met him at other times, always in Rome in the Hotel Mediterraneo and sometimes in Salvo Lima's Rome apartment, which was in Via Campania, I think, running across the Via Veneto.

Calò gave out money and received it, always in cash, as was the custom. These were funds coming from kickbacks that were then distributed, as we know, among the political parties and several of the Cosa Nostra bosses. Still more could be stashed away in Switzerland. For the payments of the so-called 'straightening up' (read 'protection money') he turned to the IOR deposits.

But theirs wasn't only a financial relationship. I know from my father that he was in touch with Calò during the kidnapping of Aldo Moro. The story has many twists, but we can make a brief summary. There was a part of the Mafia that was also interested in seeking to free the statesman. In particular, this initiative was undertaken – so my father said – by the cousins Ignazio and Nino Salvo, in agreement with a part of the Sicilian Christian Democrats, especially the secretary Rosario Nicoletti and Salvo Lima. In order to undertake a kind of preliminary investigation, they called in none other than Pippo Calò, who knew the Roman scene very well. In fact, their faith was well placed because through his contacts with the Magliana gang it seems he succeeded in discovering the hideout in Via Gradoli where Moro was being held captive by members of the Red Brigades.

But then at the last minute something happened. My father said that the highest national levels of the Christian Democrat party had intervened to stifle interest in the matter.

It was a move that affected not only political circles. Even my father's traditional points of contact were showing they were against the plan to free Aldo Moro. He had shared the information in his possession both with Signor Franco and with his friend Lo Verde/Provenzano. Both of them advised him to go no further and halt the operation. Similar advice came to him from the Gladiò sphere, of which he was probably a part. The terminus of this counter-order, namely Pippo Calò, was informed by my father in person, who told of the decision in a meeting set up for this purpose. (On the subject of the Mafia's interest in securing the release of Aldo Moro, which was then aborted, there exist numerous accounts from the 'collaborators with justice', the most credible being from the *pentito* Francesco Marino Mannoia.)

Ustica and the Murder of Roberto Parisi

The Moro Case was not the only trouble Don Vito found himself involved with in his ambiguous role of politician in close contact with the secret service world. It will be up to the judiciary eventually to discover whether Ciancimino belonged to Gladio's counter-espionage set-up, but the following is Massimo's account of the events that unfolded in June 1980.

MASSIMO: About 9.30 one evening in Mondello we were out to dinner at the Circolo Lauria club. Then at a certain point a man came up to us who said he had an urgent message from Attilio Ruffini, who had been Minister of Defence until a few weeks previously. This message bearer told my father that Ruffini urgently required a meeting. The ex-minister was his great friend and carried great weight in the Sicilian Christian Democrat party.

What happened that evening in June 1980? It was the Ustica air disaster, the Itavia DC9 that disintegrated in mid-flight with eighty-one people on board. It was only later that the flight tracks of the Libyan MiG and the French secret services became known, but my father was told about it that night.

But this event also has a private side regarding *Ingegnere* Roberto Parisi, director of ICEM, the company that – thanks to my father – held the contract for Palermo's public lighting, and who was also the owner of the Palermo football team. His wife Elvira and his only daughter Alessandra were on that internal flight from Bologna to Palermo that went down near the island of Ustica. I can remember the sadness my father felt when he decided to tell his friend about the events that happened in the skies over the island that evening. His feelings were genuine, but he was also rigid in insisting that Parisi shouldn't think even for a minute about raising his voice in protest.

Roberto Parisi came to a terrible end. He was found dead one cold morning in February 1985 a couple of steps from his works in Partanna Mondello. Five killers surrounded him and finished him off, together with poor Giuseppe Mangano, who earned his living as his driver.

My father had been in prison for three months and so Parisi found himself without his protector. If Dad had been at liberty, he might possibly have been able to save him that time, as in the past, when the Mafia wanted his head to punish him for not maintaining agreements made solely on the word of honour.

Parisi's death caused terror in political circles and especially in his business associate, who went straight to Giovanni to arrange an urgent talk with my father to ask his advice, given Parisi's death, about what to do about running the ICEM business. He seemed beside himself, telling my brother and me (I'd just come back from Rome) that he was prepared to sell up everything so as not to end up like his partner. He also said that he'd been to Salvo Lima, who'd advised him, 'Go to Vito, speak with his sons.' He was really out of his mind.

I calmed him down saying that I'd bring forward the next meeting with my father in prison. When I saw him back in Rome in Rebibbia prison, I gathered he already knew the reason for bringing the meeting forward. His reply was clear: 'Tell Pierluigi to stay calm and continue running ICEM as normal because that wasn't the cause of the problem. But my advice is not to take any decision regarding the recent acquisition of the Mozia fish farm.'

He told me about the case of 'Icemare', a fish-farming enterprise situated in the Marsala 'Stagnone' that Parisi had taken over with the verbal agreement that he would sell it back as soon as Mario Niceta had resolved his liquidity problems and the firm's reorganization.

When the time came to reverse the apparent sale, Parisi had put forward demands outside the verbal agreement. He mentioned having undertaken investments and payments that had contributed to the growth of the firm's value and wanted these to be taken into account. Perhaps he wasn't totally wrong, but with those people reason counts for nothing. Only brute force, poor *Ingegner* Parisi.

All Together Now, With Feeling

The other political 'Big Chief' in this gang that succeeded in keeping hold on the reins of an entire population and its own interests, at home and abroad, was Salvo Lima. In contrast to Vito Ciancimino he was the classic affable Christian Democrat, always with a smile and – in his own way – open-handed in the sense that he knew how to distribute 'resources' wisely, taking care that some 'leftovers' percolated right down to where politicians rarely take a look. 'Eat and have others do the same' was his creed, a philosophy that was at the base of the immense client system that was able to guarantee the survival even of the less fortunate and a powerful electoral force for his party. This was the machinery of a consensus that lasted for nearly half a century: Lima and Ciancimino at the top of the pyramid, great dispensers of wealth, favours and immunity even to 'friends' in the other smaller parties, in particular the Republicans and Social Democrats, who were always ready to support him even in the more difficult situations. What legitimized the two leaders in the role of political bosses, beyond belonging to the great Christian Democrat family, was their ease of access to the 'grand bazaar' of Cosa Nostra. Indeed, even good old Salvo Lima had his saints in paradise, taking care nevertheless to keep a good distance from the high-tension wires and remain as far as possible within the ambit of so-called 'formal institutional correctness'.

He managed to obtain this by recourse to a political strategy carried out almost certainly behind the official lines and without raising his voice or doing anything that could attract the attention of the media spotlight. Few words in public, many contacts in private. In fact, Salvo Lima's public rallies could be counted on the fingers of one hand. He preferred receptions where he didn't have to speak to invited members of the electorate, or hotel conventions, such as those put on for him by his supporters and financial backers, with cousins Ignazio and Nino Salvo at the head, followed by the thousands of entrepreneurs and property developers we've met in Massimo's and Giovanni's accounts.

In short, he wasn't exactly what you would call a sparkling politician. There'll be no fundamental works of his for the record in the history of the Sicilian people. As we've said, his great ability was that of satisfying as many people as he could, and his clients certainly didn't go to him for tracts of political philosophy. Public opinion in Palermo was the expression of a minority that was destined to remain such. Even when Salvo Lima's star was beginning to decline, given the problem of continuing to defend a system ever more scandalously compromised by the Mafia, he never changed his stamp. In the mid-1980s, the Christian Democrat party ushered him sideways into the European Parliament, but Salvo hadn't a clue what the big issues were and all he could offer the electorate was condensed into: 'Sicily needs Europe and Europe needs Sicily.' The beginning and the end of his great political programme.

The *pentito* Tommaso Buscetta, who outlined in his testimony the greater part of the accusations collected at the trial of life senator Giulio Andreotti (for decades head of Lima's political camp and then Ciancimino's as well), told the judges that Salvo was the son of a 'man of honour' in a Central Palermo 'family', but this allegation hasn't been borne out. But on the friendships and connections of the man who was many times mayor and assessor of Palermo, however, there's less doubt, especially as his political history speaks for itself.

One common misconception, anyway, needs to be exploded: it wasn't the Andreotti faction that brought the Mafia into the Christian Democrat party. That political embrace had happened earlier, from a time when the party had no factions but rested on the coexistence of retainers of block votes, then called the 'bigwigs'.

The association between Don Vito and Lima was solid and, at least at certain times, showed no signs of backfiring. There was an almost physical continuity in that block of power. There was a tried and tested mechanism that fitted every situation. For example, there were the privileges. Is it a matter of chance that Lima's house in the so-called 'Via Roma Nuova' was bought by the developer Ciccio Vassallo, the very same person we've seen visiting Ciancimino's house? Furthermore, thanks to Palermo's mild climate, Lima spent a good part of the year in the Mondello summer residence in Via Danae. That road was a veritable icon of political power. Within a few metres it contained the homes of the most famous leaders: Ciancimino, Lima, Lauricella and Rosario Nicoletti, the respective secretaries of the Italian Socialist Party and the Christian Democrats. But it was also the symbol of their later collapse when on 12 March 1992 Cosa Nostra decided to close the account with the past and start a new strategy of terror, beginning with Lima's assassination just a couple of steps from Via Danae.

There was the ritual of morning coffee in Via Danae. Ciancimino went every Sunday morning, shortly before noon. They spoke calmly, without the rush of weekdays. It was an atmosphere more suited to securing agreements, but also for offering opinions on facts and events and, above all, trying to understand them. In 1982, for example, the main topic was news of the arrival of General Carlo Alberto Dalla Chiesa in Palermo with the dreaded function of Anti-Mafia Prefect. The presence of one of the highest-ranking Carabinieri officers sent to reclaim Sicilian politics – as was said by Giovanni Spadolini, then head of the government – was seen as a disaster. Vito Ciancimino has left the following comment: 'The fear of Dalla Chiesa's arrival developed into an out and out collective psychosis.' Such was the total opposition that the Prefect was left totally powerless and in deadly isolation. 'The General,' continues Don Vito, 'was so marginalized that everyone expected his resignation. I remember that Mario D'Acquisto [then President of the Region] told everyone that he'd heard from Spadolini that the General wouldn't have special powers because everyone was against it.' In fact, Dalla Chiesa never received the special powers he'd been promised and was killed exactly one hundred days after his arrival in Palermo. Vito Ciancimino recalled what he, Lima and Nino Salvo said on that occasion: 'I couldn't understand the reason for that murder. It seemed a waste of time given that, under the conditions imposed on him, Dalla Chiesa couldn't have caused us a pennyworth of harm. Lima, his eyes glowing with hatred, dropped his proverbial reserve and said to me, "For certain Romans he was more dangerous and ill-tempered in retirement than he was as a Prefect with special powers."' According to Don Vito, what Lima meant precisely was that Dalla Chiesa's demise was more useful in Rome than in Palermo.

MASSIMO: From 1983 to 1985 my father was in the eye of a hurricane of investigations into his accumulated wealth and in particular his Canadian property investments. The inquiry was led by Giovanni Falcone, who was extremely well informed on how the politics-Mafia system worked thanks to the testimony of the *pentito* Tommaso Buscetta.

In this period my father found himself in great difficulty because that particular investigating magistrate didn't fit into the framework that for years had characterized the judiciary's activity.

Before Falcone things were very different in Palermo. After his second arrest and while he was fighting once again to stop his property being seized, he told me that he was used to a clear relationship with the heads of the various judicial offices.

He said that those days, where everything happened in the light of day, had been the best ever. They created the habit of a close and almost family-like relationship with the top spheres of the magistracy, based on travels, dinners, celebrations and meetings in Salvo Lima's house. My father named many names, several of whom are still employed at top levels of the magistracy. He called them 'approachable', each one with his own narrative, relatives, weaknesses and needs.

During the 1980s, however, many certainties began to disappear because the magistracy was slowly changing its colours. So it was necessary to put strategies and counter-measures in place in an attempt to nullify the repression, which was mainly fed by the violent turn that Cosa Nostra had chosen to take in its power-mad dream that it could take on the state. There were many VIP victims: the *vicequestore* Boris Giuliano, the Region's President Piersanti Mattarella, the prosecutor Gaetano Costa, the judge Rocco Chinnici, General Carlo Alberto Dalla Chiesa, the regional secretary of the Communist Party Pio La Torre and many others. In the face of all these killings, my father kept emphasizing his conviction that all that bloodshed could only bring more trouble. Perhaps he hid behind the consolatory justifications of Lo Verde/Provenzano, whom he continued to see on a regular basis. Provenzano was always ready to criticize the line taken by 'that madman Riina' but never decided to oppose it. When similar consultations occurred with Signor Franco, he too was pretty immovable and cynical, ready to speak his mind but never to intervene.

I asked my father which were the magistrates he considered 'friends' in some way, and what he told me I've handed over to the prosecuting magistrates who have me under investigation. The picture of the past is in the description of the private relationships we've seen above. But that wasn't all. At the beginning of the 1980s an inquiry was started into the Canadian investments. Falcone had managed to trace back the transfers between the UBS and the Canadian bank and so discover the properties that had been bought in Montreal. He had also discovered traces of Michel Pozza's presence in Palermo. The lawyer had stayed at the Hotel Palace in Mondello and my father had paid the bill.

Falcone had prepared the paperwork for the request to the Canadian authorities to seize his property, but my father managed to get to know in time what was happening in the Courts of Justice and so at the last minute was quickly able to sell up, thus removing the property from any requisition order by the instructing judge. According to what Dad told me, it was the prosecuting magistrate Giusto Sciacchitano who passed on the inside information.

Even the investigation into the so-called 'Palazzo di vetro',

he said, was 'adjusted' in some way. The story is well known:
it was a matter of fixing the sale of a high-rise business complex in receivership. The Salvo cousins were plotting under the
table to favour certain friends. The uproar over the matter
brought about an inquiry by the magistrates that – it's now all
history – ended surprisingly in the matter being shelved.

Then came the inquiry they called 'Contracts and the Mafia'.
This was the period between the end of the 1980s and the
beginning of the '90s. The connection was made by the Carabinieri but it was never developed as it should have been by
the prosecutor Pietro Giammanco and his staff.

It was also the period, after my father had been sentenced
to internal exile outside Rotello in Molise, in which the investigation began to grow in support of the request to take precautionary measures and, yet again, the seizure of his assets.
My father asked his friend Lo Verde/Provenzano if there was
a way to block the investigations. 'Now they're after the money,'
he said, 'and we can't afford any mistakes. We need to move
carefully.' He also met Provenzano to voice his disappointment
over the judge involved with the precautionary measures,
Beniamino Tessitore. Lo Verde told him that in that moment
everyone was worried about exposure, adding, 'Masino Cannella's in charge of liaising.' This particular detail struck my
father, who was surprised by the Cigar's sudden prestige: 'Shit,
Masino's gone up in the world.'

A few days later Cannella met my father and gave him assurances that there was a sure way, ' already successfully tried, for
stopping the seizure of our friend Giovanni Pilo's assets, which

seemed to have completely disappeared'. It was necessary, however, to follow a clearly defined path, and bring in several friends.

One of these was Prof. Pietro Di Miceli, a celebrated business consultant in Palermo who we knew by name only and who they said was close to certain Masonic circles and the secret services.

It was natural, therefore, for my father to want to know more about this man, and he turned for information to Signor Franco, who confirmed the choice and also mentioned the consultant's excellent relations with the Palermo magistrates. And so it was that Di Miceli was invited to a meeting that took place in Rome at our house in Piazza di Spagna and this served to establish the criteria to be adopted for obtaining a watertight case in his favour.

Following this meeting, Prof. Di Miceli said that he'd spoken with Tessitore, who'd pressed him to go ahead and given him the formal task in the tribunal's name of producing a report on the origins of my father's assets.

After several weeks, the report was submitted. The excellent work of the experts acknowledged that my father's effects came from a legitimate source, equal to twice the sum that was the object of seizure. [Di Miceli would later be put on trial, accused of protecting Don Vito, but was found innocent.]

6

The Fall

It was a long and laborious road that led Vito Ciancimino towards a slow but inexorable and disastrous decline. It was not in his character to give up easily and he was well in with a group of political retainers in a strong social and electoral consensus. It's enough to recall the private war he started with Angelo Vicari, then chief of police, when he questioned Vicari's choice of words at the time Vito was elected mayor of Palermo. 'A scandalous appointment,' said Vicari. Don Vito dragged him into court, making perhaps the worst decision of his life, seeing that it was also the Vicari affair that contributed to his early resignation.

In the early days, the power wielded by Giovanni Gioia and Salvo Lima was the shield behind which he could shelter in that it guaranteed a balance with the Mafia, but that came to change with the Corleonesi muscling into the Palermo scene. This rustic clan was depicted universally as a gang of criminals motivated by an atavistic hunger that caused them to be arrogant and greedy, wanting to 'make up for' the wrongs they suffered in the past when the self-importance of the politico-Mafia power base of 'the capital Palermo' had alienated Liggio and his *viddani* ('peasants').

Don Vito was able to act as middleman for, and somehow keep a check on, the Corleonesi's unbridled appetites, insisting on the 'equal shares' system we've come to know, based on the prerogative of a fixed percentage for Cosa Nostra and the kickbacks that went to financing the politics.

That this system was never seen as a crime by the one-time mayor is shown by several handwritten pages Don Vito submitted to the prosecutor Giancarlo Caselli in 1993 when Caselli went to interrogate him in Rebibbia on the hypothesis that he might start a clear collaboration after the tumultuous parenthesis of the so-called 'Deal' that began the day after the Capaci massacre. The philosophy of the kickback system has never been as clear as it is today: 'I've no sense of guilt over the kickbacks,' wrote Don Vito, 'because I received them from, and in the main could account for them to, my RESPECTFUL POLITICIANS (Ministers) who were THE STATE. AT THAT TIME THE STATE FUNCTIONED IN THAT WAY AND EVERYONE KNEW IT, FROM THE PRESIDENTS OF THE REPUBLIC DOWN.'

This is what a politician could write who had spent thirty years as a leading player in criminal activity in a power block that seemed unassailable, despite the accusations that reached even the highest levels of institutional power, the Anti-Mafia Commission included. This is how a 1963 report from the Italian Communist Party (*The Mafia and Palermo*) described the system that linked the Sicilian Mafia-political family system:

> And so we find Giuseppe Brandaleone as city assessor; his brother Ferdinando as Provincial administration assessor; Vito Ciancimino as city assessor and Filippo Rubino, his brother-in-law, as Provincial administration assessor. The Gioia family is 'well' placed: of the two brothers-in-law Gioia and Sturzo, both married to daughters of the ex-President of the Cassa di Risparmio bank, Senator Cusenza (deceased), one is an MP and the other an assessor for the Province. Barbaccia, the MP's brother, is an assessor with the Tourist Board. 'Full employment' for the Guttadauro family: one brother is a city councillor, the other brother, Egidio, is provincial representative on the Province's Tourist Board; the son of this same Guttadauro is a Provincial councillor, and also a Christian Democrat aligned with the Reina group. And furthermore, Vito Giganti, the 'foreign' member of the City Council, and his brother Gaspare, Provincial delegate to the vocational schools.

The Death of Michele Reina

For decades the system survived every accusation. It was more difficult, however, to resist the internal dialectic that didn't speak the institutions' reassuring language but rather the bloody one of the 'Sicilian berets' (typically worn by the peasants, here the Corleonesi) who were always more interested in feeding on speculation and the public purse. Dangerous winds were blowing inside Cosa Nostra: they were winds of war. The struggle between Palermo and the Corleonesi reached a point of no return, and so began the killing spree that was immediately targeted on the politicians as well, with the death of the Christian Democrat Provincial Secretary, Michele Reina (then the acceptable face of the party), in 1979 and that of the President of the Region, Piersanti Mattarella, the following year.

In the collective imagination, the killing of Reina was taken to be a direct consequence of Don Vito's 'intimidatory politics'. The murdered politician's widow Marina Pipitone made no mystery of her aversion to Ciancimino and an unofficial source has told of a vitriolic encounter between the two during a visit of condolence that was interrupted by the peremptory tones of Signora Marina, who told him to 'Go away, I don't know how you dare show yourself here!' In Don Vito's writings there's no mention at all of the Reina affair. There's only a bland portrait of his murdered colleague, whom he depicts as a politician absolutely dependent on Salvo Lima. Don Vito recalls having heard him on the morning he came to be murdered: 'He was in very good spirits and I remember we were joking a good deal on the phone. That same evening the murderer came. We were thrown into consternation.'

Don Vito's eldest son Giovanni maintains that the hostile attitude of Reina's widow was a result of the 'press campaign that influenced her and led her to think my father was the cause of Michele's death'.

GIOVANNI: 'Giovanni, they've killed the Christian Democrat Provincial Secretary, Michele Reina.' I heard the news from a female friend. We were at the house of friends, she was watching television, I was playing cards. We immediately stopped the game and all crowded round the television as it was giving a special extended edition of the news.

I knew Michele Reina because I'd seen him at our house many times. He was a big jovial kid and it struck me badly to see him on the television screen slumped back in the driving seat, his faced disfigured and covered in blood. I thought my father could easily have been in his place, seeing that they were fellow party members and held positions of the same importance.

I rushed home and found my father in his dressing gown pacing up and down the large drawing room in the dark with his hands behind his back, as he always did when he was worrying about something. He said to me, 'They shot him like a dog, poor Michele. I saw him only two days ago and he was his usual happy self, now he's on a slab of marble in the morgue. The crime's been claimed by terrorists of the extreme left, can you imagine it? It makes you laugh, not even your local village idiot would believe it.' As if speaking to himself, he observed, 'He wasn't even killed for his role in politics. Everyone knows that Michele depended completely on Salvo Lima. How many times have I heard him say he couldn't give a definite answer until he'd spoken to Salvo? If politics was the case, then they should have whacked his boss Lima, not him.'

'Then why did they kill him?' I asked.

'Well, I think it was Michele's front men,' he replied, ' in order to get their hands on his money. Not even his wife knew how much there was. You'll see, poor Marina'll get only a few crumbs and they'll take the largest slice of the cake.'

He was so convinced of his hypothesis that took no further precautions and continued to live life as he normally did.

Massimo Ciancimino has given a very different explanation of Reina's death to the magistrates.

MASSIMO: My father was shocked to hear from Lo Verde/- Provenzano that Michele Reina had been killed as a favour for him. 'For me?' he asked. But he didn't want to go into it any further because, he said, the help that certain people give is sometimes a disaster and only brings trouble. The real truth is that Totò Riina considered Michele Reina untrustworthy and uncontrollable and maintained that he was moving away from Salvo Lima's party line. There wasn't a day went past without Reina consulting my father. On the question of a tender my father had OK'd a couple of big decisions on the advice of Reina's councillors and this managed to piss Salvo Lima off. All this wasn't to Totò Riina's liking. There's this to be added as well, said my father, that the less there was of Michele Reina, the more they could launch the rising star of Mario D'Acquisto.

This is one version. On the other hand, Provenzano held to the hypothesis that Reina's murder had been committed in my father's interest because Michele had been in contact with the MP Rosario Nicoletti and together they were ready to start a new faction to make overtures to the left, which would have created difficulties for my father's group. He wasn't convinced by this version because, he said, there was already an agreement and a friendship between the two and they'd already begun to work together.

The Death of Piersanti Mattarella

The President of the Region was assassinated on 6 January 1980 in front of his wife. In the annals of Sicilian criminal history this murder has always been seen as an act of Mafia terrorism. But the investigations led by Giovanni Falcone have left a less clear picture of the matter. They suggest an ambiguous plot with one possible motive grounded in Mafia-political interests (contracts) and another suggestion hinting – and perhaps more than hinting – at the presence of secret forces – the secret services and far-right terrorists – that would shift the motive towards a more elaborate hypothesis, such as the desire to interrupt Piersanti Mattarella's political overture to the Communists.

Vito Ciancimino's explanation in 1992 is surprising. It was given during the period of his rapport with the Carabinieri at the time of the so-called 'Deal', when he was still undecided whether or not to trust the authorities. He had already put down in black and white a disturbing paragraph in his book *Le Mafie* that he was then writing:

> In Sicilian political life Mattarella was what Moro was in national politics. Once, after one of his many admirable intuitions, I told

him that only De Gasperi and Moro could stand next to him in comparison. Smiling good-naturedly, he replied: 'Don't let on to a soul and, if you ever happen to, then you must also add, "*Si parva licet componere magnis*." [If one can compare small with large, Virgil, *Georgics* IV, 176].' He was certainly destined to play significant roles in national politics. And I can bear witness to the great distress he felt over Aldo Moro's death; I'm sure that, in whatever position of responsibility he held, he would never have neglected to seek out whoever were the instigators behind Moro's murder. And here, as I see it, is the context surrounding Mattarella's death. For the Establishment (with a capital E) he was a dangerous man, indeed it was as well he never became a part of it and that was the way it was. Perhaps Gladio or some irregular group had a hand in it.

In the same extract, Don Vito pays little attention to the Mafia's path of protection money, because of his belief in the hold of the 'system' from which almost no one deviated. 'The sharing out of profits has gone on since the time of the Celts and in Palermo since the time of the Phoenicians.'

The Ciancimino family's rapport with the Mattarella family was a complex one that went back a long way to the start of Don Vito's political and economic fortunes, when he began his activity in the transport business with railway wagons thanks to a state concession when Bernardo Mattarella, the father of Piersanti and Sergio, was a government minister. But with Sergio Mattarella there was never a good feeling. Only with the other son was there a good understanding, even if a general opinion (rising from investigations) plants the suspicion that it was some 'fault' of Don Vito and his dangerous friendships that brought about the tragic fate that the young 'president of good government' met with in Sicily. As proof of this special rapport between the two, a solidarity that went beyond alliance, there's a note by Ciancimino on the subject of a cartoon by Bruno Caruso that appeared on the front page of *L'Ora* on 1 December 1970. This showed a group portrait of local notables beside the 'famous bandit' Liggio and below them the caption '*Long Live Sicily*'. Don Vito writes:

In the cartoon published in *L'Ora* newspaper, the following were depicted: Giovanni Gioia MP, Bernardo MATTARELLA MP, the lawyer Girolamo Bellavista, the public prosecutor Pietro Scaglione and myself (Vito Ciancimino). In the background stood the figure of the famous bandit LUCIANO LIGGIO. Gioia, Bellavista and the heirs of Scaglione (since murdered) and myself have started an action against the *Ora* newspaper and the artist Caruso, who drew the cartoon. The heirs of Mattarella (since deceased) did not deem it appropriate to start an action. The Hon. Giovanni Gioia had an altercation on the telephone with the most authoritative of the Mattarella children, namely the Hon. Pier Santi, about the lack of a suit on the family's part, in order to persuade him to start an action along with the rest, but obtained only an evasive response . . . Given the well-known friendship between the MATTARELLA family and myself, the Hon. Giovanni turned to ME to PERSUADE Pier Santi. I spoke to Pier Santi and he convinced me that he could not nor should not

start that action. I reverted to Gioia and said that Pier Santi was
RIGHT not to go to court. Gioia asked me the reason. In a firm
manner I replied that I would never tell him or anyone else. And
so it was and so it shall be. I have to assume that the Hon. Sergio
Mattarella knows the TRUTH of the conversation between his
brother Pier Santi and myself.

Years later when, disappointed by everything and everyone at
the end of seven years in gaol, he was to set about writing 'the
whole truth about Ciancimino' with his son Massimo, he would
come back to Mattarella's painful and tragic end, urged by his
son to tell the story of his relationship with the secret services
and in particular with Signor Franco, who we have encountered many times before.

MASSIMO: My father knew from Signor Franco that Mattarella's
killers weren't Sicilian Mafiosi but came from 'henchmen' in
Rome, part hoodlums, part terrorists . . . extreme left or extreme
right . . . I don't remember which. It was a real anomaly for the
habits of Cosa Nostra, which never ever delegates important
operations to anyone. So he was certain the secret service was
involved, but couldn't understand the lack of a trusted killer
from Cosa Nostra. So he asked Lo Verde/Provenzano how come,
on the occasion of such an extraordinary and violent killing,
they hadn't observed the usual prudence of keeping everything
under wraps and on their own territory and had shared out
important secrets with organizations that had completely different ends from those of the Mafia. He was told that it was a

matter of an exchange of favours. This was Provenzano's reply and my father didn't go any further, because that's what he had decided to do since the time of prosecutor Pietro Scaglione's murder. Back then in 1971 my father had asked Lo Verde if Cosa Nostra had killed his close friend the magistrate, but he had been evasive and even embarrassed. From that moment he had sworn never to ask any more questions.

In more than one meeting Signor Franco had spoken to my father about an exchange of favours with regard to Mattarella's murder and he had sought confirmation among circles of the forces of law and order that agreed there was secret service involvement.

Answering with Weapons

It may be curious, but it is the case that in the period before the Mafia killing spree Vito Ciancimino slipped out of politics, announced his loss of interest in it to all and sundry and, instead, his overwhelming attraction to business. 'I'm moving into finance,' he told the newspapers. And perhaps there was some truth in it, to judge from Massimo's accounts of the alleged Milanese investments through the companies of Marcello Dell'Utri, Francesco Paolo Alamia and the connection with Roberto Calvi. This series of links was documented by the newspapers at the time, when Ciancimino was mentioned as an associate of Francesco Paolo Alamia. Don Vito later denied any financial participation, but did confirm his collaboration. 'I'm a consultant,' he said.

But at the beginning of the 1980s Don Vito is again pawing the ground and energized in his adherence to the centrist party line of Attilio Ruffini, then a minister. Less than three years had passed since the Anti-Mafia Commission's infamous judgements had branded him a living symbol of the links between Mafia and politicians. Ciancimino thought perhaps there was a road to rehabilitation. But that wasn't to be the case: a mechanism had been started inside the party that would lead to his marginalization, eventual collapse and prison, a consequence of his political isolation that was decreed in a 1984 press statement by national party secretary Ciriaco De Mita. To the journalists who had protested to him about the excessive power the one-time mayor had enjoyed inside the Christian Democrat party, he replied sharply, 'We've kicked Ciancimino out.'

Don Vito's last attempt to raise his head again, before his demise at the regional Christian Democrat congress in Agrigento, was on 15 November 1981 in the salon of the Hotel La Zagarella, when he sent out a clear Mafia-style intimidation to the whole party. It was launched on behalf of Cosa Nostra, which was concerned about losing its influence on politics and, as a consequence, its control over the 'small change', the money. Ciancimino's veiled threat made use of an allusion to terrorism, which he spelled out in a firm voice: 'Someone has maintained that the Red Brigades intend to mount an offensive in Sicily. At this point, we who are the authentic interpreters of the conscience, dignity, passion, history and, above all, the courage of the Sicilian people, make a clear declaration that we will not give in to provocation. This is a sinister and cowardly war. And whoever calls upon us to fight with weapons, will find we have weapons. And whoever wants to sow the seeds of death, will find death themselves.' The threatening inference was even clearer coming from someone who lived in Sicily, an area that was completely outside the political and strategic interests of extreme-left terrorism. The Region had never been the theatre of any action by the Red Brigades, perhaps because a politico-military evaluation of the area could see that it wouldn't allow the presence together of two 'military' structures with such a strong hegemonic connotation. But the threat caused a stir only in the media, and had no influence on Ciancimino's fate, which was already sealed.

The Agrigento Congress

Don Vito himself has pointed to the 1983 Christian Democrat Congress in Agrigento as marking the beginning of the end: 'The long road that would take me to prison started precisely at the Agrigento congress.'

The climate in which the party's regional session took place was unsettling: the deep wound left by the polemics which were triggered by the Anti-Mafia Commission's reports, the declarations by its chairman, and the after-effects of the 1964 Bevivino Commission into irregularities in Palermo's administration had still not healed. Salvo Lima continued to steer things from under the safety of the huge Christian Democrat umbrella, while Ciancimino had no similar protection inside the party. He was on his own, and so he remained. No faction was ready to accept him onto their lists and, by its efforts alone, the Don Vito group would never have reached the quorum necessary to obtain representation in the party's governance. Not even Lima, who in 1976 had brought him into the bosom of his huge family, could manage to save his old friend-and-enemy who had turned out to be useful to him on several occasions.

In order to describe the previously unheard of 'rigour' of that assembly, we need do no more than read Don Vito's own words: 'The Agrigento Congress took place under the banner of moralizing the party's life and it was even decided that membership should be checked by notaries. This made sure that there would be no more false membership cards, generally numbered to be 95% of the total of those enrolled.' With his usual debunking sarcasm he notes: 'Every membership had to be renewed, a complete farce, needless to say.' His political isolation signalled the end of Vito Ciancimino, a kind of green light to the judiciary that was already pressing forward with investigations into the past fifteen years of city administration.

First there was the judicial communication, then the notification of impending investigation, from Giovanni Falcone, the inevitable consequence of revelations from the collaboration of Tommaso Buscetta, the ex-Mafia friend of Lima who pointed to Ciancimino as the hub of the illegal system rooted in Palermo. At the same time came the first search of the villa in Via Danae in Mondello, as Massimo recalls.

Don Vito knew very well there was a domino effect and where it could lead: to prison and the seizure of his assets. He was aware that he was about to battle for his life – life being money in his eyes – a much more difficult battle than those he had fought over the preceding years. His friends began to grow scarce out of fear of being caught up in the judicial offensive, his accomplices slipped away, and the attacks by *L'Ora* brought the by now shaky image of the political man close to death's door. In the wake of the Anti-Mafia Commission, the newspaper's editor Vittorio Nisticò had already published a headline: 'This man is dangerous.' So who knew what would be written when – although still not charged – Ciancimino was sent off under the flashbulbs of the major national newspapers into internal exile in Patti Marina. The flash pan exploded at the beginning of November 1984 with his arrest for association with the Mafia, the crime introduced to the Penal Code only two years earlier on the wave of the killings of Dalla Chiesa and Pio La Torre, the Communist Party Regional Secretary who, even after his death, was able to damage Cosa Nostra, ensuring the acceleration of the bill into law on the seizure of assets that now bears his name.

The Arrest

Vito Ciancimino wrote vividly about the day of his arrest on 3 November 1984.

I'd come back from internal exile in Patti, in the province of Messina, before the sentence that was to be given on 5 November. That day is one of my clearest memories. It was three o'clock in

the afternoon when a police superintendent came to the house
and told me that the commissioner wanted to speak to me. I
tried to put up a little resistance, but my intuition told me not
to and off I went with him. At police headquarters I was told
the judge's sentence and from that moment everything happened
very quickly. By eight o'clock I was on the train for Rome,
my destination the Roman district prison of Rebibbia. I was in
solitary confinement until 25 November, the date of my second
examination by the judge.

He would have all the time he needed to think and reflect
and understand where it was he had gone wrong. Falcone
had discovered his Trojan horse in Canada, a story we have
heard in detail from Giovanni: his trip over to Montreal and
New York, the transfer of Swiss francs from the UBS for the
purchase of the Canadian shopping centre. This was the right
trail. 'Follow the money and you'll find the Mafioso,' was
Falcone's motto.

Alone and without friends, Don Vito didn't give up hope
in miracles. You never knew what might happen. The
encounter with Giovanni Falcone wasn't a dreadful ordeal:
the magistrate harboured the secret hope of inducing him
to collaborate and so left an open door in a cordial manner.
He told him of the suicide of Rosario Nicoletti who in 1984,
after a detested but rarely disowned past among the 'young
Turks', was a regional deputy. And he told him of Nino and
Ignazio Salvo's arrest, perhaps precisely in order to make him
reflect on the importance of these events, which were by now

equivalent to a complete dismantling of the system that had seemed so indestructible.

But what Don Vito wrote in his notebook doesn't make one think of a man resigned to his fate; nor does the account he gave to the magistrates in the years following his second arrest in 1992.

When I was in Rebibbia in 1984 [he said to Public Prosecutors Gian Carlo Caselli and Antonio Ingroia when they were questioning him in 1992] the order was understood that any contact between myself and the Salvo cousins was forbidden. But from my spy hole I used to see them passing and we exchanged a few words of greeting. Then from a distance I saw them in the interrogation room. But once, because of some error or because the thing had been arranged by Nino Salvo, he and I found ourselves together in the shower room. Straightaway he said, 'Do you now know which people in Rome Salvo Lima was telling us about after Dalla Chiesa's death?' 'Wasn't it the Communists?' I said. Then he replied, 'You haven't got it,' and accused a politician of making the decision on the deaths of Dalla Chiesa and La Torre. Seeing how shocked I was, Nino retorted that Dalla Chiesa knew a great deal about the skeletons in various political closets.

Don Vito's testimony can appear to be a little spare in parts, beginning with the apparent ease with which 'by chance' he finds himself in the prison showers with Nino Salvo, despite the judge's express prohibition. Chance or negligence on the part of prison officers? According to Massimo Ciancimino, things happened in a quite different way.

MASSIMO: From the moment my father's 'fall' began, we saw a continual whirl of activity around him: investigators, but also people I find difficult to place among the panorama of the authorities. One of the most stalwart visitors to Rebibbia in that period was Signor Franco. During the years preceding the arrest, we've seen how both he and Lo Verde/Provenzano acted as my father's real advisers. For the first time, however, Signor Franco had to perform this role for a man no longer free and influential, but for a prisoner who was by now subject to depression and, therefore, to the temptation to collaborate.

I tried myself to persuade my father to talk to the judges and these attempts went on for some time, right up to the 1990s. If they didn't succeed it wasn't because Giovanni Falcone wasn't cooperative – indeed, he always kept his word, about allowing my father house arrest in Rome, for example – but because of my father's indecision. He was afraid of getting us, his sons, involved in the consequences of any eventual collaboration.

This is why Signor Franco made sure he was never short of any help, even when he was in Rebibbia. Indeed, I learned from my father afterwards that the meeting with Nino Salvo was by no means a coincidence, but engineered in some way by his friend, who was certain that the chance of talking with an old acquaintance would bolster him up and give him the strength to suffer prison in silence, without compromising anyone. In fact, what he was advised was 'absolute calm and silence, because things will be adjusted without the need of involving anyone at all'.

Giovanni's Escape

Don Vito's ups and downs with the judiciary have left a mark on his children, especially Giovanni and Massimo. The eldest son was investigated and only escaped arrest by a miracle, the youngest had to turn his life around to tend to his father's needs.

For Giovanni, the terrible afternoon of 3 November 1984 was one he can't forget, with his father in handcuffs and himself obliged to flee without knowing what future awaited him.

GIOVANNI: When I came home, the police were already there. The house was like a battlefield because it was being laid waste by a search that was under way. The only room spared was that of my grandmother Adele, who'd been ill and bedridden for some time. My father was creating a scene because the police commissioner wasn't there: 'If he wants to see me, why doesn't he come to my house like everyone else, including his predecessor? It's he who wants to speak to me, not me to him.' Given the fact I was a lawyer, he gave me the task of dealing with the police to find out what was going on. I was told in no uncertain terms that there was a warrant for his arrest and it would be served on him at Headquarters. I passed this on and he knew that he was obliged to go. I remember he went into my grandmother's room to say goodbye: he was very fond of her because he knew how much he owed his mother-in-law for having looked after her grandchildren right from birth.

Outside police headquarters there was a crowd of journalists, photographers and television cameramen. It was difficult to move and obviously we couldn't avoid them. A copy of the warrant of arrest was given to my father and he began to read it closely. After a while I saw his face turn white, he was drained of colour and his forehead broke out in sweat. Then he collapsed onto a bench.

Very slowly he gathered himself together and placed the warrant in his briefcase, fixing me with a straight look in the eyes as if he wanted to tell me something that he couldn't say publicly under the eyes of the surrounding police. One of them told him that he would be taken that evening to Rebibbia, the prison in Rome. In those minutes an infinite number of strange thoughts went through my mind, or perhaps they were simply ridiculous, given the situation I found myself in. I couldn't remember ever having been to the circus with my father when I was a child, or to the cinema or funfair; he wasn't even there among my friends and relatives on the day I graduated. I thought of the many times he'd missed the opportunity to be with me.

We exchanged looks and I couldn't understand what he wanted to tell me. Then he suddenly seemed to lose it, because he said, 'Giovanni, move away.' I thought he wanted more room on the bench, so I shifted over a little. But he went on, 'I said move away.' By now I was at the end of the bench, but he still didn't seem satisfied. And then he added, 'Please find the pills in my bag, and take a good look because they're probably at the bottom, perhaps in between the pages of the warrant they've served.' When I had the legal document in my hand, I saw that one sheet was folded over, as if he'd wanted to leave a sign. I read it and saw that I was accused of being an accomplice in the (illegal) export of capital as the formal owner of the properties in Montreal. It was a crime for which I could be arrested. His 'move away' could only have one meaning: 'Get away, get out of Italy.'

I walked off saying in a loud voice that there was my mother to see to. 'I'll see you in Rome, when there's the hearing.' The concern for my mother was no lie. I found her lying on the sofa and her cousins looking after her to see that she wouldn't faint. But the *coup de grâce* came from me: 'I have to leave immediately, otherwise I'll be joining Papà.' I rushed to the stash of money hidden behind the three empty sockets. It had survived the police search, as had the other hiding place for bankbooks behind the kitchen tiles. I took all the money my jacket and trouser pockets could hold, hurled myself down the stairs and at that moment, through a gap in the outside gate, saw the police cars arrive. I disappeared out the back and straightaway took a taxi to the airport in time to catch a flight to Rome.

On the flight I noticed two politicians from Palermo whom I'd often seen at my father's famous meetings at home. The news of his arrest had already been broadcast on the afternoon news. While they clearly recognized me, they pretended not to see me. The first visible signs of the legal storm that was to hit the Ciancimino family were beginning to show. That same evening in Rome I was able to get to Milan and then, around ten o'clock, took a night train to Switzerland which the waiter in a dreary Milanese pizzeria had mentioned was one of those where the border controls were not too strict. In the end, all went well despite the unfortunate presence of a busybody in the compartment who had the great idea of asking the customs officials why they hadn't yet checked our passports. I only got away with it thanks to my deathly white face and the intervention of the busybody who said to the officers: 'We can leave him in peace, he's off for treatment, you know. He's not well.'

My ordeal in Switzerland was a long and tiring one. In an attempt to mount a defence and furnish documentary evidence for my lawyers, I even had to go to Canada to see if I could obtain records of the sale. The only one who could help me was Michel Pozza, who'd organized the whole operation, choice of notary included. I went to his house, but his wife Liz told me he'd been murdered the year before. I asked if I could speak with Sam, the boss I'd met over dinner with Pozza. He too was dead, but only because 'he ate like a horse, although already overweight', as Liz explained. She also advised me to get out of Canada 'immediately, because you're running serious risks here'. All I could do was go back to Switzerland but the next available flight was the following day and so I had to sleep in the airport, as it was too risky to go to a hotel.

My exile in Switzerland lasted several months, time for Judge Falcone to study the papers he'd requisitioned in Montreal (he'd got there before me!) and fix a date for questioning. It was my mother who told me the date with the good news that the judge had given assurances that it would all happen without a single day in gaol. As ever, Falcone was true to his word. I told him what little I knew, but in exact detail: I explained that my father had been advised by several entrepreneurs in Milan and identified the photo of the man who'd organized the Canadian side of things: the unfortunate Michel Pozza. Falcone knew I was being honest and he was quite paternal. 'You see?' he said, 'Now you've taken a great weight off your shoulders, you'll feel a lot better. Your counsel should have had more faith in the law and not forced you to stay so long out of the country.' The remark embarrassed my legal team who were present at the hearing. Before allowing me to go, he authorized a first meeting in prison with my father, adding, 'When you get back from Rome come in and have an informal chat.' After the necessary technical period, I was clear of the legal troubles that, from that moment on, concerned only my father.

But how much my life had changed, how different it was counting each passing day. As soon as I came home what hit me most was the strange silence that enveloped the house, specially the large drawing room, once full of people coming and going and raising their voices. After Baffo's arrest no one showed their face any more. The politicians, the businessmen and everyone who used to come to ask a favour seemed to have vanished into thin air. Some, besides sloping off, did more, as in the case of the former minister Calogero Mannino, arrested for having links with the Mafia in 1995 and subsequently completely acquitted. At the same time my father was again in Rebibbia, the prison where Mannino had also been sent. I was hurt by the words he used, and still remember them, when outlining his defence for the journalists given permission to interview him in his cell: 'The thing that most upsets me is being forced to stay in the same place as Vito Ciancimino finds himself. This is a humiliation too hard to swallow.' Reading Mannino's words I had a feeling of nausea and wondered why he hadn't felt the same humiliation the time I saw him with my own eyes in our house, laughing and joking with my father in perfect harmony.

I thus became aware of the great isolation into which we had been plunged. Even my mother told me sadly that no one had showed up at Christmas time, except for Gaspare, the good soul for whom my father had once found a job.

Impunity in Handcuffs

For the people of Palermo, the arrest of Don Vito was a historic date. No one would have bet even a penny on the possibility of being able to see the great man in handcuffs on the television screen. Massimo himself speaks with a sense of incredulity about the day of the first search: 'It took place at the same time in the houses in Mondello and in Via Sciuti on Judge Falcone's orders. We were in the same state as a boxer who's taken a deadly blow on the chin.'

It took only nine days for the spectacle of the unravelling

to be complete: on 12 November 1984 Nino Salvo, the symbol of impunity (since the 1970s), entered the gates of Rebibbia. It was a time of rebirth and renewal for the law-abiding citizen. A time of hope offered by a group of judges barricaded in the small fortress of the Law Courts and by a handful of plain-clothesmen who, for once, obeyed the law and not the inside protectors on guard. At that moment, how far away seemed the time when – on account of an unwritten rule of institutional etiquette in the offices of the police and Carabinieri – it would be discussed whether the questioning of a politician, especially one in public office, should go to a 'cop' or the prosecutor of the Republic in person. And so at the same time as abstruse rules could be discussed, the best servants of the state, chosen among that group of 'madmen' without official robes, as they were called, vanished during the course of a killing spree that has no equal in the contemporary history of civilized Europe.

The fact is that, through one of those unforeseeable accidents that change the course of history, a group of special people came together at the same time, in the same place, that were capable of taking extraordinary steps. The stakes were very high: what was in question was the very survival of the extremely well tried and tested 'system' at the top of whose pyramid were the greedy wheeler-dealer politicians and Cosa Nostra's butchers.

The dates of the continuous series of killings illustrate the fundamental stages of a journey that can be mapped out in blood: journalist Mauro De Mauro (1970), Public Prosecutor

Pietro Scaglione (1971), Carabinieri colonel Giuseppe Russo (1977), Christian Democrat secretary Michele Reina (1979), journalist Mario Francese (1979), head of the flying squad Boris Giuliano (1979), judge Cesare Terranova (1979), President of the Region Piersanti Mattarella (1980), Carabinieri captain Emanuele Basile (1980), Public Prosecutor Gaetano Costa (1980), Communist Party secretary Pio La Torre (1982), General Carlo Alberto Dalla Chiesa (1982), police officer Calogero Zucchetto (1982), judge Rocco Chinnici (1983), Carabinieri captain Mario D'Aleo (1983), police commissioner Giuseppe Montana (1985), *vicequestore* Antonino Cassarà (1985), one-time mayor and Christian Democrat Giuseppe Insalaco (1988), businessman Libero Grassi (1991), one-time mayor and Christian Democrat Salvo Lima (1992). And so on to the final blows of the Capaci and Via D'Amelio massacres that brought an end to the most representative exponents of the Palermo 'Anti-Mafia pool': Giovanni Falcone and Paolo Borsellino.

One aspect of the business is represented by the no-holds-barred struggle that Vito Ciancimino conducted, trading blow for blow, with Giovanni Falcone. The former mayor had the worst of it. We have seen how the political isolation the judge succeeded in imposing on Don Vito gave him the space for the legal initiative that was once blocked by the environmental conditions of a sick society. And so the powerful Ciancimino in handcuffs opened the way for a kind of liberation: from that moment on not even the Salvo cousins and Salvo Lima were untouchable.

Rotello

And so, as used to be meted out to the common Mafioso, Don Vito came to know the humiliation, first, of internal exile, followed by a ban on domicile in Palermo. After a year's detention in Rebibbia and the Cavallacci di Termini Imerese and one month in a Patti hotel awaiting sentence, it was decided his place of exile should be the tiny village of Rotello in Molise, at some distance from Campobasso. It was a real trauma for the Corleonese politician used to a quite different judicial treatment:

> I was released on 22 November 1985 and in police headquarters was handed an expulsion order with the injunction to leave Sicily by midnight on 24 November, the destination Rotello, where I remained in internal exile until 4 October 1988. I spent the day of the 23rd at home, after a night in my own bed, in confusion and bewilderment: anything could take me by surprise, even life itself; it was as if I were seeing everything around me for the first time. In the company of two of my sons, I left Palermo the next day for Rotello, where I settled into a *pensione* called La Rustica. Here I stayed until January 1987 when I moved into a small apartment in the old part of the village. I remember the lady who ran the *pensione* as a woman of stimulating beauty and razor-sharp intelligence, one of those who wear the trousers in the house.

From Don Vito's memories comes the clear knowledge that he was able to bond with Rotello's inhabitants, a bond that was fed by long chats in the open and interminable games of cards. 'Of those years,' he writes in his diary, 'lived in the tranquillity of Rotello, I remember the daily task of signing on at the police station, not being able to go out after eight o'clock in the evening and my nostalgia for Palermo.' While there, Don Vito was continually kept company by his sons, who took turns every fortnight, and, less frequently, by his wife.

MASSIMO: I was forced to serve the sentence of internal exile as well, even though – at least not then – I had no previous record. At first, the whole family was mobilized to take fortnightly or even twenty-day turns. Even my mother, who couldn't really boast of a very happy marriage, often came to Rotello and became friendly with many people in the village.

However, I was Dad's favourite. Or perhaps it would be more correct to say that that was my destiny? As usual I was paying the price for being the youngest of the brothers and the least occupied with a career. This is why Baffo chose me. But also because, he said, my brothers 'were less good company'. He was soon bored and showed signs of any impatience. But it was as if I, on the other hand, had nothing else to do but live in that hole of two thousand inhabitants and spend whole days reading long novels and watching television.

But I was useful, not to say indispensable, for his needs. I shuttled backwards and forwards from Palermo and kept in touch with the lawyers and those at the time who had mobilized themselves to neutralize the judicial proceedings for the seizure of his assets.

He was often coming and going as well. I remember he had dozens of meetings in Palermo, all authorized by the judge at the precautionary measures tribunal. Here too was a trick that, I recall perfectly, made Falcone suspicious. Every time he saw me, in fact, he would ask if my father was in town and, when I said yes, he would say: 'What's this, is he always in Palermo?' He made an official complaint about it. The fact was that Di Miceli helped my father in some way to obtain the permission. Indeed, it was in his role as legal consultant that he was able to stand as the reason for the many authorizations granted. Officially my father came to Palermo almost always to meet consultants and lawyers, but at the same time he saw and took advice from his friend Lo Verde/Provenzano. In essence he continued to direct his affairs and control his system from Rotello perfectly in tune with Lo Verde and Signor Franco. I don't recall ever seeing Lo Verde in Molise; in fact I can exclude that possibility. But I can confirm with absolute assurance that more than once I saw the very elegant Signor Franco arrive in his chauffeur-driven Alfa. Each time it happened my father gave me some task so that I wouldn't be around while they talked.

The exile in Rotello left its mark on me. I think it was the time of greatest conflict with my father. Perhaps it was because we were like two prisoners who were condemned to live together rather than by choice. The close contact magnified our differences with a build-up of aggression that only he – naturally – was allowed to offload, and always on me. I was his son and had to put up with it without saying a word.

The car journeys from Rotello to Palermo were a nightmare.

I was at the wheel, but he thought it was he who was driving. He'd marked out a schedule and this had to be followed. He'd repeat the same orders he used to do in Palermo: 'Get the car ready.' This meant, as usual, that by juggling the air conditioning and parking in the shade, I saw that the car wasn't too hot or too cold. Then he had established that I wasn't to eat during the trip because 'food is heavy and dulls the reflexes'. The stop at the motorway service station was only for coffee and a quick pee. And the iron rule was to keep to the cruising speed he'd calculated after a close study of the various types of possible impact. Every car that overtook us was driven by a dickhead, just like me. At a certain point, he'd fall asleep, while still keeping that dreadful instrument of torture going that was the tape deck doling out its deadly dull music. That was the moment for putting my foot down a little on the accelerator that was otherwise supposed to keep us under a 100 kph. He'd wake up at Villa San Giovanni while we were waiting to embark on the ferry for Messina. And what I was afraid of would always happen: he'd look at his watch and start to make a scene because I hadn't observed 'his' speed limit. The outburst always came in the same manner: 'How fast have you been driving, you little dickhead?' 'No, Papà, it's never been above a hundred, like you said.' 'Do you really think I'm as much of a dickhead as you are?' He'd get a piece of paper and a pen and begin some complicated calculation that ended like this: 'We've travelled so many kilometres in x hours, therefore we've reached an average of 120 kph. But in order to maintain this average it means you've been touching top speeds of 150.

Therefore you are a total dickhead. Do you want to kill me?'
And then the canonical conclusion: 'It's you who's my enemy,
not Giovanni Falcone.'

GIOVANNI: Rotello really was a tiny and out of the way place.
Only one restaurant in the single inn that had only one room
with a bathroom, which was taken by my father. My first turn
to keep him company was towards the end of November. I'd
arrive in my car, but didn't use it because in fact Baffo forbade
me to leave him. His hypochondria had become worse following his imprisonment and there was no Raul De Preux to
reassure him, only the young doctor in the village. So there
was nothing for me to do but sit for hours in the bar watching
the old men playing billiards. My only real company was a
young man my age, a phenomenon on the green baize, with
whom I had a conversation now and then.

There were only two days to go before a prearranged
changeover and I was in the bar watching a film on television
that I'd waited days to see. It had just started when the owner
of the inn came to call me on my father's behalf. I tried to play
for time: 'Tell Papà I'll come straight after the film.' But she
replied he wanted to see me immediately. Knowing the man,
I went straightaway.

From the peremptory nature of the request, I imagined that
I was heading straight for one of his outbursts, but found him
unusually in a state of good humour and even considerate:

'Tell me the truth now, have you been very bored keeping
me company all this time?'

I replied as diplomatically as I could: 'Well, I've not exactly enjoyed myself, but spending a fortnight in the place isn't a great tragedy. I can manage it.'

'OK, listen: I saw on the television that the weather's good tomorrow. They tell me there's a seafood place on the coast not far from here that's really good for its fish. So take the car and off you go, you could set off about ten. OK? That's settled. Tomorrow you take the car and off you go to the seaside. Now, if you want, you can get back to the television.'

The invitation seemed odd, seeing that the previous days I hadn't been allowed to leave him alone, not even to go to a supermarket that was only a few kilometres away, and now, in complete contrast, I could be off for almost the whole day. But the real surprise the following morning was to see him all dressed up in grey slacks, blue jacket and matching tie. I pretended not to notice and said nothing. He again told me I could stay away even into the afternoon.

I didn't go to the coast, which was too far away, but to a medieval town they told me about that was much closer. This change of programme meant I could get back much earlier than envisaged. Arriving back at the inn I noticed a blue high-performance car I'd never seen before and unusual for that town. Then I had a flashback that took me back to an evening a few months earlier at the Hotel Plaza in Rome.

My father had just been arrested and I was waiting for permission to have a second meeting with him in Rebibbia. I'd seen him that day and was feeling a little upset. I couldn't get to sleep and so was getting dressed again, even though it was past midnight, in order to go out and stretch my legs when the telephone rang and the hotel porter put a call through.

A male voice, polite but firm, asked me to come down for a brief chat.

'Who is this?' I asked, feeling put out.

'I know who you are, you're Giovanni Ciancimino, and this morning you had a meeting with your father in prison. Please come down, it'll only take a few moments.'

I went out of the hotel and saw no one until a blue car came up within a few centimetres of my legs. I glimpsed the driver after he'd lowered the window. He couldn't have been over forty, he had a clear complexion and was wearing a blue overcoat and enormous glasses.

'In you get, I don't want to talk in the street.'

I recognized the voice I'd heard on the phone, but I was a little concerned.

'Come on, get in. If I was here to do you any harm, I'd have done it by now.'

I got in the car while the stranger started it up and, as a conciliatory gesture, offered me a cigarette.

'Really, don't you think before any cigarette, you might introduce yourself?'

He replied that his name and profession had no importance whatsoever, but what he had to tell my father did. He took pains to make it clear that he didn't belong to any criminal society and that he was making contact on behalf of some 'bosses', some very powerful people. At my brusque reaction he became more precise:

'When you next see your father you must tell him to keep calm and not to worry, because the situation could improve substantially. But it's important that he doesn't do anything stupid. Don't ask him anything, he'll understand perfectly. He's a very intelligent man and there's no need for anything else to be said. You tell him what I've just told you, obviously taking the necessary precautions and being careful no one overhears you.'

At the next meeting I told my father everything, leaning close and speaking in his ear. He became furious and told me to return with these words alone: 'I don't want any of my children used as intermediaries for any reason whatsoever and that this will never happen again. The people he represents have no problem contacting me, even in here.' I saw the stranger again and passed on the message. We never saw each other again.

Until Rotello, that is, because that car parked below the inn was the same as the one that evening at the Plaza. I knew that something clandestine was going on and didn't go into the *pensione*. I waited in the bar, watching who was coming in and going out. Then I saw an older gentleman emerge dressed in dark clothes with a hat and a scarf who went to sit in the passenger seat. Then the man himself appeared. I recognized him immediately without a shadow of a doubt: it was the same as the man at the Plaza. He looked around, got in the car and set off. I could deduce that he wasn't the one who wanted to speak to Baffo, but the other man.

I confronted my father with my revelation that in the village I'd recognized the man who'd passed on the message to him in Rebibbia and therefore demanded to know what was going on, seeing as I was no longer the young boy who was subjected to a threatened kidnapping fifteen years earlier.

He gave me this reply:

'It's not a question of age. Even if you were fifty years old I wouldn't ever tell you who those people were and what they'd come to do in this out-of-the-way place. It's enough for you to know that there are people who have my interests at heart because they don't see why only I should have to pay for everyone else.'

I went back to Palermo with a sense of bitterness, convinced that the legal storm that had hit my father hadn't changed his character one bit.

MASSIMO: Anyway, the exile in Rotello came to an end a year earlier than the sentence decreed because from October 1988 my father was able to benefit from the law that abolished internal exile and was substituted by the new ban on domicile.

This meant that once he left Rotello he couldn't go to Palermo and he went to live in Rome, first at the Hotel Plaza and then in an apartment in Piazza di Spagna.

This providential legislative reform didn't drop out of the sky. My father never lost an opportunity to seek the help of old friends in an attempt to remedy his situation. More than once he'd spoken about it with Salvo Lima and in his own home had met his colleague in the same faction, Mario D'Acquisto, then undersecretary in the Department of Justice.

There they decided not to go down the usual route of the Tribunal for Precautionary Measures in Palermo – which would have attracted notice and criticism – and chose instead the route of a provision at national level.

7

1992: End of the Equilibrium

From 1989 to 1993 Italy was swept by a wave of Mafia violence the intensity and nature of which it had never known before. It is true there had been Mafia wars before, one in the 1960s and another in the 1980s, and between them the 'killing spree' that did away with the best of the state's public servants, of Sicily's political class, entrepreneurs and journalists committed to resisting Cosa Nostra's overweening power. Now for the first time in Sicilian history, Mafia bosses even dared target 'Holy Mother Church', assassinating Father Pino Puglisi, parish priest of Palermo's Brancaccio quarter, who was highly committed to combating the Mafia and the area's clan bosses; they also gave an 'adequate response' to Pope John Paul II's speech against the Mafia, which he delivered in Agrigento on 5 May 1993. Earlier they had limited themselves to a theatrical, but bloodless, intimidation of Cardinal Pappalardo when the inmates of the Ucciardone prison boycotted the order of Easter mass in 1983.

The Mafia reached the height of its destructive violence between the summers of 1992 and 1993, when Totò Riina stepped into the role of strategist of a totally new group identity for Cosa Nostra, that of a political terrorist organization that had no hesitation in spreading death and terror – using methods we have since come to identify with those of al-Qaeda – with the aim of influencing the laws of the state, bending them towards granting impunity to the Mafia organization.

It is incredible the metamorphosis that the Sicilian Cosa Nostra underwent in that brief period, abandoning the fundamental principles of its 'ideology' – violence used only as a last resort and always exercised in a clinical manner without involving innocent bystanders – to turn to indiscriminate reprisals in a strategy of terrorist bombings more in the 'Lebanese' manner. This was a change that, to the present day, no investigation has fully managed to explain, despite the rich harvest of information and testimonies from the numerous collaborators with justice.

Something of a reconstruction has been accomplished by the courts of law, but not all the black holes of the various phases of the period have been filled. And that is because on each occasion an external agent has intervened to blur the outlines. What can be said with certainty is that this ugly story, offered to the general public under the label of 'A deal between the state and the Mafia', cannot be filed away as a matter of mere criminality. What can be glimpsed beyond the mountain of court evidence, the testimony of witnesses, beyond the clues examined during the course of exhaustive hearings, is the disquieting presence of forces moving in the opposite direction to the search for truth.

We will probably have to agree with those who maintain that the instrument of the law is inadequate for understanding these events, because by its nature it cannot operate in the absence of incontrovertible proof: it is said that truth in a court of law does not always coincide with the truth of the facts themselves. But an effort to understand according to the rules of history, morality and politics should not be denied. Parliament's records hold the necessary documents for beginning the journey of historical review. Also in the light of what is suspected and feared, that the 'Deal' has in no way been shelved, nor in the short run could it have been, at least as long as the problem of Cosa Nostra members in prison still remains. At the outset of this unnatural pact between 'cops and robbers', the robbers were given a promise that a truce in terrorist activity would open up benefits in exchange. The moratorium was put into effect and has now lasted for sixteen years, but those serving life sentences have had them reconfirmed by the Supreme Court of Cassation and a strict regime still operates, albeit left open to individual interpretation of the rules and regulations, which means they are not applied equally for everyone.

Some twenty years have passed now since Cosa Nostra launched its battle for survival, trusting in its power to blackmail a political and institutional class historically compromised by the long-unpunished collaboration that preceded it. In 1989 Giovanni Falcone was the anomaly who instigated the crisis in the mechanics of this peaceful coexistence between state and Mafia. The judge was farsighted and knew that it was the right moment to launch the final battle against the Mafia. The international situation would never be more favourable: the fall of Communism in the West brought about the end of any 'Red peril' and rendered more or less useless the anticommunist stance under which every hush-hush union with the Mafia bosses was justified and seen as a bulwark against the arrival of 'the Cossacks'.

And so Falcone made his move, strong as he was under the protection of a government minister – Claudio Martelli – who was determined to stamp out the indecent *éminence grise* of the business Mafia and its political allies.

But Don Totò had his own problems: the *pentiti* were destroying Cosa Nostra, Anti-Mafia legislation was finally turning to tackling its illegal wealth and, above all, people saw that Giovanni Falcone's Maxi-trial was standing up against all the attacks of politicians who supported the status quo: first-degree sentences were creating panic among the members of Cosa Nostra, while 'Maxi-2' and 'Maxi-3' were in preparation, as well as trials against compromised politicians.

Falcone therefore had to be defused. First they tried to blacken his name, then came the bombs. The judge was subjected to an anonymous letter campaign, which the press came to call '*l'estate del Corvo*' ('the summer of the Raven') after the anonymous signatory, which accused him of allowing the *pentito* Salvatore Contorno to return to Palermo to do away with his enemies there. These accusations were supposed to help 'justify' Cosa Nostra's bloody vendetta. In June 1989 they attempted to blow up the judge's seaside villa on the rocks at Addaura using seventy-five sticks of plastic explosive. It is said the attempt was only foiled by a stroke of luck: the men in his bodyguard found the sports bag of explosive while carrying out a routine search. For years this was the accepted version, even at the level of the courts, but in recent months this has come to be questioned, even denied, by surprising new evidence coming to light – twenty years after the facts – that points to a corps of strange institutional figures who in June 1989 were already in the deadly spider's web that was tightening around Giovanni Falcone.

We shall have to wait for the conclusion of investigations by the Public Prosecutor's office in Caltanissetta to know if the sweeping manoeuvres of the secret services in Palermo in June 1989 had anything to do with the moves to undermine the judge's authority, apart, that is, from the attempt to blow him sky-high. There is a line of inquiry that leads directly to describing the attempt at Addaura as part of a kind of 'inter-departmental war' among the secret services going on in the background. This would take the shape of an authentic spy narrative with the 'bad guys' trying to eliminate Falcone and the 'good guys' trying to foil the attempt, as in those Hollywood films where the evil and cynical CIA meets the FBI defending the Constitution.

As we know, Falcone was later forced to leave Palermo. Claudio Martelli sheltered him politically by appointing him Director of Penal Affairs at the Ministry of Justice. But this was not enough to save his life. He arrived in Rome on 13 March 1991 exactly at the time – as we came to know in the following years – Cosa Nostra was getting ready to launch its final attack on the 'State that didn't honour its agreements'.

Totò Riina had lost face personally with his broken promises. For years he had assured Cosa Nostra members of the certainty that 'everything would be seen to' and that after the storm the calm of the good years of the past would return, when the Mafia would again enjoy total impunity.

But the facts gave him the lie. It was the Supreme Court of Cassation that put the headstone on Cosa Nostra's 'line of strategy' with its final guilty verdict on the nineteen life sentences for the bosses and the hundreds of years in prison for the organization's big and little fish. The person they found 'guilty' for all this was Giovanni Falcone, because from his new office in Via Arenula he also put in motion the final deadly counter-measure to suppress any attempt at sabotaging the Maxi Trial. He had upset the officially approved mechanism that allowed the First Penal Section of the Supreme Court of Cassation to hear practically all the appeals of the Mafia and terrorist trials. He instituted a principle of rotation that took away that section's exclusivity of hearing Mafia trials. In fact, the Maxi Trial did not go to the court presided over by Judge Corrado Carnevale, whose adherence to the formal letter of the law had, in the past, resulted in important trials being dropped.

The End of Falcone

But the good news of the Supreme Court's sentence also marked the beginning of the end for Giovanni Falcone. At the very moment of the judge's final victory the conditions were in place for Totò Riina's counter-offensive, with Riina now Cosa Nostra's supreme godfather, primarily because the role played by the other Mafia boss, Bernardo Provenzano, was always a cautious one; he never wanted to stick his neck out, not even in the slightest gesture of disagreement. Don Binnu did not agree with Riina's suicidal choice – as Massimo Ciancimino makes very clear – which he saw as counter-productive and contrary to Cosa Nostra's nature, which was 'based on pacts and Christian Democracy'. But he never said a word to his colleague; rather, he formally agreed to every decision until – according to Massimo's account – he could liberate himself (collaborating with Vito Ciancimino and the Carabinieri in the capture of the dictator-boss) and take charge of the organization himself to turn it once again towards the reassuring line of 'collaboration' with the state.

On the day of the Supreme Court's verdict Falcone's death warrant was signed. On 30 January 1992 Totò Riina's whole world was crumbling because the confirmation of those life sentences put the stamp of failure on a course of action that had brought the whole organization to ruin and made it a prisoner of the boss's errors of judgement. So Riina was an emperor with no clothes, no longer in possession of the protection that in the past had characterized the Mafia's power. Not only had no one in power, politician, magistrate or anyone else, succeeded in 'seeing to' the historic trial against the Mafia, as had been promised, but what had also been made clear by the confessions of the *pentiti* was the truth about Cosa Nostra's secrets and, above all, the troubles of its greedy, lying bosses who had committed perjury. It was the end of the myth of the 'men of honour' as being 'just men' and 'defenders of the oppressed'.

Meanwhile in 1992 Vito Ciancimino was living in Rome in an apartment on the small rise of San Sebastianello overlooking Piazza di Spagna, having been investigated for the umpteenth time about the Mafia and contracts, then arrested and released in 1990 by the Supreme Court that quashed the warrant for his arrest. Because the trial for links with the Mafia (the one presided over by Falcone) had not yet passed sentence, he was out on bail awaiting the final verdict. That his lucky star was in decline was seen in the continual attentions of the prosecuting magistrates and the scant amount of credibility offered him by the politicians. The Christian Democrats' greatest hope was finally to remove his name from the party's history. The former mayor had already experienced the humiliation of prison in 1984 and had spent all his energy and friendships – publicly acceptable or not – in trying to escape the tentacles of justice that were reaching for his much talked about illicit wealth, a small part of which had been uncovered (in Canada and Switzerland) by Giovanni Falcone. He had served more than three years of internal exile on his own in Rotello, comforted only by the unwavering friendship of Signor Lo Verde/Provenzano, the reassuring presence of Signor Franco/Carlo (who, as we have seen, was always ready to hand out suggestions and advice) and by the constant attentions of his sons, Massimo in particular, who was gradually assuming the role of his father's 'tutelary spirit'.

In fact, that winter of 1992 we find the young man who was not yet twenty-nine nearly always present in Piazza di Spagna.

Don Vito was now dedicating himself almost exclusively to writing his memoirs: a voluminous diary composed with the express intention of defending his honour by attacking the judges, journalists and 'all those involved in Anti-Mafia nonsense'. This unscrupulous personal history is filled with evasions and omissions that try to show that his system made everyone equal, there was no right and left, and there were no heroes. He calls Falcone a biased judge, and depicts Dalla Chiesa's death as the settling of a score among the powers that be. His ideological defence of the system's payoffs and kickbacks is openly shameless. Well before the explosion of the '*Mani pulite*' ('Clean Hands') operation and therefore well before Bettino Craxi's famous speech of self-defence in Parliament ('*Così fan tutti*' – 'Everybody's doing it like this'), Vito Ciancimino almost claims that politicians have the right to gather illicit finance, in line with the theory fashionable today that 'if everybody's doing it' it's no longer a crime. How different his reactions and explanations were to his son Massimo in the 2000s, just before his death, by now convinced that he should 'tell all' at the insistence of a young man who now feels his name bears a heavy weight and understands that the only way to lighten the load is real collaboration between his father and the judiciary.

The End of Salvo Lima

Unwittingly, Don Vito introduces the hypothetical readers of this diary (offered unsuccessfully to publishers, journalists and investigators) to the climate that was about to shake up the First Republic, devastated by shockwaves from investigations into corruption in the North and Mafia and politics in the South. This explosion was produced by two deadly fuses going off almost at the same time: Antonio Di Pietro's investigations in Milan and, in the South, the period of bloodshed beginning with the murder of Salvo Lima, the Christian Democrat's pro-consul in Sicily, and man of the Mafia, Vito Ciancimino's inseparable alter ego, born politically in the shadow of a wise and farsighted Palermo Mafia and switching later to a forced coexistence with the Corleonese Totò Riina. And Provenzano? He clings on to 'his' Don Vito, the friend he knew and appreciated when he was a child and who would never disappoint him.

Salvo Lima was killed on the morning of 12 March 1992 in Via delle Palme, a couple of steps from the Via Danae in Mondello we have come to know as Palermo's centre of power. He was overtaken in his car, together with party members Alfredo Li Vecchi and Nando Liggio, with whom he had had a ritual morning coffee, while they were driving to the Hotel Palace to see to the final details of preparations for Giulio Andreotti's visit to Palermo, which was part of the electoral campaign for the voting on 4 and 5 May. It was a terrible scene, a horrendous death after a chase that ended up beside a rubbish bin. The former mayor and Euro MP had tried to play a desperate card: he stopped the car in the middle of the road and ran off, followed by the two motorcyclists whose faces were masked by full-face helmets. His run came to an end after a few strides when he fell on his face and his silver hair turned red with blood, directly below the stinking container. The killers made sure the job was well done and slipped away on their red Enduro without a glance at the two men in the car who were waiting for the worst, eyes closed in terror. They were saved by Lima's decision to abandon the car and try to escape on foot.

The news of Lima's death was an atomic bomb. Even more than Ciancimino the Euro MP – who had chosen the ambiguous 'A friend in Strasbourg' for his slogan – was the living symbol of the untouchable. No one had ever succeeded in pinning a charge on him of having links with the Mafia, not even Falcone, who had learned of his origins from Buscetta: 'Son of Vincenzo, a Cosa Nostra man of honour'. But without any proof the information was worthless.

It was Falcone who first understood the gravity of the situation: he telephoned Paolo Borsellino in Palermo to tell him 'all equilibriums have gone up in the air, anything can happen now'. So much for any equilibrium: Lima dead and Ciancimino out of it, waiting for his verdict. No one could guarantee anything for any one any more, while the political world went into a tail spin, not knowing how to get out of it.

Salvo Lima's murder was undoubtedly a Mafia job, and immediately appeared as a split between Cosa Nostra and the politicians: it was enough to see the pallid faces of the state nomenclature who rushed to Palermo and lined up in the front pews of the basilica of San Domenico during a rather muted funeral ceremony that took place without the presence of the head of state, Francesco Cossiga.

The picture was totally clear to Vito Ciancimino, barricaded in his golden cage in Piazza di Spagna. 'Anything can happen now' brooded Giovanni Falcone obsessively in his bombproof office in Via Arenula, a stone's throw from the famous Spanish Steps of Trinità dei Monti, beside Don Vito's Roman retreat. And indeed it did. From that tragic morning in March in a developed Western European country, the unthinkable happened: a criminal organization launched a military offensive in order to force the Italian state to loosen its grip on Mafia repression. It declared war in order to negotiate a peace, as the collaborators with justice later explained when speaking of the strategy of Totò Riina, the 'supreme commander' – on the run for over thirty years – the godfather of Cosa Nostra; but it was 'not all his own work'. So the Mafia bombed the motorway near Capaci in order to free itself from the uncontrollable and unshakable Falcone and fifty-six days later repeated the act in Via D'Amelio with Paolo Borsellino, exactly at the same time as Don Vito was trying to negotiate a difficult reconciliation, accepting the overtures of the special Carabinieri's ROS section, as we hear in detail from his son Massimo.

Remembering the origins of his political adventure, Don Vito recalled that his reins were constantly curbed by his belonging to the Mafia, reins which were shrewdly held tight for decades by the Signor Lo Verde/Provenzano that Massimo discovered in the magazine he was flipping through in a barber's shop.

The balance sheet before Ciancimino's eyes in March 1992 was not an edifying one, even if his legal troubles seemed small potatoes when compared with those grey hairs covered in blood shown in the news flashes by the reporters who rushed to Via Danae in Palermo. Going back in his mind, Don Vito jotted down a few sparse recollections:

> I got to know Lima when I joined the 'great family' (as we say) of the Christian Democrat party. On this matter I have to say that, coming from a socialist family and brought up in a culture that was strictly non-church (when giving a funeral oration for Bernardino Verro, Corleone's socialist mayor killed by the Mafia, an uncle of mine named Calogero ended his speech by saying, 'You won't go to the paradise of the priests but to the paradise of the just'), I thought that all Christian Democrats believed in God and abided strictly by the Ten Commandments. I was immediately disabused of this and came to the conclusion (an arrogant one, if you like) that I was far better than they were by a long chalk. Anyway, I found myself at the 'dance' and continued to 'dance', so only have myself to blame. My father told me to keep strictly out of politics. I didn't follow his advice and the results are there to see, and how.

In line with his habitual tendency for self-exculpation, offloading the blame for his life's disasters onto to fate or someone else, Vito Ciancimino offers a fatalistic view of his more than questionable past decisions, almost as if he wanted to emphasize that there was no other way of doing politics.

The killing of Lima, however, opened a new chapter in Don Vito's life. He knew that the body left among the rubbish bins in Mondello was a terrifying message for the entire political class, especially that in Sicily, which had once lived happily with the 'Goodfellas' of the Mafia. He understood that they were coming close to a final reckoning and that nothing would be as it was because the rules of the game were changing and the Mafia no longer had any intention of being beholden to politicians and their Byzantine ways and means. He was extremely unsettled and preoccupied. His sons bear witness to this.

MASSIMO: We were in Rome and heard the news on the television. My father was really shaken up; I'd never seen him in that state before. He went up and down the rooms as if searching for a thread he couldn't find. The television continued to broadcast extra bulletins, but he was already past them and searching for a key to decode what had happened.

'It's crazy, what's the sense of all this? Where's it going to lead? This is a sign to the politicians, certain connections are dangerous . . . I warned them many times . . . I didn't expect this . . . Who could have imagined anything like it?' Then he turned to me, as if he'd only that moment become aware of my presence: 'Get me an Ansiolin tablet, lock the door and don't leave the house.' He shut the door of his room and didn't come out for more than two hours.

In the end, he gave me an order: 'Tomorrow you go to Palermo to speak to your brother Giovanni. Explain the situation to him and tell him to get in touch with Lima's family and say that my presence at the funeral wouldn't be wise. If there's anything at all they need, however, they shouldn't hesitate to contact me.' He entrusted this task to Giovanni, because he was a great friend of Lima's children, especially his daughter Susanna and her husband.

GIOVANNI: Of all the politicians that came to our house, Salvo Lima was the one I knew best. He was extremely courteous and friendly. Despite being one of Sicily's most powerful men, he didn't throw his weight around, unlike many of the less powerful, who were arrogant and proud.

My father too, who showed little consideration for his fellow human beings, considered Lima a sharp and intelligent rival. He respected him because – he said – in contrast to the usual run of politicians he 'kept his word'. Certainly he also had a grave defect, that of supporting the camp of Giulio Andreotti. When my father fell from grace because of his judicial troubles, Salvo Lima – unlike the cowards elsewhere – never turned his back on him.

As soon as I learned what had happened in Mondello, I called my father. His voice sounded funereal, he already knew everything, and he silenced me in a few words: 'Salvo didn't deserve an end like this. They're just butchers.'

After the funeral, which I didn't attend in order to avoid newspaper gossip and exploitation, I went to see him in Rome. I'd seen him some time before and he was unusually cheerful and full of the joys of life. But after Lima's brutal murder he seemed another person, so much so that – before anything else – he asked me what point the work was at on the construction of the chapel in the Capuchin cemetery. Then he wanted to know if many people had attended the funeral and which politicians had been able to go. I had the impression that in his mind the list would help him to know which direction the affair might take.

He began to walk up and down the hall, his face dark and thoughtful. He assumed the stance he took up when mulling things over: one hand touching his beard, the other behind his back. Then he stopped and said: 'They bumped him off in the worst of ways, giving him all the time in the world to know he was about to die. I hope when it comes to my turn they send people who are quick and more efficient.' Then, still walking up and down the hall, he went on: 'Salvo once asked me, in an ironical way, blowing smoke out from the cigarette in his ever-present holder, what I thought of Mafiosi. I replied right away, without even giving it a second thought, because I'd already thought of an answer long ago. I told him that in my opinion they were a bunch of dickheads with the unfortunate habit of using a gun. Salvo gave a hearty laugh and changed the subject.'

I had the feeling that for the first time in his life he was truly afraid of being killed and ending in the same way as his friend Salvo Lima.

Enter Signor Lo Verde

'He's gone mad,' Don Vito told his sons, commenting on what he considered was certain to be an initiative of Totò Riina. In fact it was only Riina who was capable of decreeing Salvo Lima's dramatic end. There had been similar occurrences in the past, when the Mafia opened its 'political campaign' with a series of attacks on prominent people: first Michele Reina, then Piersanti Mattarella, followed by the Communist Pio La Torre, the opposition's representative who stuck his neck out more than anyone in the fight against Cosa Nostra. Don Vito was chewing things over, knowing very well the methods of Totò Riina's 'Corleonese line' had earned him the nickname of 'The Beast'. What could he do? The decision wasn't difficult, almost obligatory, as his youngest son explains.

MASSIMO: The day after Lima's death I followed my father's wishes and set off for Palermo. I remember the crowd of reporters, photographers and cameramen who had descended there, all sent by their respective desks and titles. There were also a good many traumatized politicians, consciously and decisively giving out a sense of security that even the blind could see was shaky. Palermo appeared to have gone crazy, a city under military siege, partly because the state was used to countering the Mafia only with this kind of response, more choreographic than anything of substance, and partly out of necessity given the presence of numerous public figures in Palermo for that prominent event.

I went home to my mother and brothers in Via Sciuti. My cousin Pino Lisotto, who lived on the floor below, was also there. We know already how susceptible he was because of his reticent character. You can imagine his reaction when faced with a huge and terrifying event like that.

He took me aside to fill me in on these fears, his own and

those of many of Salvo Lima's friends, who were paralysed at the thought of what could happen to them. He told me he'd been contacted very discreetly and cautiously by a Dottore Nando Liggio – one of the eyewitnesses who survived the ambush in Via Danae – and by the Hon. Sebastiano Purpura, widely considered to be Salvo Lima's right-hand man and, therefore, a party to any context that concerned him. They both had good motives to fear for their lives and so were searching for reassurance and advice about what action to take. The pistol shots in Mondello had achieved the desired effect: the intimidation of an entire political class. 'The two of them,' said the extremely worried Pino, 'are terrorized, they don't know what to do and won't leave the house for anything. They'd like to meet your father to get some advice and information on how this business came about. They don't know what's hit them, if it's a matter of things coming from a milieu of mutual friends or if the hand's come from other quarters.' He concluded: ' They'd be willing to jump on a plane to go to Rome and speak to him.'

When I came back to Piazza di Spagna I found Baffo calmer, but by no means cheered up. I repeated word for word the conversation I'd had with Pino, but he didn't want to hear any of it: 'There's no reason at this particular time for anyone outside the family to come and see me in Rome. At most, Lisotto can come if he wants.'

My father had been released on bail pending the final verdict on his links with the Mafia. Even though he was free to come and go as he pleased, we didn't move from the house for almost a week: the time necessary for him to evaluate coolly, without any flood of anxiety, what was the best thing to do. In the end, when all the noise and media attention had died down, he decided to go to Palermo on the grounds – a purely theatrical pretext – that he had to consult his lawyers. But the real motive was otherwise: he was going to Palermo to ask advice from his friend and protector Signor Lo Verde/Provenzano. The meeting happened quietly, apart from the usual tried and tested precautions in arranging the appointment. After a few days, Binnu and my father saw each other in one of the places that in the past had housed the Mafioso, a fugitive from justice since 1963, namely Via Cannolichio in Mezzomonreale, in the direct shadow of the Norman cathedral.

I don't know what exactly was said on that occasion. But I do know what my father told me several years later, once he'd decided to put his story down in writing. In the circumstances he came to know what was building up inside Cosa Nostra, such as Riina's crazy plan and the new hard line they were all set to follow after Lima's death. What he heard from Provenzano revealed, if not in detail, then certainly in broad outline, that Riina's insane plan was definitely fed and suggested – as Don Binnu made no attempt to hide – by 'someone who's pumping him way above himself'.

He spoke plainly of 'insanity', did Signor Lo Verde, who either couldn't or wouldn't oppose the strategy of bloodshed. But he took a precaution, sending his wife and two children back to Corleone, putting them safely out of any judicial consequences of what was about to happen. And that wasn't the only reason for such a decision. On his own, without the obligations of helping his family, Provenzano had freedom to move about. In fact, from that moment on, he began to circulate with more autonomy, to the point of showing up in Rome more than once, especially when Riina's 'insanity' became the reality of terrorist attacks. I later learned that the meetings served to monitor and decipher developments from those critical moments. He came to the house or to Via Vittoria, which crossed Via del Babbuino a couple of steps from Piazza da Spagna, where a friend of my father's, the businessman Romano Tronci, had put a flat at his disposal. Dad had even given Lo Verde the keys to it, and also to Signor Franco/Carlo who, after Lima's death, had again established contact on a pretty frequent basis. They often met to try to evaluate the direction that events were slowly taking.

As he did with Lo Verde, my father expressed to Franco his doubts about the 'authenticity' of what was happening. He was in turmoil; he couldn't understand why Cosa Nostra should suddenly decide to betray its own nature, which was one of non-belligerence towards the authorities, and set out on a road of political terrorism, which it had always avoided in the past. There seemed no explanation or motive behind a decision that, at the end of the day, seemed self-destructive. He asked Provenzano more than once about what irrational calculation had prompted Lima's death. Of one thing he was certain: Salvo's death wasn't in Cosa Nostra's interests and therefore the Mafia was performing favours for some outside entity. What could it be? I don't think my father had a straight answer from the person he was speaking to, beyond vague references to the usual shady people around Riina who were 'filling his head with nonsense'.

It's Terrorism

The days passed quickly, without Don Vito getting a handle on what was going on. He could only see that the worst was still about to happen and no one could consider themselves safe. On 23 May 1992 the ground literally shook: five hundred kilos of TNT were used to kill Giovanni Falcone, the judge who was Cosa Nostra's sworn enemy. With him died his wife, Francesca Morvillo, who was also a judge, and three of their bodyguards: Antonio Montinaro, Rocco Di Cillo and Vito Schifani. In the collective imagination the Capaci massacre will forever remain Italy's 9/11. Even today, eighteen years later, the images of the Punta Raisi motorway blown apart and the cars thrown hundreds of metres still give rise to feelings that are difficult to control. And to this day we ask ourselves about the extent of the damage created by the absence of one man, a judge like Giovanni Falcone.

For Don Vito this was absolute confirmation that something dark was going on inside Cosa Nostra and the country at large, that a violent battle was being drawn up between the politico-economic powers behind the shield of fighting the Mafia. In his diary, Ciancimino recorded his interpretation of the Capaci massacre, which he saw as the latest stage of a strategy set in motion by Salvo Lima's murder. According to Vito, Giovanni Falcone's power would have become unstoppable had the judge come to head the National Prosecutor's Anti-Mafia office, the new legislative instrument already approved by Justice Minister Martelli and in an advanced stage of being put into place. Falcone, wrote

Don Vito, 'acted as if he had been charged with forming a new government for the Republic . . . And according to us he actually wanted to form a new government, that is, create the Republic's real power, that is, to command the Republic through the new Super Prosecutor's office.' And because of this, Ciancimino continues, 'he worried all Italy's magistrates, including those in his own [Anti-Mafia] pool . . . but above all he caused concern among that part of the political power that distrusted him and his godfathers. Perhaps this is the key to the death of Dottore Falcone. At this point the words come to mind of the magistrate Dottore Vito D'Ambrosio, when he spoke of the attack Falcone suffered at his villa [the bomb attempt at Addaura]: "If it wasn't the Mafia, then it was the secret service. There's no alternative." But at the service of whom?'

The same doubts, the same dark construction of events, formed the basis of the frequent meetings with his 'advisers' Signor Franco and Signor Lo Verde, two people who, during the course of that not readily decipherable period, played the ambiguous role of sources that only rarely gave replies with any certainty, as they had no wish to stick their necks out. And so Don Vito, ever more concerned, did everything to suggest a rather more complex view of the attack attributed exclusively to Cosa Nostra.

MASSIMO: 'It's terrorism, not the Mafia.' So my father went about saying, ever more convinced of the existence of someone or something that was directing the Corleonesi towards a bloodbath. He'd even agreed to talk about it to the newspapers, well aware that his hypotheses would be seen as attempts on the part of a Mafioso trying to protect his own flock and turn attention away from Cosa Nostra. But he said clearly that behind these crimes he felt a hand other than the Mafia's, while recognizing its role as the logistical base for carrying them out.

But it was impossible to explain the decision behind the timing of Falcone's death, or the necessity of an atrocity carried out in such a spectacularly senseless manner. My father held that it wasn't within the Mafia's capabilities to deploy such a large amount of force to achieve a result that could have been obtained by using the more traditional means. 'Falcone often went out and about Rome and often without his bodyguard. I saw him many times in La Carbonara, the restaurant in Campo dei Fiori, and they knew this. Then why that scenario?'

According to him – as he repeatedly said after Salvo Lima's death, and even more after the Capaci massacre – 'Another body is arming the Mafia's hand'. How many times did I hear him say, 'This is not their own work.'

I also remember another meeting, one of those tricks destiny plays, between my father and Giovanni Falcone. I had a good relationship with the magistrate, and he knew that in the past, when he was investigating my father's assets, I'd tried to push him into collaborating many times. This was a difficult task because not all of us, his sons that is, were convinced that this was the best path to take. He was always very reluctant himself, which is understandable when you consider that, right up to the end, he was in close touch with Provenzano, who was certainly against any thought of collaboration, and with Signor Franco/Carlo, who was also a brake on any such move.

This chance meeting occurred in the middle of May 1992 on an Alitalia flight from Palermo to Rome, the last Falcone took, because the return flight he took on that Saturday of the attack on 23 May was in a plane from the Prime Minister's office.

My father's relationship with Falcone was a little less friendly. However, that time they had a meaningful exchange of words even if they were spoken jovially and with a smile on their lips.

'Good morning, Signor Ciancimino.'

'Good morning, *dottore*. How are you? I see you don't miss out on good Roman cooking, perhaps you're overdoing it with the *spaghetti alla carbonara* . . . How's life with Andreotti going?'

'I've chosen the lesser evil . . . it's become too difficult to work in Palermo . . .'

Who knows, if they had had the opportunity to speak more often, perhaps my father's life would have changed. And perhaps mine as well.

8

The Deal: Part 1

Capaci's TNT shook the whole country and provoked an unprecedented wave of indignation and opposition to the Mafia. Sicily came out onto the streets, and favour towards the politicians was at an all-time low. The funeral, with the bitter polemics of the widow of Vito Schifani, chief of the bodyguard, moved the whole world. Tales emerged of the difficulties faced by the Palermo Anti-Mafia pool, the isolation that Falcone faced, opposed as he was not only by the political world, but by his colleagues and superiors as well: his diary is an act of accusation against the Public Prosecutor Pietro Giammanco, who was one of the many causes that led the prosecuting magistrate to leave Palermo. He would be removed in the space of a few days, following the firm stand taken by nearly all Palermo's State Prosecutors. At the same time, all the suppositions began to loom up that have regularly tainted the investigations into Sicily's contorted problems. There is always an attempt to throw things off track, a missing piece, some proof missing: Falcone's computer, for example, was tampered with and left with only a part of its memory.

It was in this climate that investigations into the Capaci attack began. It was not exactly the right one for a stern reply to the Mafia. The state seemed to be floundering, even though with a spurt of dignity Parliament managed to overcome its previous paralysing divisions and lobby interests in order to elect Oscar Luigi Scalfaro as President of the Republic. The general confusion is understandable: the investigators themselves didn't know which way to turn. Never before had they found themselves up against an attack by the Mafia that was so heavy and so virulent. Faced with the babble of public opinion and the shameful loss of political power, it was clear that something had to be done, anything at all.

So a special Carabinieri corps moved in, namely two officers of the ROS group: Colonel Mario Mori and his trustworthy collaborator Captain Giuseppe De Donno. They decided to 'seek out sources, starting points, news', anything that could 'take the investigators profitably inside of the Mafia structure'. In simple terms, this meant finding some source at a good enough level to conduct a 'dialogue with the enemy'.

And so the story of the so-called 'Deal' began, even if the Carabinieri do not acknowledge it, and deny the thesis that they were leading players in the search for an 'agreement' with the Mafia in order to bring about a truce.

Worthy of the best screenplays for a spy movie, the story of this very complex affair spreads out over many years from precisely 1992 and is given for the most part in the proceedings of two trials: the first over the fact that no search was carried out for Totò Riina's hideout, for which Mario Mori and Captain

Ultimo were charged and acquitted. Both men were initially national heroes for having captured the head of Cosa Nostra, and then immediately afterwards found themselves in the dock, accused of having made a deal with him so that no search warrant was served on him which, according to many, would have brought to light something that could not be made public. Perhaps this was the famous 'papello', the list of Cosa Nostra's requests to the state: special terms and benefits for those detained, the abolition of a strict regime, guarantees for the restoration of seized assets and even, together with all that we shall see, a review of Falcone's Maxi-Trial.

The first to speak the fateful word 'papello' was the *pentito* Giovanni Brusca, when he revealed the existence of the 'Deal' and said that Totò Riina had 'presented the papello' to the state.

The other court setting is Colonel (now General) Mori's second trial when – along with Colonel Mauro Obinu – he was charged with aiding and abetting Bernardo Provenzano as a fugitive from justice. Originating principally from the accusations of another officer on the force, Colonel Michele Riccio, the case is still being heard in Palermo. The two defendants have always denied the accusations, but in this setting the *coup de théâtre* of Massimo Ciancimino's revelations burst onto the scene while the court was about pass judgement on the two officers in the dock on the basis of Riccio's accusations: 'In 1995 I was stopped from capturing Bernardo Provenzano, a fugitive from justice for forty years.' But why should Mori, who had captured Riina, have placed obstacles in the way of arresting Cosa Nostra's Number 2? This question lies at the heart of the

enormous affair of the 'Deal'. The implication is that Provenzano – Vito Ciancimino's great puppet master – was an inte-
gral part of the agreement with the Mafia and, after the
'fortunate' arrest of Riina, which saw the end of the leader's
hard line, he became the guarantor and mediator of a 'pax
mafiosa' that still holds to this day.

This interesting narrative is worthy of a novel, but fits into
the context of a very real and slippery trial. It is told now by
Massimo Ciancimino, who uses his father's memories, but also
supporting documents found among the thousands of pages
Don Vito filled up obsessively with the intention of appending
them as verification to the book of the truth he was working
on from the year 2000 with the help of his youngest son, with
whom – finally – he had established a more intimate and emotional relationship. A large part of this story, therefore, took
place in the past, beginning with the Capaci massacre, but came
to Massimo's knowledge only a decade later.

MASSIMO: I met Captain Giuseppe De Donno one morning
at Fiumicino airport five or six days after the Capaci bombing.
I knew him from way back because at the time of my father's
first investigation by Falcone, he was the one who had carried
out the house search. On that occasion a certain feeling was
created because of his courteous manner towards the family.

We were at the check-in and said hello to each other. He
asked me if I was going to Palermo and if I was on the same
flight as he was. In the end he said, 'Well, if it's possible perhaps we can sit together.' With the help of a hostess, who found

the seats for us, we were able to do so. The main topic of conversation was, naturally enough, the Capaci bomb attack and our memories of Giovanni Falcone. I passed on to him what my father thought of the whole business, and told him his doubts about the strategy that didn't seem to him to be the work of the Mafia alone. I also recalled the good relationship I'd established with the judge, when I was seeing to all my father's needs, and my attempts to get him to collaborate.

From these recollections he took the opportunity to introduce a proposal: the possibility of meeting my father informally. At the time I didn't understand and told him that the Carabinieri had all the room they needed to reach him: 'You only have to send him the usual notification card asking him to appear.' But he came back with, 'No, that's not what we want. Any eventual meeting would be in a different guise, not an official one, but more discreet.'

It seemed a difficult thing to me, even if De Donno had already given me to understand that it was his superior officer, Colonel Mori, who was able to give the go-ahead for the operation. 'You have to take into account the mentality of a man like my father,' I replied. 'In his way of thinking, there's no way he'd meet the Carabinieri unless he received an official request. I can only say that he prevented me from doing my national service precisely because I'd shown an interest in serving it in the force. Why on earth should there be a Carabiniere in the family? But could I at least know the reason why you want to see him?'

'To try to put an end to this butchery that even your father says is more terrorism than Mafia. And because of his past activities and his experience, he's without doubt a privileged channel through which to try an approach.'

I saw him again that afternoon in Palermo. We met at the Ribaudo kiosk near the Teatro Massimo and the Carini barracks, the headquarters of the Carabinieri's operations division. We began to walk and talk about things in greater depth. He explained to me that inside the force, and in harmony with other authorities, they wanted to find an alternative path to the official policy in order to bring a stop to the escalation in Mafia crime that had then culminated in the Capaci bombing. He broached the subject of capturing the Mafia's notorious fugitives from justice, even if he agreed with me that getting behind bars those bosses still at large wouldn't be enough to secure a final victory. I bided my time and assured him that I'd speak to my father. He advised the utmost secrecy and gave me his telephone numbers, even his mother's, where he was about to go.

I went back to Rome almost immediately after the weekend. When my father learned the details of my strange encounter, which – thinking about it now – I doubt was by chance, he seemed neither particularly surprised, nor prejudicially against, perhaps because De Donno had made reference to his legal position, for which my father had already tried his traditional channels of prominent friends. Probably he was thinking of the possibility that a contact with the authorities could help him in his personal battle with the courts. He told me that he'd consider the matter and would soon give me an answer.

I think that at the back of his mind he was already thinking of conferring, as was his custom, with his points of contact, Provenzano and Signor Franco. He met with the former after a day or two. He came to our house in Piazza di Spagna. The same happened with Signor Franco/Carlo. He came the following morning at 11.45, as punctual as ever, a few hours before the appointment already planned with De Donno. He wore a linen suit, casual but elegant shoes, tie, no bag, and the usual glasses. My father had asked me to switch on the air conditioning in the living room and not to go out.

I followed the ritual, meeting Signor Franco at the door, ushering him into the living room and kept him company in the vain hope that – while we exchanged a little gossip – I'd learn something of this strange person. We spoke of the Mafia and of Tangentopoli (as the endemic corruption in Italy had come to be christened) that was spreading such concern amongst the authorities. I tried to extract a comment from him on Andreotti's reaction to the presumed involvement of the Russian secret services in the Capaci bombing. He replied with a smile, just as my father was coming into the room. The conversation went on without me for half an hour, then they arranged to meet the following day. You didn't have to be Sherlock Holmes to deduce that my father had been given the go-ahead, both by Lo Verde and by Franco, to hear what the Carabinieri had to propose.

The meeting with the Captain was fixed for three o'clock that afternoon. Half an hour before I went out of the house to meet him in Piazza di Spagna. I thought he'd be arriving

via the underground but instead I saw him draw up in a white
Fiat with a civilian number plate, even though Piazza di Spagna
was closed to normal traffic.

We had an espresso in a bar in order to spare him the torture of a cup of the notorious Ciancimino coffee. None of us
drank it, so we rarely used the coffee machine, with the result
that it was worse than a kick in the stomach. I didn't want
Giuseppe to end up like the other guests who I'd seen pull a
face at the first mouthful, or those others who, remembering
past experiences, declined the offer with the excuse that they'd
given up coffee for health reasons.

Look Who's Here . . .

The first appointment between my father and the Carabinieri
came about at three o'clock on that hot afternoon of the first
week in June 1992. 'Look who's here?' was his opening greeting
for De Donno. The last time the two had met was exactly two
years earlier when the officer had notified him of a court order
for his remand and asked him to accompany him to Headquarters. The time elapsed wasn't much, but the circumstances
were completely different: the captain was nervous, even if he
was putting on a brave face, my father self-confident as if
wanting to say that he'd seen things correctly at the time, pre-
dicting to the officer that the investigations into contracts
'wouldn't be going anywhere'.

He took delight in goading whoever he was speaking to, did

my father. So that De Donno's 'How are you? I hope you're well' received the acid comment 'I would be, but for you.'

I left them alone for a couple of hours. When they'd finished I walked a short way with the captain to find out the result of the meeting. 'It went better than we thought,' he said. 'He's taking a couple of days to think about it. He thinks the same as we do; we have to come up with a solution to avoid more bloodshed.'

The two days became three, the time needed to see both Lo Verde and Signor Franco. The meeting with the former had already been planned for discussing what to do about certain public works contracts, among them a flyover in Palermo and a distribution network for methane gas in Caltanissetta. He came to the apartment in Via Vittoria where my father usually received the 'ambassadors' of Provenzano and Pino Lipari, technical people who were delegates for the public works sector. This apartment at number 5 on the second floor was used as a kind of guest house, with dark panelled ceilings and furniture to match. Nothing more than a small apartment: entrance hall, living room, one bedroom and a bathroom in the garret.

I only knew about the appointment a few minutes before. This was a precaution my father always took: he told me to open up the house and air it, then wait for Lo Verde in case he'd forgotten to bring his keys. He had brought them, however, arriving alone and on foot from the Via del Corso side. After the ritual friendly punch, he asked me to notify my father.

Back at our flat I found him busy dressing, an activity I was always heavily involved in. 'Get me the light trousers hanging in the wardrobe . . . and watch that nothing drops out of the pockets . . .' He wanted his golden pillbox with a turquoise stone set into the lid, a present from his old friend Bernardo Mattarella that he carried about with him everywhere. I also handed him his gold money clip that was a present from Mamma and had been touched for good luck by the miraculous hands of Uncle Mimì, the exterminating angel of any sign of the evil eye.

He ordered me to 'get the uniform' – that's what he called his dark suit, which he used to wear with a white or blue linen shirt – and the leather case with his many spectacles and a pair of pencils and notebooks. He was always tense when he had to meet Lo Verde, changing his route continually, even going past the place to shake off anyone tailing him. At the main door to the block, it was my job to open up and hand over the keys. This time he told me, 'Wait for me at home. Depending on the replies I get, you'll have to call your friend, the captain.'

He came back to the flat about three hours later, without saying a word. He asked me to help him change out of his clothes and, feeling tired, he wanted to rest. After a little he called me in and, while he held one or two sheets of paper, he asked me to arrange a meeting with De Donno for the following afternoon. I followed his instructions to the letter, but also the captain's: I phoned from a callbox at some distance from the house.

The appointment was fixed for 2.30, a time that meant anyone coming in wouldn't be seen, as the porter's lodge was closed from 1.00 to 3.30. I waited for De Donno down on the street and, as usual, led him into the living room where I'd closed the windows, switched on the air conditioning and put on a selection of background music to block any listening device. My father was obsessed by the thought of bugs, hidden microphones and anyone snooping on them. Thinking about it, it was thanks to Signor Franco's good advice that the only ones never intercepted were my father and Bernardo Provenzano.

This time the captain stayed for about an hour and a half. I don't know what exactly was said, but I do know that immediately afterwards we had to go. My father said we had to get to Palermo, but impressed upon me not to tell anyone of the journey, not even our relatives. Instead, he decided we'd stay in a hotel, the Astoria Palace in Via Monte Pellegrino to be exact, which was also furnished with the best air conditioning. We arrived there the following day after a difficult journey plagued by the excessive heat and the traffic jam on the motorway caused by the damage of the Capaci explosion.

My brother Roberto came to the hotel with an envelope left in my name with the porter in Via Sciuti. It was a letter from Signor Lo Verde to fix the day for the next appointment with my father. At the same time, my father discussed with Roberto – who's a lawyer – the legal difficulties linked with the confiscation order. The subject focused on the contacts with the business consultant Pietro Di Miceli, the mysterious figure we've already met in the guise of 'fixer' of the different problems relating to seizure of my father's assets. [This accusation is one that was made by Massimo Ciancimino during his testimony to the Palermo Prosecutor.] I'd met him many times myself in

Rome and even cooked a meal for him. My father held him in
great esteem.

But such attention to detail never surprised me, because of
the deployment of forces my father put in place to avoid the
confiscation of his assets: men from Cosa Nostra, the secret
services and truckloads of sweeteners heaped upon the magistrates. Besides, this obsession had been the principal moti-
vation of his adventurous acceptance of contact with the
Carabinieri beyond, perhaps, his secret wish to put himself
back in the political game.

Following the 'pizzino' request, the meeting with Lo Verde
took place on Wednesday 17 June 1992 in Piazza Unità d'Italia
in the offices of Mario Niceta, a mutual acquaintance of
Provenzano and my father's. They were the premises of a finance
company occupying the mezzanine on the same block where
my brother Giovanni lived on the sixth floor.

Lo Verde had suggested two dates: 16 and 17 June. He preferred the second, which fell on the Wednesday, when a small
local market was held in Piazza Unità d'Italia. The crowds would
have played in favour of Lo Verde's anonymity and, above all,
of my father, who was the more recognizable, given that in
Palermo the other was no more than a fleeting ghost. These
precautions, however, were the norm: meetings were arranged
when porter's lodges or offices or doctor's surgeries were closed
or out in isolated villas that were easily controlled.

At the agreed hour we left my brother's apartment (he was
on holiday) and went down to the offices of the Parabancaria
where Lo Verde/Provenzano was waiting for us. After the

initial greetings I went back upstairs and waited for about three hours. I later learned that among the subjects in the air, namely the Carabinieri, Riina and the proposals for mediation, they also discussed the possibility of my going to work in the very same offices, an eventuality that was fortunately averted.

Cinà, the Intermediary

This is the moment when what was to be 'the Deal' took shape. Beyond organizing the date of the meeting, the job of Provenzano's first 'pizzino' was to communicate a general invitation to Don Vito: 'If you think that speaking with these people will bring us some benefit, then don't miss out.' Once they were together face to face, Ciancimino and Lo Verde spoke plainly everything they had to say. And Don Vito – as Massimo came to learn in the 2000s – laid out his idea clearly: that the only way to bring a stop to the killing was to end Riina's freedom as a fugitive. But Provenzano didn't see it in the same way or else, faithful to his incurable optimism in reason, he preferred to think that there were less drastic solutions. Perhaps he considered Riina to be more reasonable than he was and not so careless as to let the Carabinieri's ready hands fall on him.

'In essence,' explains Massimo, reporting his father's words, 'Provenzano ingenuously thought that Riina might consider that the authorities' desire to come to the table and make a deal meant his new strategy was a success.'

*

MASSIMO: He passed up on Provenzano's line that in effect was asking him to open up contact with Riina. My father categorically refused any possibility of dealing directly with him. But Lo Verde always had a solution for everything and so proposed an old acquaintance as a go-between for Riina and my father: the neurologist Antonino Cinà, the man chosen by Luciano Liggio when, by means of Ciancimino's good offices, he tried to play the card of obtaining a retrial after he had been handed a life sentence. Provenzano even organized the means of contact with the physician. Through Pino Lipari's wife, I learned where and when to see Cinà and set up a meeting for my father. I was told to go the next day and meet him at 3.30 in his San Lorenzo surgery.

I asked the nurse to inform the doctor that Massimo had arrived. I was seen straightaway, even though there were a good many people waiting. We arranged that he would come to meet my father after 8.00 at my brother's flat in Piazza Unità d'Italia, as he was still away on holiday.

Cinà arrived at 8.15; they spoke for about half an hour and said they'd see each other again the next day at lunchtime.

The day after Cinà passed on Riina's assent to go ahead with the Carabinieri, but also to try to find out their real intentions and get some reassurance themselves that a trap wasn't being laid and that they weren't playing on different levels. The doctor received the necessary assurances and the surety that the next step would be speaking with Colonel Mori to hear how they wanted to establish dialogue and what they could offer in return.

We went back to Rome and, with the usual precautions (never the same public callbox and always far from the house), I got in touch with De Donno offering him a meeting with his superior officer also present.

I Fear the Greeks . . .

MASSIMO: They arrived in Piazza di Spagna one afternoon shortly after 20 June 1992. This I'm sure of because it hadn't been more than a week since the meeting with Dr Cinà on the 18th. I was waiting for them on the street and saw them coming on foot. The colonel was wearing a red polo shirt tucked into light slacks. I accompanied them into the house and showed them into the living room that was suitably prepared with air conditioning, music and cold water. Then I went to tell my father. 'What's the colonel wearing?' he asked me. 'Has he got a jacket on or not?' When he heard the colonel was wearing an everyday polo shirt, he chose the following outfit: a short-sleeved linen shirt, glasses without the patch – given the presence of a formal guest – his bag, pencil and notebooks.

'Good afternoon, Colonel.'

'It's a great pleasure, thank you for seeing us.'

'I'd like to be able to share your pleasure, but perhaps it's somewhat premature: *Timeo Danaos et dona ferentes* ['I fear the Greeks. even when bearing gifts', Virgil, *Aeneid* II, 49]. Although it may seen strange to you, you're not the first Carabinieri to come to my house. I'll say more: I've even been on close terms with a general and, with my blessing, he could say he was my great friend.'

His aggressive stance was designed to intimidate the two officers he was speaking to in order to put the crucial question: 'Let's be clear, Colonel. First, notwithstanding the good intentions of our friend the captain, I'd like to know who's sending you, and how far you both have credibility because, as you can well imagine, this isn't the first initiative of this kind I've conducted, but it could be the last, seeing the delicate nature of what's on the table. So don't come proposing any nonsense to me about your capacity to have any real influence over Palermo's Public Prosecutor, because, to judge from the results of your reports into contracts, at this moment I don't see you having any strong influence there.'

Mori and De Donno then played the weak card of a high-ranking ROS officer's involvement in the operation.

Rognoni and Mancino

The discussion was reconstructed in later years. What has remained in Massimo's mind is the recollection of a verbal duel that allowed the Carabinieri's 'good intentions' to shine through, and little more, while Ciancimino attempted to check if the paramilitary's initiative was autonomous or enjoyed real political support. Don Vito put the people he was talking to on guard against the good faith of 'those on the other side' and against the success of any possible offers. He admitted to the colonel that he had little belief in what he was doing and let him know he was doing it because it was a path 'suggested as the only one that was able to achieve quick responses and even possible results'. Obviously he did not cite the source of this suggestion, but we can accept that it was Provenzano. If not him, then who else? Don Vito had no faith in Riina: 'That man's got a revolver instead of a head.' But what exercised him most was the political support. 'Because, dear Colonel, let's not take anything for granted: either this kind of operation has guaranteed support in high places or you're going nowhere. And I don't expect an answer; I'll find that out for myself.'

In effect, that's what happened. After having said goodbye to the officers with the promise of meeting again soon, he received a visit from Signor Franco that same evening.

MASSIMO: I've never known what they talked about. I can only imagine that my father was somehow reassured by the talks. Probably he'd received the answers he was looking for. Many years later, while we were gathering his recollections for the book, he told me that he'd received assurances that there was support for the Carabinieri initiative. Signor Franco himself told him 'the Hon. Rognoni and the Hon. Mancino knew about it'. (The two politicians have categorically denied this.)

As soon as Signor Franco went, he told me to get ready to leave the next day for Palermo and that he'd give me an envelope to give to Pino Lipari's family. The mission also included a message for Dr Cinà and a meeting at his house in Mondello. It was at that moment he was landed with the nickname of 'Iolanda' from the name of the street where he lived, Via Principessa Iolanda.

Operation 'Papello'

We have come to the heart of 'the Deal'. The letter Ciancimino sent to Cinà was only a prelude, an invitation to Cosa Nostra to enter into the details of the agreement, which the men of honour held to be indispensable for ending the terrorist atrocities. It was perhaps the most delicate phase of the entire business: from the tenor of the reply hung the continuation or not of the contact. And the nature of the requests hung on the possibility that the Carabinieri's offers would hold up. Up until that time, beyond the promise to help Ciancimino 'with his business', they had been rather vague, and centred on the 'unconditional surrender of the main fugitives, including Riina and Provenzano, in exchange for humane treatment' for their families. This condition was placed alongside a much more appetizing reference to 'the application of more favourable laws in the area of cases to do with the seizure of assets'. It was this glimmer that was to open the threshold for the list of items contained in the so-called 'papello'.

MASSIMO: Everything took place during the last week of June 1992. I met Dr Cinà twice in Palermo and it was during the second meeting that we arranged to meet again the following day at one o'clock, with him telling me in advance that he'd give me a letter I was to pass on immediately to my father.

This news didn't fill me with joy, because it would upset my plans for the weekend, which were to go to Panarea, as I did every year, for the feast of St Peter and St Paul on 29 June. They celebrate the event on the island with an extravagant display of fireworks that is a spectacle definitely worth seeing from a boat in company with friends.

The appointment was in front of the Bar Caflisch in Mondello where, at the time, everyone gathered for an aperitif. Cinà couldn't even park for the huge amount of traffic and gave me the sealed envelope for my father as he drove past. He told me to hand it over soon with his warm greetings. I gave it to him the day after and as we know now it contained the 'papello'. He told me to put it on the bed along with the numerous other papers that made it seem like a ministerial desk. I left him to his rituals and made off for the beach – after having notified, as prearranged, both De Donno and Signor Franco. I took myself off to Fregene, longing for the other beach on Panarea where I hadn't been able to go.

This notorious 'papello' has been the obscure object of desire of all fans of Italian spy stories. It's a term that's entered everyday vocabulary, a little like 'pizzini', thanks to the enormous media clamour it aroused. For years we have asked ourselves – and investigators and magistrates have striven to find out – if this 'piece of paper' that in some way demonstrated the 'shameful link' between the state and the Mafia did in fact really exist. Massimo Ciancimino himself was attacked and criticized for being a 'loudmouth' each time he mentioned having this 'piece of paper' in his possession. It seemed as if he were just making an exaggerated claim with the aim of launching covert messages of intimidation. These attacks always ended with the challenge to produce the proof.

On the one hand, Mario Mori's two trials had done nothing to disperse the mysterious nimbus around the 'papello' which, in turn, had been introduced by the *pentito* Giovanni Brusca who referred to its existence by the winning term that was familiar only to Sicilians. In actual fact, a 'papello' was a piece of parchment containing obscene light verse in dog Latin that was given to first-year students in Sicilian universities in exchange for the payment of a certain 'tax' that ended up in the pockets of the 'seniors' who organized the various faculties' freshers' rag. In the case of this 'papello', the 'tax' was to be paid to the Mafia by the state in exchange for a civil co-existence with no terrorist atrocities.

On the other hand, its existence is still denied by the Carabinieri involved in those events of 1992, in the sense that they continue to maintain that they never received any written proposal via Ciancimino. Colonel Mori declared this when Brusca revealed its existence, and continued to maintain it during his trial. Indeed, according to ROS, 'the Deal' never even existed, given that the initial contact was limited to the attempt to 'seek out sources, information, starting points for investigation' in order to capture the heads of Cosa Nostra and put a stop to the chain of bloodshed. So much so that, according to the ROS officers, it was really they who were the first to express surprise at Ciancimino's willingness to become the go-between for them with no less than the inner heart of Cosa Nostra.

Massimo had the 'papello' in his hands in a sealed envelope, but never read its contents. He was able to do this exactly ten years later while working with his father on the 'book of the truth' .

MASSIMO: When we were working on reconstructing the details of events in 1992 I asked him what was on that sheet of paper. He looked at me and gave one of his little smiles, saying, 'Go and get the third volume of the *Encyclopaedia of the History of Sicily* that's in the living room.' They were the usual books for show, part of the furnishings. I brought the volume to his bedroom, and he opened it in a decisive manner at a couple of pages about the middle of the book. He took out a sheet of paper and showed it to me: twelve points on twelve numbered lines. I knew what it was straightaway, the same one I'd only glimpsed before: this was the notorious 'papello'. 'Excuse me,' I said, 'but how long has this thing been lying here?' 'Since the day of my arrest in December 1992.' We were now in 2002, busily working on excavating his secrets, the 1992 'pizzini' from Provenzano, but also those of the 2000s following on from 'the Deal' in which he was no longer the leading player, because it had been brought forward by new political bodies.

The points in the 'papello' were written in block capital letters, but I'm not certain it was Riina's writing. But I do know for certain that the document came from him:

1)   Revision of the Maxi-Trial sentences

2)   Annulment of article 41b of penal code [strict regime for convicted Mafiosi]

3)   Revision of the Rognoni–La Torre law [the crime of having Mafia links]

4)   Reform of the *pentiti* law

5)   Grant benefits of dissociation – as per Red Brigades – for those convicted of Mafia offences

6)   House arrest for Mafiosi over 70

7)   Closure of special prisons

8)   Sentences to be served near homes of family members

9)   No censorship of family letters

10)   No preventative measures for family members

11)   Arrest only if caught in flagrante

12)   No fuel tax [for Sicilians], as per Val D'Aosta

Attached to this sheet was a yellow Post-it note written by my father: 'Delivered, FREELY, to Colonel of Carabinieri MARIO MORI of ROS.'

He explained to me how some of these requests were the same thing; others were impossible as propositions and perhaps a few – with some retouching – might have met with agreement. I asked him if the reference to the abolition of a tax on fuel, on the Val D'Aosta model, was his own suggestion, the consequence of a stay in the area that had provoked some reproach in his mind. 'Those people,' he said, 'have got a casino concession and tax-free petrol. Whereas with us, a region with some political autonomy, they've closed the casino at Taormina and denied us the tax break'. I was still doubtful that the matter had been aired in the letter to Cinà, the one that preceded the arrival of the 'papello'.

But it's good to look back to those days at the end of June 1992; they were so full of activity with consultations and expectations. There was a perfect triangulation on the Rome–Palermo axis between him, Lo Verde/Provenzano and Franco, the last two regularly informed on developments with the Carabinieri. I believe there was even a double means of communication: a direct one between my father and Franco, and between my father and Lo Verde; and direct, though unofficial, between Franco and Lo Verde, but 'mediated' between Franco and ROS: the former saddling my father with the part the Carabinieri clearly didn't want to play, as had happened when it was a matter of getting to know the identity of the institutional body offering political support for ROS's initiative. Or in the case of the 'pizzino' with which Provenzano/Lo Verde warned my father that 'the same people we're now talking to,' that is, the Carabinieri, 'have rented an apartment opposite yours; they've placed an officer there to listen and keep watch.' It's incredible that Provenzano knew the same classified information (police surveillance of the Ciancimino home in Palermo from a building in Via Sciuti) that my father learned from Franco.

The meetings intensified. After I had brought the 'papello' to him in Rome, there was certainly one with Franco in Via Vittoria. My father asked for the keys and placed them in the inside pocket of his briefcase. He ordered me to wait at home and not to go out 'because perhaps you'll have to call the captain for a new appointment'.

'Furthermore,' he added, 'tomorrow I think it'll be useful for you to go to Palermo again.'

'Whatever for?' I blurted out.

He exploded back at me, 'Why, dickhead, have you got more important things to do?'

He came home a couple of hours later, looking rather tired. He immediately confirmed that I'd have to go back to Palermo the next day: 'Arrange a flight for yourself for ten o'clock. I have to give you an envelope but I'll see to it this evening, I'm too shattered right now.' I assured him that I'd do everything as he wished, including booking the flight under an assumed name, just as De Donno had also advised. He also told me in advance that we'd be going back to Palermo immediately after I came back to Rome, because – as every year – he had to go to the Capuchin cemetery for the anniversary of my grandfather Giovanni's death.

The next morning at seven o'clock he burst into my room, saying, 'The envelope's ready and it's on the living-room table. Now get a pen and paper and I'll dictate the instructions for you: go to Dr Cinà's surgery, he must read this letter in your presence and then give it back to you: however, you then give it to his lieutenant [Pino Lipari] and when you get a reply you can come back. Avoid being seen in public, especially if you have to meet that captain friend of yours.'

Everything went according to plan. He decided to take the

aeroplane on Saturday 11 July to avoid any difficulties along the motorway, which was still closed. The timetable was full of appointments and, apart from my grandfather's anniversary, there was the matter of meeting both Franco and Lo Verde again.

First he saw to his friend Provenzano, with whom he'd still not had an opportunity to discuss the 'papello'. I had given the letter personally to Pino Lipari with the request for a meeting and, within the space of a few hours, I'd taken possession of the reply in a 'pizzino' from Provenzano himself. The meeting again took place in the offices of 'friend Mario' in Piazza Unità d'Italia. On that occasion Lo Verde shared my father's perplexity over the 'unacceptable proposals' contained in the 'papello'. In any case he asked him to go ahead and try to find some possible points for mediation, an idea that he'd anticipated in the letter where he'd confirmed the appointment: 'I think that this is the moment when we must all make an effort . . .' In the same 'pizzino' Lo Verde reveals that Riina is stressed out: 'Our friend is under great pressure. Let's hope that the reply arrives in time . . .' And with this, he hoped that they'd be able to 'talk together' before anything ugly happened. This meeting took place probably around the middle of July.

At the same time my father also saw Franco: we met him – he was driving a blue Mercedes accompanied by another person – in front of the house we'd rented, which was also in Mondello, on the road that leads to the sanctuary of Santa Rosalia, after leaving the villa on Via Danae.

They stopped a moment to speak and I saw that Signor Franco handed him a sheet of paper: it was the 'papello'. I've always asked myself about the reason for handing this over: it was certainly a copy because he tore it up and put it in his pocket, a sign that it had no value. I've always doubted that Franco brought it to Palermo at the request of my father, who had no wish to travel about with such a 'bomb' in his pocket.

9

The Deal: Part 2

There have been a good many nods and winks and ironical looks over the 'Deal'. The representatives involved of the powers that be – already named by collaborators with justice before Massimo Ciancimino – have always rejected strenuously the suspicion they were taking part in a dialogue between the state and the Mafia in 1992. The trial in Florence over the Mafia terrorist attacks up and down the peninsula in 1993 admitted the presence of anomalies when putting the pieces together for the time, but it attributed the ROS Carabinieri's attitude to a normal anxiety for results when faced with a state that was impotent under Cosa Nostra's savage blows.

Then the discovery of the 'papello' made the history of the Mafia over the last twenty years an even more behind-the-scenes one, characterized by a previously unthinkable plot between organized crime and secret forces: bombs, atrocities, bugging, *pentiti* and part-time Mafia foot soldiers. On the other hand, something truly out of the ordinary had to have been going on: too many coincidental clues among the many witness statements, some expert, that supported the working hypotheses of the investigations in the ongoing trials.

We have the example of Don Vito's son, for instance. He has been denigrated, branded a kind of 'telltale' and mouthpiece for his dead father. But he is not the only one to speak of intrigue. In the days before suspicion, other voices have said the same thing, and have recently been added to in the present.

Let's take this business of the 'papello'. We have already heard Massimo Ciancimino's statements, but they are not the only ones. His brother Giovanni is a moderate man, unlikely to want to grab the limelight, and he too has testified under oath. His narrative more than confirms his brother's.

GIOVANNI: After the Capaci massacre and certainly before Via D'Amelio, I took off for Rome to see my father. During the course of a long conversation, during which he showed himself to be particularly trusting, he told me these exact words: 'An important pathway's been opened up, so I can perhaps manage to resolve my affairs. Some people in high places have given me the job of negotiating with the people on the other side in order to stop this becoming a bloodbath. It's something that could make things easier for everyone.'

I argued furiously with him about this, because I also knew that, going right back to the Rotello days, when he repeatedly assured me of being a Mafia victim and of having nothing to do with them, he had been lying.

Some time after the Via D'Amelio atrocity, I went see him in Addaura where he was living at the time. He asked me to take him on a trip in the car to Monte Pellegrino and, during the journey, he asked my opinion on a number of legal matters. He wanted to know in general what the preconditions were to obtain a retrial and then, with regard to the Rognoni– La Torre law, he asked about the mechanisms that governed how far penalties were retroactive or not. In more detail, he wanted to know what chance there was of overturning the Maxi-Trial verdicts and getting a retrial and also of obtaining an interpretation of the Rognoni–La Torre law that could block the seizure of assets held before the law came into force. At the same time, referring to the negotiations he'd spoken to me about in Rome, he said, 'That business has gone ahead, the other side has made requests to the people in high places.'

During the trip, he pulled out of his pocket a sheet of paper, handwritten in block capitals, and studied it as he was asking for explanations and – although the light was poor and it was only for a few seconds – I was also able to see it.

My father never told me who these highly placed people were, but he was certainly convinced by what he was doing, so much so that he became angry when I assured him that the hypothetical points put forward were practically impossible to attain. I have to add that I'm well aware of the confidential good rapport that my brother Massimo enjoyed with Carabinieri Captain De Donno from the period following my father's arrest in 1990. During the course of '92 I learned from Massimo that, together with a colonel, the captain had to go and meet our father in Rome. I later learned, again from

Massimo, that this did take place, but when I asked my father
about it he was very evasive.

Clues and Witnesses

Other witnesses that have only recently come forward agree
with the interpretation that contact existed between the ROS
and Vito Ciancimino. Confirmation has been given by the
former Attorney General, Claudio Martelli, and by Liliana Ferraro who, in 1992, took over Giovanni Falcone's job in the office
of Penal Affairs at the Ministry of Justice. Both of them testified at the Mori trial, confirming ROS's interest, in the period
following the Capaci atrocity, in obtaining Vito Ciancimino's
collaboration. In particular, Liliana Ferraro has said that,
although she doesn't remember the exact date, she received a
visit by De Donno at the Ministry.

'He told me that he had made contact with the son,
Massimo Ciancimino,' she said, 'and that through him he was
hoping to be able to hook in, or had already hooked in, I don't
remember very well, Vito Ciancimino. And finally he asked me
if it would be the case to mention the matter to Martelli, as
Minister, because he was also asking for some political support for the operation they were undertaking. I replied that I
didn't consider the Minister's involvement practicable, but it
was the right moment to mention it to Dottore Borsellino immediately, adding that I'd therefore be ready to inform him myself.
Anyway De Donno spoke to me of Ciancimino's possible

collaboration, but never of any deal. He added that the initiative was coming from the section to which he belonged.'

A later investigation into 'political support' involved Luciano Violante, who was then head of the Anti-Mafia Commission. Vito Ciancimino asked Mori if he could meet him because the other potential offers of support (from Mancino and Rognoni, according to what Signor Franco told Don Vito) did not seem too trustworthy to him. Above all, for his own needs (that is, seeing to his legal battles) he thought Violante's intervention essential as he was 'the only one who could give any guarantees of support at that historic moment' (it was the beginnning of the Tangentopoli scandal) and the only one able to 'take action with the magistracy'. But Violante declined Mori's invitation for an informal meeting with Ciancimino, suggesting he take the official route, which was a written request for an official hearing. The request came later, but when it should have been taken into consideration, Ciancimino was already under arrest.

This long and complicated narrative of 'the Deal' comes punctuated by Massimo Ciancimino's recollections but also by documents today in the possession of the Public Prosecutors of Palermo and Caltanissetta: his father's handwritten notes, legal papers and the endless diary that outlines his memoirs, the 'posthumous confession' Don Vito thought to write when close to the end. Physically worn out, debilitated by seven and a half years of custody (1992–9), disappointed as well by his friend Provenzano and the phantom Franco, this man now out of power

thought of pursuing a little vendetta on the cynical political
system by writing 'his truth' with the help of his son. He
certainly showed all his cards, such as the 'papello', but also those
'pizzini' that helped magistrates to decipher the fifty-six days –
from Capaci to Via D'Amelio – that were not enough to stop
the worst events. The cards remained well hidden for years in
the Piazza di Spagna apartment, located in the ninth volume of
the *Encyclopedia Treccani* in a space specially created by gluing
the last page to the hard cover. They are printed here (Provenzano's spelling errors and howlers corrected in translation):

> My dear *Ingegnere*, I've learned that you have given my analyses
> to the Professor, let me know if and also how you think I can
> go and see him; if you think that speaking with these people will
> bring us some benefit, then don't miss out.

> M has told me that we can see each other on the 16th or 17th;
> Wednesday would be more prudent. Let me know in good time.

This is a message from June 1992: Provenzano is asking about
a medical check-up with a 'Professor' named by his friend Vito.
Then he declares his willingness for Ciancimino to continue
talking with the Carabinieri. M (Massimo) will make the
appointment.

> My dear *Ingegnere*, I received the news that you have collected
> the prescription from the dear Doctor. I think this is the moment
> we should all make an effort, as we've already discussed at our

last meeting, our friend is under great pressure; let's hope the reply arrives in time, and that there's time for the two of us to speak together. I know you have the good habit of going to the cemetery on your Father's anniversary. If you remember you spoke to me about it. We could meet there to offer up a prayer to God together.

Or, as per last time, at your convenience at our friend Mario's. We need to know because we need time to organize ourselves.

This comes from July 1992. The prescription collected is the 'papello' and the 'Doctor' is Cinà. The effort asked for is that required to make Riina's brazen proposals acceptable, the Corleone boss being described here as 'under great pressure' by whoever is filling his head with 'rubbish' .

My dear *Ingegnere*, it's been communicated to me that the same people we're now talking to have rented an apartment opposite your house.

They've created an office to listen and watch in. I saw that the last time you slept in a hotel, and wanted to know if you'd also been informed. We must be cautious, also for fixing the day of the next meeting. I'll let M know.

I've heard nothing about the Gas. If the problem's been resolved, let me know how.

This 'pizzino' is from the first half of July. Lo Verde/ Provenzano is warning Vito that his house in Palermo is under Carabinieri surveillance. He asks for caution, even in deciding on the way to arrange the next meeting.

> My dear *Ingegnere*, M has told me that given the events that have happened it isn't prudent to meet Thursday 23 as we said the last time we saw each other. I spoke to friends we have in common, they told me that when M comes to Palermo he isn't alone. I know the boy is careful. I think something isn't right and wonder if you want to continue to speak with these people. Let me know. May the Good Lord protect us.

Here we have come to events after Borsellino's death. At the previous meeting Don Vito and Lo Verde had made an appointment for 23 July. Obviously the attack in Via D'Amelio causes it to be called off. However, Provenzano warns his friend that his son (M) is followed when he travels. The old boss also warns him that something's not right and asks him if, after Via D'Amelio, he still intends to continue the contact with the Carabinieri. That the climate is not of the best is underlined by the closing phrase.

MASSIMO: It was an effort managing my father's secret correspondence. He handed me a sealed envelope, usually containing half a sheet of paper with a cryptic message. The addressee was nearly always Signor Lo Verde; sometimes it could be delivered to Pino Lipari, other times it had to be handed to the boss personally, and then I had to ask Lipari to rustle up an appointment. The ritual was always the same: the envelope had to be opened in front of me after a check to see that it hadn't been opened by anyone else, including me. The envelopes were sealed with adhesive tape for this reason. They read it in front of me and, after having torn it up, they gave it back to me to take to my father, together with the reply, which was delivered to me the same day.

There was a secret code for identifying the sender, but I never knew what it was. It's certain, though, that before opening the envelope my father already knew who it was from.

When I gave him back the 'pizzino' that had been read and torn up, more often than not he burned it in the kitchen. But if he had guests and wanted to avoid the smell of something burning, he would rid himself of it down the toilet with several flushes.

The incoming letters, those not his, therefore, were treated with surgical care: he opened them wearing latex gloves, read the contents and immediately made a copy. He had a fear of leaving fingerprints. He checked while I made the copy, cut it out and then got rid of the original by burning it himself.

Via D'Amelio

Sunday 19 July 1992 is a day that has entered Italy's collective imagination. The attack on Judge Paolo Borsellino ricocheted from Palermo and had all of Italy transfixed by the images of

Via D'Amelio looking like a street in Beirut. The bodies of the
magistrate and the young officers of his bodyguard – Agostino
Catalano, Emanuela Loi, Vincenzo Li Muli, Walter Eddie Cosina
and Claudio Traina – were reduced to shreds and even scat-
tered among the trees. It was an apocalyptic scene that took
the country back to that strategy of tension we had believed
was buried along with the victims of the bombs in Milan,
Bologna and Brescia and the Italicus train atrocity, to name
but the worst cases that stick in the Italian consciousness.

While we have to wonder about the origin of the brutal
attack, there will be someone who can offer the right key to
deciphering what went on. Among the possible candidates are
surely the leading players in the underground negotiations
entrusted to Palermo's former mayor, Vito Ciancimino.

It escaped no one, least of all Don Vito, who had already
expressed total pessimism about the operation's success, that
the Via D'Amelio atrocity buried all possible dialogue between
the Mafia and the state. A few days before the 19th – as
Massimo Ciancimino recalls – '... having come back from
Palermo he told me to call Captain De Donno to set up an
appointment with Mori, because he had to respond to the
colonel'. Don Vito's negotiations in Palermo had not produced
the desired effect of softening Riina's demands in some way.
As far as Massimo understands it, not even the work of
'polishing' the text Dr Cinà handed over produced the desired
result, which was bringing Cosa Nostra back to reason. It is
obvious that the venerable Ciancimino had pondered the matter
a great deal, with Signor Franco's help as well, and was trying

to identify the points where there could be some movement and a possibility left open for some compromise. In a note written in Don Vito's hand that he gave his son as an 'enclosure' for the book of memoirs under construction in the 2000s – which Massimo has handed over to the judges – he writes the names of Rognoni and Mancino, regarding them as political support for 'the Deal' (as he seems to have understood from Signor Franco), but adds 'Attorney General' almost as if to indicate the authority figure without whose contribution it would be impossible to attempt any move on from the demands in the 'papello'. He explains that reopening the Maxi-Trial would only be possible by going through the European Court in Strasbourg and hypothesizes a reform of the justice system 'in the American style' with an 'elective system'. He guesses about the possibility of passing a law that abolishes 'preventative custody' 'unless caught in the act' and, in that case, 'summary trial'. All in all, a package that had a politically presentable dress, coupled with the standard reference to Cosa Nostra's timeless dream, a 'Party of the South'.

MASSIMO: The reactions my father had gathered in Palermo weren't enthusiastic. I had an inkling of it on the plane as we were coming back to Rome. 'You'll see,' he said. 'They'll tell everyone to go fuck themselves because the proposals were unacceptable and even unpresentable.' I saw he was particularly on edge because he would soon have to communicate the other party's intransigence to Colonel Mori. We were still before Via D'Amelio in time, but Provenzano had already shown he was completely lukewarm about the 'contropapello', the counter-proposal my father had spelled out for him during the Palermo meetings. In a subsequent meeting, Provenzano made Riina's official position even more clear: he was absolutely immovable on the 'papello'. My father explained this intransigence only in the light of what Provenzano wrote in the 'pizzino': 'our friend is under great pressure'. However there was someone who was fanning the flames in order to keep temperatures high and prevent 'the pistol that Riina had instead of a brain' from being lowered. Faced with these walls of intransigence, my father's comment was this: 'Either they've gone completely mad or their backs are well covered.'

Dottore Borsellino's tragic fate closed every channel of communication. The last fleeting meeting with Colonel Mori and De Donno took place one or two days before 19 July; it lasted a few minutes, enough for an update on any possible good news that might have come up. But the only news that came was of Via D'Amelio and that was most certainly not good.

It was confirmation, as if any were needed, of my father's conviction that there was no possible approach with Riina. With its unacceptable demands, the 'papello' was the most demonstrable piece of evidence of his lack of intent to negotiate. Obviously, contact with the Carabinieri dropped off, but not with Provenzano or Signor Franco.

He put out a flanking movement in Signor Lo Verde's direction especially because he represented for my father the only pathway open to extract Cosa Nostra from Totò Riina's rule and introduce a more moderate leadership. In a few words, it meant neutralizing Riina, having him arrested, thereby transferring command to the more 'reasonable' Lo Verde/-Provenzano.

It wasn't an easy undertaking, but it succeeded through the good reasons put forward by my father. According to what he told me, the meetings that took place in July and August were blunt and direct: 'The moment's come to take some responsibility; the technique of burying your head in the sand's no longer an option. Binnu, you helped create this monster and now have a duty to come up with a solution.'

A New Strategy

Following what Massimo Ciancimino says, in Signor Franco's meetings with Don Vito he also became convinced that the above prospect was the right direction. In the end, a return to the peaceful coexistence between state and Mafia squared perfectly with Mafioso DNA, and Bernardo Provenzano represented the man most able to oversee a return to the old politics of operating under the surface and regaining the social consensus that had become prejudiced by the senseless terrorist strategy.

But why should Don Binnu have accepted collaborating in Riina's capture? Massimo explains it in his father's words: 'He didn't agree with the atrocities. He was hoping to return to an old-style politics, to operating below the surface in a way that facilitated business and, above all, worked towards getting the guarantee that he would be able to act, move and travel about in peace even though he was a fugitive.' This was the famous safe-conduct pass that created so much scandal.

MASSIMO: On 25 August my father asked me to get in touch again with Captain De Donno and Colonel Mori to arrange a meeting that took place in our Piazza di Spagna flat. To put it briefly, as he later told me, the nature of the relationship with ROS completely changed. My father's offer was no longer 'delivering some fugitives' but collaborating in the capture of Totò Riina. This was an extreme attempt to re-enter the game in which he expected to find the solution to his legal troubles.

What arguments did he use to convince the men he was talking to? My father explained to the Carabinieri that, apart from Provenzano, whoever eventually came to succeed Riina would also be very dangerous. And at the same time, Provenzano was the only one able to lead them to the place where Don Totò was in hiding. Therefore the only safe solution possible of guaranteeing the end of terrorism against the state was immunity for Binnu, whom he held to be 'the only thinking head' on the inside of the organization. This was said to the Carabinieri, to Provenzano, and also Signor Franco, who was kept constantly informed.

The following weeks slipped by without any great upset, perfectly in line with Don Vito's strategy. He had no interest in moving any faster without first having had a clear signal about how 'his business' was going. September and October came and went, during which time – going between Franco and

Provenzano – he slowly wove his web around Totò Riina. Contact with his old Corleone friend proved essential because Don Binnu was the single and primary source capable of identifying ' the Cosa Nostra godfather's' hideout. It was a game of chess he played on two boards: he took from Provenzano and Franco in order to give to the Carabinieri, but always with his own interests at heart, slowly divulging information as he received positive signals from them in turn.

MASSIMO: And the signals arrived with the news that Pietro Di Miceli, the business consultant and the Palermo Public Prosecutor's chief expert in the case over the seizure of my father's assets, was bringing his investigation to a close with a favourable conclusion. [Di Miceli would later be put on trial for making a false report, a charge on which he was declared innocent.] I remember exactly that, later on, Captain De Donno phoned me to tell me about an article in the magazine *Panorama* of mid-December under the headline 'Seizure of Ciancimino's assets soon to be blocked'. It was this that finally convinced my father to enter into the heart of the operation.

Previously in November, he'd already received more than a hint from Provenzano about the area where Riina could be found. It was quite an extensive stretch that ran from Monreale to the port of Palermo. My father then asked De Donno to get some topographical maps of this zone, together with the telephone directory and lists of users for gas, water, lighting and some land registry maps with the intent of analysing them with Provenzano. The subsequent sifting of this material led

them to identifying a much more limited area from Baida to
Via Leonardo Da Vinci. Originally contained in a carrying case,
a yellow plastic tube, the map was reduced in size to two sheets
of A3, which my father placed in a large envelope, together
with a card, telling me that it had to go to Palermo for Lo
Verde to examine.

The envelope came back with some news: my father had me
look at the map on which Provenzano had circled an exact
area with a felt tip and marked out several users of light, water,
phone and gas.

At this point, everything was ready: it was a matter of getting this information to the Carabinieri. A kind of protocol
had been agreed about the mode of capture in such a way that
the family wouldn't be involved in the operation and also
allowed to get to Corleone after 'cleaning' the house of all that
was 'dangerous': written material, documents, notes and any
fingerprints. But there was also another motive for adopting
the protocol, which was the desire to make the capture toler-
able, to send a message to Riina to say that he hadn't been sold
out in any way, but that it was a case of a 'necessary sacrifice'
in order to save what could be saved. It was a recognition
almost of the honour between brothers-in-arms.

The Trap

So the relationship between Don Vito and the ROS Carabinieri
apparently proceeded peacefully: Mori and De Donno waiting

for the maps that would put them in a position to tighten a noose around Totò Riina's hideout and the venerable Ciancimino drawing it all out with the clear intention of gaining encouraging signals – if not actual assurances – of the paramilitary's benevolent interest in removing the preventative measures that were putting his 'cash' at risk. It was the autumn of 1992 and there was not very much time left for salvaging Don Vito's assets.

Obviously this is a reconstruction of events based on what Massimo has offered to the magistrates. It may not be the case that things went exactly like this; indeed – according to the ROS officers – they were completely different, starting with the capture of Totò Riina 'in which Vito Ciancimino had absolutely no part to play'. Primarily this was because of his sudden arrest, which occurred on the afternoon of 19 December, just as he was preparing to go out to attend a dinner.

It is precisely this unexpected arrest, the result of a warrant from the State Prosecutor's office that revoked his release on bail (given despite his conviction for links with the Mafia) while waiting a final verdict from the Supreme Court of Cassation, that throws a sinister shadow over the end of the 'forced cohabitation' between Ciancimino and the Carabinieri. One school of thought, and by no means a minority view, maintains the idea that it was not by chance the former mayor found himself in Rebibbia and in that particular moment. It was as if someone wanted him out of the way.

MASSIMO: As my father claims, he was caught in a trap from the moment he was persuaded to ask for the return of his passport, which had been withdrawn when they began investigating him for the crime of having links with the Mafia. It's a strange story, full of coincidences and inexplicable influences. It starts with the message from Lo Verde/Provenzano that, once the capture of the 'mad man' (Riina) was cut and dried, then he should perhaps find himself out of Italy, both to give himself a safety margin, and also to limit the risk of being seen by people who could have linked their close relationship with Totò Riina's 'betrayal'.

Besides, my father liked the prospect of having his passport back. He couldn't believe in a return to full liberty. The ability to move about without limits or bureaucratic restrictions was true freedom for him. In this sense, he thought he was hampered if he couldn't hold a passport.

So for this reason he accepted the offer from ROS to help him obtain the document. I remember the moment well and how all those around him were against the initiative, which left him open to the suspicion that he was preparing to flee the country. Against it were important barristers such as Professors Campo and Siracusano, his lawyer Giorgio Ghiron, and his sons, three of whom had graduated in law. To them it seemed like a suicidal course. But he was determined to go ahead nonetheless, entrusting the task of filing the petition to his lawyer, Avv. Ghiron, even though he had his doubts. Afterwards, when he became aware of his error in prison, he called the Carabinieri's suggestion a trap. According to him, ROS had urged him to be incautious in order to have him arrested and keep him out of circulation, once they had the information they wanted from him.

On the other hand, he had the necessary documents if he'd wanted to leave the country. He had an identity card that would allow him to do so, as well as a false passport, which was not in his own name. Signor Franco obtained it for him immediately after Salvo Lima's assassination in March 1992, in case he found it necessary to leave, particularly for reasons of safety. I don't know if it was a Tunisian or a Turkish passport, but the Carabinieri didn't know about it. To the assumed name, a very odd photograph of my father was added. I can't forget the afternoon he had the photograph taken. First of all, he went to a hairdresser near the apartment in Piazza di Spagna who really made him look a sight. It was a shock to see him when he came home in a wig and false beard, much thicker than his natural one. At home, a photographer sent personally by Signor Franco was waiting for him. But the false passport was never put to use. He would have done so only for personal safety in a real emergency. In the heat of the moment of Lima's murder he would say repeatedly: 'We're all in danger now.'

GIOVANNI: On the occasion of a meeting in Palermo or Rome, I don't remember which, following Ignazio Salvo's murder, my father had something to say to me: 'They've let me know that I should apply for a passport.' I was confused because I thought such a request both inopportune and detrimental at the very time he was waiting for the result of his appeal against the first-degree sentence for his links with the Mafia.

However, at his insistence, I asked a trusted member of his defence team, Professor Orazio Campo, to write the petition.

But he categorically refused because he, too, thought it inopportune and, above all, it wouldn't be granted. As far as I know, it was then filed by a lawyer in Rome my father had engaged separately.

When they arrested him on 19 December I had many opportunities to remind him of the fateful consequences of the enterprise and he had many opportunities to rage about how he'd been betrayed and sold out.

This passport business and ROS's interest in Ciancimino's preventative custody has been the subject of an actual mini-investigation by the Caltanissetta Prosecutor's office, following several statements made during the transmission of *AnnoZero* by the former Attorney General, Claudio Martelli, who was remembering his 'request in 1992 about the seizure of Vito Ciancimino's assets'. By mistake, the former minister placed it in June '92. In fact, as Liliana Ferraro (at the time Martelli's closest collaborator) clarified in Caltanissetta, the minister's participation in it was in the following October. She testified that it was to do with 'a matter concerning Vito Ciancimino's assets and ROS's intervention.'

'I reminded him,' the testimony continues, 'that the problem he was talking about had instead arisen in autumn 1992, a little before he himself as minister presented the latest proposals for completing the plan of action against Cosa Nostra to Parliament's Anti-Mafia Commission. With regard to the Hon. Martelli's recollection, repeated here today, another memory occurs to me, in that I seem to recall in the same autumn of

1992, at the time of one or two meetings with Colonel Mori in which investigative talks were certainly spoken of, together with the method of executing them and of an eventual extension of those who could be admitted to them, the figure of Vito Ciancimino and his wish to recover his passport came up. As far as I remember, and as far as it concerned me, the matter had no follow-up, as I had no direct jurisdiction over the subject, but obviously I informed the Minister for Justice right away.'

Martelli echoes this: 'I remember that when Dottoressa Ferraro informed me of these talks I was indignant at the idea a passport should be given to Vito Ciancimino, who rather should have been having his assets seized. Having informed myself that the issue of a passport required the authorization of the Attorney General's office in Palermo, I intervened – I think directly – speaking with [the] prosecuting magistrate Siclari.'

When Don Vito came to be arrested, Massimo wasn't with him. He was still in Palermo with the maps given him by Lo Verde/Provenzano to pass on to his father. The envelope remained in his hands, while Don Vito left with the understanding they would see each other again in Rome after a couple of days. But the police arrived before that. The news of his arrest reached Massimo while he was still in Palermo.

MASSIMO: I wasn't expecting anything of the kind, and as a result was completely bewildered. I called Captain De Donno to find out more, but he seemed more confused than I was.

He told me: 'I don't know anything about this, I swear. I was on my way to his house because we had a meeting, but I couldn't get there because I could see there was an operation under way. All around it was full of police. I don't know anything else; I'd nothing to do with it.'

I got to Rome straightaway, also to prepare the requests for visits with the lawyers. They told me there was no problem because I could see him right away, seeing that the arrest was in consequence of a verdict and not of an investigation under way, in which case there was a period of isolation.

But before being able to visit him in prison I heard his voice on my mobile. My father was able to call me using the cell phone of De Donno, who was sitting beside him in Rebibbia. That call had a particular aim: the Carabinieri weren't going to miss out on getting their hands on the famous maps and told me through my father that I had to give them to the captain. I gave them to him after a day or two. I really would have liked to keep a copy, but De Donno said it was wiser to get rid of everything. I was persuaded to do so when my father also asked me.

10

The New Mediators

Totò Riina was captured in Palermo on the morning of 15 January 1993. He was in a little runabout driven by his friend Salvatore Biondino, having just come out of his secret address in Via Bernini. It wasn't yet nine o'clock and his trusted driver was taking him to an important meeting of the Cosa Nostra *cupola*. The *pentito* Giovanni Brusca would later say that on the agenda for discussion that day was taking up the boss's programme of bloodshed again, after the imposed cessation to see what the authorities' reaction would be to the slaughter in Via D'Amelio.

Don Totò never made it to that gathering; Captain Ultimo's blitz was swift and faultless. In less than two minutes the boss was lying face-down on the ground and then bundled into a Carabinieri decoy car while the drivers crowding the Motel Agip roundabout on the ring road thought they were witnessing a kidnapping. Taken by surprise, confused, traumatized, but also a little relieved, once he was sure he was in the Carabinieri's hands and not those of his Mafia enemies, Riina was taken to a small room in the Bonsignore barracks and photographed beneath the portrait of assassinated Carabinieri chief Carlo Alberto Dalla Chiesa, in whose memory Ultimo gripped his wrists.

Vito Ciancimino had been in prison almost a month, his presence there sealing the definitive end to the mediation the ROS Carabinieri had requested. But Don Vito was keeping an eye on events and he knew that he had to try to salvage what he could of that initial ambitious project. The sight of Riina's face behind bars gave lifeblood and euphoria to the authorities' initiative and, in contrast, marginalized his own role. The only way to 'keep on his feet' was to formalize his collaboration with the judges.

He made this specific request to the Carabinieri, who somehow tried to steer him into the protective enclosure of those turned state witnesses.

Don Totò's Hideout

According to Massimo Ciancimino, Don Vito reached an agreement with the Carabinieri about a management of the facts whereby the deal's initial phase that took place before the Via D'Amelio attack would not be made public. Don Vito's son says his father prepared a kind of handwritten memoir that offers the 'agreed version' of these various stages – from the meeting on the aeroplane with De Donno up to his arrest – and put it in a document voluntarily handed over to the magistrates (at the time he began to talk to magistrates Ingroia and Caselli in the Public Prosecutor's Office) during the course of a search while he was in prison.

Is it because of their mutual distrust that the magistracy never thought it necessary to formalize the umpteenth attempt at getting Don Vito to collaborate? The question remains open, but Massimo thinks not, when – on more than one occasion – he underlines the fact that the judges paid little attention to what his father was telling them. One thing, however, was not invented, and that concerns the whole investigation about the Carabinieri's failure to make a search of the Via Bernini hideout.

What did happen there? It was simply that the apartment where Riina lived with his wife and four children, two boys and two girls, was not searched for eighteen days; furthermore, a few hours after the lightning strike, the CCTV cameras that monitored the main door of the Via Bernini apartment block day and night were taken down. This action, which the Carabinieri have always said was a 'mistake', has given rise to endless polemics and, primarily, a trial (against Mori and Ultimo, both later acquitted) when several collaborators with justice revealed that Cosa Nostra 'cleaned out Riina's hideout' and that the boss's wife was given the opportunity to make it to Corleone with absolute calm, taking the contents of the safe with her. The curious aspect of the whole affair is that neither at the trials for Capaci and Via D'Amelio in Caltanissetta, nor in Florence (for the bombings in Rome, Milan and Florence in 1993), nor even in the hearing to discover the 'truth' about the hideout, was Don Vito ever called upon as a witness on any side. Essentially, notes Massimo Ciancimino, 'A trial was held to ascertain the existence or not of a deal between the Mafia and the country's authorities without ever interrogating the mediator in that deal. Isn't there something not right here?'

MASSIMO: Locked up in his cell, number G8 in Rebibbia, my father continued to watch as events unfolded and couldn't help but see his suspicions confirmed that the 'game' was now being played well above his head. Everything he had forecast so often came to pass: the area where Riina lived was the one Signor Lo Verde had circled on the maps which I myself handed over to Captain De Donno. But the newspapers were talking of the fundamental contribution to the boss's capture by the *pentito* Balduccio Di Maggio, a Mafioso (later *pentito*) from San Giuseppe Jato, who gave himself up to the police in Borgo-manero in Piemonte, declaring his willingness to collaborate for the express purpose of obtaining Don Totò's arrest. All this my father took as a 'diversion', a shield for concealing and protecting Provenzano's 'betrayal' of Riina and my father's involvement in it.

For a certain period, links with the Carabinieri continued. There were frequent investigative hearings with my father in prison. Mori and De Donno were present during the official questioning by Caselli and Ingroia after Riina's capture that led to the possibility of collaboration, which then failed without anyone giving the reason beyond unspecific justifications about the contradictory nature and unreliability of his earlier evidence. But it has to be said that, in order to make himself more appealing to the magistrates, he'd already revealed the identity of the mediator who brought Riina's messages to him, namely Dr Antonino Cinà.

In any case, it didn't take much for the idea to grow that he'd been clinically 'shafted'. The certainty of this was reinforced when we later heard about the failure to search the hideout; otherwise everything had been carried out according to the agreement made at the time with the Carabinieri. And so my father thought there must be someone leading the dance in his place. At the same time, another reasonable doubt was gaining ground: his exclusion had also been accepted by his friends Lo Verde and Franco, who were now in touch with new political sources. The further things went, my father gathered, as he said, that his 'elimination' (by means of his arrest with the passport as expedient motive) was in essence a change imposed during the course of the operation. The substitution of a 'worn-out horse' (for the man compromised by judicial difficulties, especially in the historic moment following the discovery of the 'rascal' Mario Chiesa and of Tangentopoli) by 'fresh troops'.

But it's also possible that during its long existence, 'the Deal' – originating in a 'businesslike' agreement with two officers enjoying political support – had so changed shape that its original dimensions had been abandoned: it was no longer a question of 'give and take' but one of support for a political project to save an electoral tradition that risked being destroyed by the corruption scandals. This too had been my father's idea, as it's easy to demonstrate by the simple analysis of the so-called 'contropapello' (counter-proposal) and by successive actions from his prison cell, with the help of Signor Franco and his men who came and went in Rebibbia.

A New Ferryman?

So we have a Don Vito who, even from the depths of his cell, made every effort to speak out as if he were a free man. And Franco and Lo Verde continued to be his points of contact.

But who is the mysterious 'ferryman' who took control of this incandescent magma and whose disturbing presence accompanies the start of the 'Second Republic'? Massimo Ciancimino gives one answer derived from what his father said, but primarily from Don Vito's papers, namely the notes and messages coming from Lo Verde that Massimo delivered to him in prison. Ciancimino Jr has handed these over to the judiciary and they are now part of the evidence in several ongoing trials.

In the hearing for the charges against General Mori and Colonel Obinu (for failing to capture Provenzano) the following name has emerged: 'It's Dottore Marcello Dell'Utri, the senator . . . and MP. We're talking about the person who put the Forza Italia party on its feet and in turn became Prime Minister. My father was sure of this not by deduction or a flight of the imagination. No, my father's source was Lo Verde, who had made some kind of contact with the "new politics" of Silvio Berlusconi.'

The senator has brushed aside Massimo's testimony as 'rubbish', announcing an imminent judicial counter-offensive. He has declared this to the media: 'It's all garbage, a load of bullshit, the ravings of a madman. How does one defend oneself against accusations that have absolutely no basis in reality?'

Don Vito probably never had any dealings with Dell'Utri. 'But my father,' Massimo testified, 'knew very well who he was and where he came from, at the same time harbouring a low opinion of him and no esteem whatsoever. Past events such as the investments in Milano 2, the friendship with Francesco Paolo Alamia and the construction contractors Buscemi and Bonura and the Lu.Ra.No. property company are precedents that lead perfectly to Dell'Utri's identification.'

Don Vito's son has given several pieces of support on this subject to the magistrates. But let us hear the account directly from him.

MASSIMO: These are from documents that come from 1994 or 1995, I don't remember which. They draw a clear outline of the institutional powers of that time and their mixing with Cosa Nostra circles, which was hard to avoid. They're threatening letters my father intended to send to Dell'Utri, but the real and ultimate recipient was Silvio Berlusconi, who as head of the executive was responsible for the government's initiatives (deemed ' disappointing') towards legislative provisions to comply with the demands of the Mafia, initiatives that were still becalmed in the shoals of investigations and hostage to the judges. They were an out-and-out act of

political rebellion, but of course I can't confirm that those letters were ever actually sent.

I do remember, however, that my father's criticisms were
not only over his disappointment over the lack of political initiative towards the benefit of the organization, there was a real
anger over the inadequate knowledge as to how best to exploit
the potential of the March '94 elections which brought Forza
Italia and Berlusconi to power.

Perhaps here we should glance at these fragments of text, which,
according to Massimo, were inspired by Provenzano and were
to be sent to Dell'Utri and 'to the Prime Minister, the Hon.
Silvio Berlusconi . . .'

> . . . years of prison for this political position of mine, I intend
> to give my contribution (that won't be a modest one) so that
> this sad event won't come about

> I remain convinced that if this event does come about (in the
> judicial sphere as well as elsewhere) the Hon. Berlusconi will
> make one of his television channels available

> If a large amount of time passes and I'm still not charged with
> any crime, I shall be constrained to break the silence that I've
> maintained for years and in consequence will hold a press con-
> ference not only for this small episode but first and foremost to
> demonstrate the ineptitude that has lasted since I . . .

These documents are in the hands of the magistrates right now. But let us hear Massimo Ciancimino for his interpretation.

MASSIMO: I must start by saying that I had never given a hint of any of this to the magistrates. Seeing as I was already on trial for the business of the gas company – which we'll talk about shortly – I had no wish at all to go and throw myself into the meat grinder of Dell'Utri and Berlusconi's affairs. Besides, I'd had assurances from Franco, via an emissary of his, that these documents would never see the light of day. And Franco was rarely ever wrong. In fact it was quite something for them to emerge from the oblivion into which they'd sunk, and I'll tell you the story of how that came about later on. So, at that point, with my credibility at stake, I decided to tell all. But for the moment let's continue with the documents.

Without a doubt, one of these gave details of a letter my father received from Provenzano. I am certain of this because in the summer of 1994 I had to go and get it myself from Pino Lipari's home in San Vito Lo Capo. But I had the problem of not being able to deliver it directly to my father because you can't give anything on paper to the prisoners. And so I had to read it to him while he took notes and, by the same system, he passed his thoughts on back to me. All of which I had to hand over as well to Signor Franco, who was in touch with me and already in the know.

I can confirm they contained explicit challenges, threats to the Hon. Berlusconi. He referred to a 'sad event', for the avoidance of which my father was offering his 'contribution . . . so that [it] won't come about'. What was this sad event? My father told me he was concerned for the physical safety of Berlusconi's son. I remember this because the explanation struck me as unusual, so I asked: 'What's Berlusconi's son got to do with it?' Then there was the reference to the 'Hon. Berlusconi' who 'will make one of his television channels available'. Then there's the threat that if something doesn't come about '. . . I shall be constrained to break [my] silence'.

My father later explained to me that the thing about the television channel was a kind of reminder to the Premier and referred to an old interview of his where he declared himself ready to put his communications media at the service of any one of his friends if they had need of it or entered into politics. So that was the moment to maintain the commitment, otherwise my father was threatening to 'break [his] silence'.

But all this was a film that he'd created in his own mind, a script that didn't exist. The truth was that Vito Ciancimino was in an arc of shadow from which he'd never emerge. My father's the only politician at a certain level that served out his entire sentence for the crime of having links with the Mafia. I haven't the slightest intention of defending him because while he was alive it was truly indefensible. But are we truly to believe he was the only Mafioso who'd infiltrated politics and respectable Sicilian society?

Things went ahead, however, without my father having any power to intervene: his imprisonment lasted for seven long years with his feelings of regret, his illnesses and anger when he realized the harshness of his defeat. For obvious reasons, the link with Lo Verde/Provenzano had slackened off: however geared up you might be for any trouble, it's pretty difficult to imagine any close communication between a prisoner and a fugitive, without forgetting that a Ciancimino stuck in prison was no longer any use to anyone. Even Signor Franco was now tending to delegate contact to his right-hand man, with the job more or less of monitoring his moods and keeping him calm whenever he went off at a tangent, threatening to make theatrical public statements. I also began to see him less often and to share the burden of weekly visits with my brothers.

Old Friends, New Friends

Vito Ciancimino was released from prison in November 1999. He went into house arrest after serving the entire part of his sentence for links with the Mafia, a crime that before that date allowed no concession for extenuating circumstances. However, when it came to the remaining part of his sentence for more common offences, it was possible to put in a request and obtain house arrest for health reasons.

Don Vito was not very well. He had been photographed in a wheelchair at the time of an ugly fracture to his femur. He was worried about his prostate and hypertension, which in the past had already caused both ischaemia and an ictus. For his son Massimo his coming home meant a return to his old role of assistant and general dogsbody, exactly as it had been in the long years of the former mayor's court battles and his undiscloseable contacts with the Mafia and secret service operatives.

We know little about his last prison sentence. Massimo himself admits to having slackened off his contact with his father. We can pick up on not only Don Vito's disappointment over his status as prisoner whom his friends had 'forgotten', but also his unshakable pertinacity in trying to find a definitive way out of his legal problems and in particular the sword of Damocles in the form of seizure of his assets. It's clear he wanted a return to full liberty in order to exorcize his long-standing fear of dying in prison.

But one way or another, his return home opened up the old habits of a continual exchange of information with Franco and Lo Verde. House arrest certainly could not constitute a valid impediment to meetings with the former. But the problem was more evident as he sought to resume his old rapport with the latter. The way in which the two had become distanced was traumatic: Don Vito's surprise arrest during the height of working out 'a Deal' and his doubts about the role his old friend Lo Verde had played in the decision to put him out of the way. And yet they had to make contact again.

MASSIMO: Lo Verde heard of his release in the newspapers. He sent someone to get information about the state of my father's health, but also about the conditions that governed his house arrest and the trustworthiness of the domestic servants.

I assured his go-between that there were no restrictions with the servants, except they were forbidden to admit people with a criminal record. This wasn't a problem for Lo Verde, who was free to move about with his false identity. Otherwise he wouldn't have been able to range around with long car journeys between doctors' surgeries and health clinics to deal with his enlarged prostate that was close to the inevitable operation.

He came one day at the end of 1999 around Christmas time. I don't remember if the visit was prearranged, certainly I didn't know anything about it, but my father didn't seem any more surprised than usual. It was the first time the two friends had met since the passport trap. Exactly seven years had passed since that December in 1992. I read great anger in my father's face, but also pride in regarding himself as a leading player and originator of a new Mafia strategy that had caught on in the previous years: moving under the surface, new contacts, new political referents. At bottom, he thought, all this was also the fruit of the intuitions he'd shared with Lo Verde: if Cosa Nostra had changed course, returning to the age-old choice of a 'pax mafiosa', and if this had been entrusted to Provenzano – my father thought – then he was also due the credit.

He wanted to receive him in the living room and had dressed himself up in jacket and tie, almost as if wanting to mark the distance that had been created with his old friend, but also to show that his vitality was unaffected by the years he'd spent in prison. Certainly he wasn't the same man he was in '92. He could only move about with the aid of a stick but in order not to show this handicap he had me accompany him arm in arm. His shoes were no longer the handmade crocodile-skin moccasins, nor the high-class manufactured ones seen in the shop windows of Napoleon, the famous shoe shop in Piazza Politeama; they had been superseded by a less elegant orthopaedic shoe more suitable to his needs.

They exchanged kisses on both cheeks and shook hands, but the looks were cold. I helped my father sit down on the orthopaedic armchair that came with a special electronic device that helped him get to his feet again. I was curious, very curious, about what they would say, but left the room. My relationship with him had also changed; since he'd returned home and wasn't in good health he no longer saw me as the young wastrel, his untrustworthy 'dickhead'. The idea of writing a book together had helped create a closeness between us and brought him round to divulging many confidences. But I didn't imagine for a minute I could witness a meeting like this.

They spoke for more than three hours. I never learned in detail what was said. Certainly, the health of both was high on the agenda and the common enemy they had to fight in the invincible shape of an enlarged prostate. He later told me he'd spoken a great deal about politics with Lo Verde and about a Parliament that was intimidated and had given itself up to the judges' party. He explained to me the meaning of the phrases Provenzano suggested in the draft of a letter I'd read to my father in Rebibbia; it was to be an invitation to intervene immediately (we're talking about '94 to '95) in order to bring back to normal a magistracy that had gone so far as to deliver a notification of prosecution to a premier while he was presiding at an international summit. 'The most serious and important pieces of legislation,' he was fond of repeating, 'are passed in the first hundred days of a new government, while the electoral consensus is still united.'

But then they focused on the present. Lo Verde's visit was also something of an attempt to make up for his behaviour in '92, about which he felt some guilt. And for that reason he was sitting beside his old friend as if to say: what can I do for you?

The problem was the perennial one of finding a 'political solution' that would allow my father to return to being a free man. At that moment the avenues were few: a pardon or amnesty, but it had to be done quickly. It was necessary therefore to spur some friends, Lo Verde's new friends, into action because this was the right moment. It was the start of the Great Jubilee year and a provision of clemency would have been well received both by the Catholic community and the Vatican. My father explained that it would also have been perfect if the proposal for an amnesty or a pardon had come from the centre left because, he said, 'the magistrates let the Communists do what they want'. It was a matter of finding a synthesis between opposing camps and moving quickly towards an approval.

He was very acerbic in his attitude to Dell'Utri but he recognized his capacity to exert huge power over Berlusconi: 'He's got him by the balls.'

Let's Hope They Do It In Time

Other meetings followed that concentrated mainly on their health problems, and little is known about them.

But a reply to the matters placed on the table in that first meeting couldn't wait. In August 2000 Massimo went in person to collect a 'pizzino' from Lo Verde/Provenzano's hands and addressed to his father:

> Dear *Ingegnere*, I hope you find yourself in a better state of health than when I saw you last month. I passed on your thoughts to our friend the sen[ator]. I explained that they couldn't make provisions such as the amnesty when in government and that it's the right thing to push to have the law approved.
>
> The friend told me that a meeting has taken place and everyone was in agreement. I saw that the Good Lord with the Cardinal has asked the same thing.

Questioned in court, Massimo Ciancimino has confirmed that the 'sen[ator] was Marcello Dell'Utri, although at that time he was still an MP. As regards the central part of the message, the interpretation he has given describes a 'Provenzano who has passed on my father's suggestions to his new friends about the timeliness that it should be the left that put forward the provision for clemency.' Dell'Utri denied these accusations but was nevertheless sentenced to seven and a half years in gaol for his links to the Mafia.

The matter of an amnesty was taken up again at the end of summer, 2001. This can be deduced from another message, again from Lo Verde, which Massimo Ciancimino has also explained to the magistrates. The text with its usual howlers, its habitual anarchic punctuation and typographical errors here corrected in translation, is a summary of the matters on the agenda:

> Dear *Ingegnere*, I've read what M has given me, but in order to avoid any misunderstanding I said that I'd speak about it when it's possible to see each other. I've been told by our Sen[ator] and by the new Prime Minister that they will push forward the new solution to your suffering. As soon as I have news I'll pass it on. I know the lawyer is favourable. Our friend Z has asked to meet the Senator. I read that you don't like this and it's necessary to take time. It's a matter of names for the Gas [company]. M told me that you're in hospital; I hope your health will soon improve and may the Good Lord be with you.

Here again, according to Massimo, the 'Sen[ator]' is Marcello Dell'Utri, who was busy pushing forward 'the new solution to your suffering'. 'Our friend Z' would be Enzo Zanghì, Don Vito's cousin, who wanted to meet Dell'Utri to tell him of his wish to be a candidate for Forza Italia.

MASSIMO: The postcard is from September 2001. Once again this one was given to me during the course of one of the usual rituals we had to go through with Pino Lipari or someone in his family. 'I've read what M has given me' is a blind because in fact there was little to read, as I'd given him an envelope containing fifty million in cash of the old lire. It was the 'straightening up' (or kickback) agreed upon for the work done in the Trapani area by the gas company, according to what was

established way back in 1984 by agreements between my father
and Provenzano. It was a sum that was kept low thanks to the
direct relationship between the two, even if the Mafia in
the area, and in particular Messina Denaro, regularly voiced
strident complaints.

However, I delivered this fifty million in person to Lo Verde
on the morning of 8 or 9 September, after having taken the
envelope containing the money from the office of Professor
Lapis.[Professor Lapis is currently on trial as a codefendant
with Ciancimino.] Before I left, Lo Verde asked me to come
back again in the afternoon because he would have a message
for my father. After several hours I went back to the same
address at 111 Via Leonardo Da Vinci, where a relative of Pino
Lipari lived, and where my father and Provenzano had met
many times in the past.

My father was in a hurry for a reply. He was anxious and,
perhaps, not totally convinced of the good intentions of Lo
Verde's friends. 'I feel sure,' he went about saying, 'I'll die in
prison.' And because of this he began thinking of returning to
live in Palermo. For the first time I heard him making remarks
such as: 'If I can't die a free man, at least I'll die on my native
soil.'

He was waiting for the 'pizzino' from his friend Lo Verde
and hoping for an amnesty. The year before his hopes had
already been dashed, despite the fact that the Jubilee had opened
up ample space with Pope Wojtyła [John Paul II]'s clear request
to the government 'for the concession of an act of clemency'.

In September 2001 my father was being treated in the Paideia

Clinic in the Collina Fleming district in order to have an operation for diverticulitis. Signor Franco, who was now ever present in his life, had just handed him the copy of a bill under discussion by the Cabinet's Justice Commission.

I went to see him immediately after lunch. He asked me for the usual pair of latex gloves and opened the letter in front of me. He read the contents attentively and made the comment, 'Let's hope they do it in time, if not I'll be dead first.' I remember he asked me if I'd recently seen his cousin Enzo Zanghì and I understood he was asking me because in the letter they were speaking about him in relation to his request to meet Marcello Dell'Utri.

I mentioned his cousin's bad mood over 'the continual fooling around' despite his huge commitment towards Forza Italia since 1994. He complained about not having received anything, even though he had always delivered a mass of votes, up to the very recent amazing result that had brought the centre right to win in all of Sicily's sixty-one electoral colleges. He told me he'd already asked for an appointment with Dell'Utri, tired of the lies that Micchichè was telling him. [This accusation of electoral malpractice would form part of the legal proceedings in which Ciancimino was involved.] Poor Enzo couldn't imagine that the cause of his lack of success was in fact my father, who was working behind the scenes to stop him obtaining any public office, fearing that this might be taken to be Ciancimino's return to politics. According to my father, Zanghì's candidature or his entry into office could have prejudiced approval of the legal benefits under discussion and the judges' reception of the request for the suspension of the charge that his legal team was all set to present.

While he was working himself up about Zanghì, the television – switched on to block any eavesdropping – began to transmit the pictures of the 9/11 attacks.

11

Addio, Don Vito

And so Vito Ciancimino dedicated the last three years of his life to the battle to regain his freedom. That it was a difficult, if not downright desperate battle is shown by Lo Verde/Proven-zano's vain attempts to set things into motion for his old friend's benefit. Signor Franco was also fairly well in evidence, but – according to what Massimo says – his was more a consolatory role than that of suggesting any effective strategy. He was a consoler, but also controller. His worry as a guarantor of the status quo was mainly that of foreseeing and blocking any sudden impulses on the part of Don Vito, who was ever more disappointed by his improbable saviours, and therefore prone to the temptation to open the bag and sweep up everyone in the whirlwind of a confession he saw as more of a vendetta: if Samson dies, then the Philistines go with him.

The most evident symptom of this temptation was the deci-sion, along with his youngest son, to start rummaging around in his past and his bottomless archive, part of which was cata-logued and kept in the light of day, and the other part hidden in the most obscure hiding places, such as the Treccani volumes or the *History of Sicily*, from which emerged the 'papello' and the 'pizzini'.

MASSIMO: In the past he'd written a kind of memoir with the title *The Mafias* and he'd distributed it to lawyers, judges, journalists, politicians and the police. No one had taken any notice of the work; in fact, its limitation was that in its holding back, its hair-splitting and resentfulness it seemed merely a work of exculpation. It was even offensive, both towards indisputable national heroes such as Falcone and Dalla Chiesa, but also towards powerful and untouchable politicians such as Andreotti. And yet there was something to be gathered from those pages as well, so much so that many facts and considerations come together in 'A Paradigm for Collaboration', a sort of plan set out of all the matters he had in mind to explain.

Once he was home, he took up the work again, but in a different spirit. Ten years had passed, many of which were spent in prison, and he saw that there wasn't a great deal to save. Now there was no longer the same need for caution, he thought – as he'd suggested some time ago in his letter to Berlusconi – it was time to 'break his silence'. It's then that we began to go over practically all his political life, using documents he elaborated on from memory. My role also changed: I was no longer the involuntary right hand who was kept in ignorance, but the repository for his stories. And so our relationship came to change as well.

For the first time I began to know Vito Ciancimino no longer in the role of father, which was anyway limited, but as a man and a politician. I discovered a lonely man locked up in his memories and his sense of guilt. And for the first time, he was willing to share the enormous burden of those memories of his past and his loneliness despite the presence of five children. I was looking at him stretched out on the famous bed that used to be the symbol of his power and arrogance. In that moment he was transformed into a simple image of physical decline, with his fractured femur and the after-effects of his long prison sentence.

To me he seemed torn between the instinct of an old lion ready to start all over again and the realization that the time had now passed when he could find any senator likely to intervene for him, having been warned off by his friend Lo Verde. Besides, he'd been in and out of depression for some time, associating the deprivation of his liberty with the deprivation of life. Leafing through the mountain of papers that survived him, I found a handwritten sheet that ends a long note on the efforts he spent – all in vain – to defend himself in the trials. Disappointed by yet another defeat, he writes, 'What to do, having got to this point? What other prospects are open to me besides being an impotent witness to my conviction? And my end? I've already been convicted (without any proof) for an offence that Parliament's abolished. Who do I have to await? What do I have to wait for? The slow agony of death? Why? For what reason, for whom? Waiting for God's justice? Unfortunately, neither God nor justice exist. So it'd be better to put an end to it. But when? And by what means? This is the problem to be resolved with all due speed.'

Through a cruel joke of destiny, Baffo died alone while I was away in Palermo. I'd been his shadow for years and then one night I wasn't there: right when I was getting to know him, he went away again and this time for good, without letting me take his hand. It was a blow not being there.

GIOVANNI: The last memory I have of my father comes from October. I went to see him in Rome, taking my son Marco, to whom Baffo was very attached. They were peaceful days and even his state of health was good. He took long walks with his grandson around the streets of the centre and in the evening we dined at his favourite restaurant in the Campo dei Fiori.

After a month or more, it was 18 November, the phone rang at home in Palermo. It was about eleven at night and he was phoning because he wanted to speak to Marco. I told him he was already asleep and asked if I should wake him. He told me he'd call the next day and began to speak of the guilty verdict passed on Andreotti at the Perugia trial [which was later overturned on appeal], while still of the idea that Beelzebub would get away with it this time as well. He had no great liking for the senator, saying of him: 'Sincerity's everything: one you've learned to fake that, the rest is easy.'

He did almost all of the talking and seemed particularly happy and sprightly in his mood. We said goodbye after a few minutes with the intention of speaking again soon. But about 6.30 in the morning there was a call from my sister Luciana who was agitated and told me that something had happened to my father: 'The "Russians" have called, I don't know, I don't understand, he's not well and they've called an ambulance.'

I got out of bed to get ready and, by conditional reflex, switched on the TV for the news. I turned to stone when the *Tg5* breaking news caption began to run with the text, 'Vito Ciancimino dies in Rome.' Eight years have passed and I can't get rid of that image.

Luciana phoned immediately afterwards, saying, 'He's dead.' 'I know,' I said, 'I've just seen it on the news.' She told me I absolutely had to go to Massimo's because he wasn't answering the phone and she had to dash off to Rome. We found Massimo in a state of total desperation: he was screaming, banging his fists on the walls, and asking himself why, when he was up in Rome all the time, it had to happen on the day he wasn't there. He couldn't stop thinking about it.

The three of us took the first plane to Rome, none of us speaking, all lost in our own thoughts. What came to my mind was the irony with which he exorcized his fear of death, helping himself to face it with well-known phrases. In particular he was fond of the one by the Emperor Aurelian: 'I know I must die one day, but can't bring myself to believe it.'

And I wondered if Uncle Mimì, who had been dead some time, had been able to keep the promise he made to him once when he was ill: 'Don't worry,' he'd reassured him, 'when your hour comes I'll come and get you when you're asleep and so you'll pass away with no suffering.'

The flat in Piazza di Spagna was closed and sealed with two iron bars. Four plainclothes policemen were guarding the entrance and told us that the body was in the mortuary awaiting an autopsy. In front of the barred door my sister Luciana had a fit of hysterics. She had a promise to keep: my father had asked her to dress him in a certain way come the moment of his last goodbye. He'd shown her where to find the clothes, they were hanging in the wardrobe protected by plastic bags: a blue pinstripe suit, a white shirt and a tie given to him by his father, my grandfather Giovanni, on the day he passed his *maturità* [school leaving] examination. In those moments of confusion and anger, not one of us paid any attention to the absence of the Moldovan couple – the famous 'Russians' – who looked after my father and who appeared to have vanished into thin air.

Luciana and Massimo went off to see him in the mortuary, while I preferred to remember him alive and smiling, as he had been in October. My brother and sister weren't allowed any direct contact; they saw him through a pane of glass, as in prison. They told me he looked at peace.

Immediately afterwards we were given permission to enter the apartment. While Luciana busied herself finding the clothes, I noticed that everything edible had been taken from the kitchen, including the numerous bottles of mineral water. Probably they'd made a quick search of the premises, judging from the untidy state of the books on the shelves and drawers left open, in which state my father would never have left them, captive as he was to his mania for perfection.

MASSIMO: 'Vito Ciancimino did well in life and in politics.' These were the words spoken by Father Antonio Di Pasquale, parish priest of San Michele Arcangelo, the church where my father's funeral took place on 23 November 2002. The words surprised me, so much so that I had to whisper in my brother Giovanni's ear, and also to break the hypocritical atmosphere of condolence that surrounded us, 'Then he certainly knows something that we don't.' Holding back the smile that wouldn't have been appropriate, Giovanni whispered back, 'Always the dickhead.'

I remember the faces of the bystanders; there were no big names from the political world, those who had once queued up to be invited to our house. There were a few friends: Ferruccio Barbera, Gianfranco Vizzini, brother of the more famous senator Carlo of Forza Italia, the publisher Giorgio Palumbo, the former assessor Giacomino Murana, and the lawyer Vito Gigante, a man of my father's camp. In the front row stood my mother in tears: I don't know if they were for the death of her husband or the pain of seeing me so overcome clutching the coffin that contained the man I'd clashed with so many times.

GIOVANNI: There were many more women than men at the funeral, the politicians who'd known him having preferred to send their wives. This wouldn't have displeased my father. The priest gave a long and passionate sermon, even without suppressing the errors he'd made. They were sins shared by many others who had the misfortune of not being – as we say in Sicily – 'happily placed'.

Eight years have passed since that funeral and we've been waiting for some reply to the questions put forward to investigators. We've received only silence. Despite the fact that my father's body underwent an autopsy and a great number of toxicology tests, still no one has communicated with us relatives about the cause of death.

MASSIMO: I've told the magistrates that I've many doubts about my father's death. He was well at the time, on form and intellectually quick. I'd heard him two or three days earlier and he'd been joking about the news of Giulio Andreotti's guilty verdict. In the past he'd always maintained that the senator would never spend a single day in gaol, so much so that he could say he hoped he'd die only after such an event came to pass. On 17 November the criminal court in Perugia found 'il Divo' guilty of a serious crime and then my father said, 'Perhaps the time has come . . .' But immediately afterwards, as if to exorcize it, he added, 'You'll see he'll get away scot free this time as well,' perhaps referring to the miracles performed by the Supreme Court of Cassation.

I don't want to be taken in by any ideas here, but I found the succession of events strange. Above all I haven't been able to explain away a slight mystery: on the morning of the 19th I found a missed call from my father, made around two in the morning. First question: if he was calling me because he wasn't feeling well, why didn't he turn to the two domestic staff who were sleeping in the house? From what we know, in fact the Moldovans only became aware of his death the following morning. Second question: how come the night-time phone call shows it was made at two o'clock, which is one hour later –

according to what little official news we had – than the time of his death? Third question: what's happened to the only witnesses of that night, who disappeared into the blue? And isn't it right to ask for the results of the autopsy?

When I agreed to collaborate, the judges who were questioning me asked me who was around my father in that last part of his life. I said that the people he spoke to were always the same: Lo Verde/Provenzano, whose infrequent appearances were imposed by his fugitive status, and the famous Signor Franco (or one of his emissaries), who was much more hands-on, because he had the role – I think – of 'troubleshooter'. And my father's restlessness could come under the heading of the things he had to watch and, eventually, calm down.

Signor Franco's presence has troubled me throughout all the business that started with 'the Deal' and ended with my father's departure from this life. I can't quite grasp the sense of his role, especially for what it became after 19 November 2002. We'd see him a little, and we'd speak about my case and the authorities' interference that characterized it. But I had the feeling that his presence had a different purpose and that, in the end, his pieces of advice were taking more the form of underhand threats.

Even on the day of the funeral I had the clear perception of his character's different shades. We were in the Capuchin cemetery in Palermo, when he came up to me. He spoke some words of comfort to me and an appreciation of the father I'd just buried. But at a certain point he took an envelope out of his pocket and gave it to me. I was left speechless when I opened it and read the card it contained: it seems incredible to say, but it was a 'pizzino' of condolence for me and the whole family from Signor Lo Verde, sent this time by a truly singular postman.

The End of the Adventure

The figure of Signor Franco is quite an astonishing one in his continual hidden presence as the elusive puppet master of Vito Ciancimino's entire political and business career. Massimo tells of how he saw him 'always at my father's side', this even going quite far back in time.

MASSIMO: I don't even recall the exact moment of his first meeting with Signor Franco. The fact is I always remember seeing them together. It was exactly the same with Signor Lo Verde: two presences that over time became truly members of the family.

In the last period of sharing his soul, my father told me of the man's adventurous origins. He said there were fortunate people in this world and, according to him, Franco was one of them. As ever, he didn't tell me everything, which was understandable. He almost always kept something to himself, which made his tales somewhat unclear. But from what I've understood, he linked Franco's 'fortunate career' with the

Montagnalonga tragedy, an air disaster that occurred at Punta
Raisi airport in 1972. According to his recollection, the number
of the victims was 114, and this hid a murder mystery that was
never solved: the number of bodies recovered didn't coincide
with the official passenger list of 115. In essence, at the roll call
there was one name missing and that – it seems – belonged
to a secret service agent who specialized in Sicilian affairs. The
role of this high-ranking official, who's never been identified,
was transferred to Signor Franco, who was then still at the
beginning of his career. My father told me all this, adding that
his association with this James Bond character intensified
during the time Franco Restivo was Interior Minister.

Mister Franco

MASSIMO: But everything really began during the time of the
Via Lazio atrocity (1969) when Bernardo Provenzano conquered
Palermo to the sound of his sawn-off shotgun. His unprecedented attack took place on a building site in the 'new Palermo',
the very symbol of speculative property development. The
object of Provenzano's Corleonese gang was the Palermo boss
Michele Cavataio, who was suspected of wanting to sell the
Corleone Mafia's organization chart to police investigators. But
in order to kill him, the hit squad, who were disguised as
policemen, didn't hesitate to kill three of his closest followers
as well. It was an out-and-out gun battle, Cavataio firing his
Colt Cobra and killing Calogero Bagarella.

The event upset a good many officers responsible for keeping public order who, as has often happened in our history, tried to flee into the wings with all due speed. And so my father was called to Rome for a meeting at the highest level with Ministers Restivo and Ruffini and urged to find lasting contact with the new Corleonese group.

And that's how his contact with the secret services came about. It was a relationship that was subsequently reinforced a year later in 1970 at the time of Junio Valerio Borghese's attempted coup, which saw the heavy involvement of the Mafia organization and Luciano Liggio in particular.

Even back then my father had to report on the strategies planned during the preparations for the coup, which entailed a meeting to discuss organization in Rome with the leader Borghese and the head of the regional Cosa Nostra *cupola* who, at that time, was Giuseppe Calderone.

I've always wondered if Franco was his real name. I put him down as that on my cell phone according to my father's directions, even though I have to say I sometimes heard him being called Carlo, especially when I came up close to him at the end of their meetings. This is why I have no idea which of the two names is the real one.

But I remember the two as friends very well. In Rome Franco would often come to take him out on his daily walk. He came in his blue car, looking elegant, wearing glasses, his grey hair beautifully coiffured, his dress impeccable. They talked endlessly as they walked the little streets between Piazza di Spagna and Piazza del Popolo. They had several friends in common, such as Conte Romolo Vaselli junior. And it was always Franco who led the way through both good and ill.

He never lost sight of my father, even when he ended up in gaol. Among the photos shown me by the magistrates, I recognized two of the men who worked for him: one who acted as his driver and another who came and went in Rebibbia in order to watch over my father in prison. (He wasn't in the photos shown me.) The driver had the face of the 'captain', the man who came up to me when I was under house arrest to suggest that I didn't speak about any 'delicate matters' and last year actually came to my own home in Bologna to threaten me.

The last time I saw Franco was in 2006. He hinted that I should get out of Italy because things were going to happen that in some way could involve me, so with my family and a reliable lawyer I went to Sharm el-Sheikh. A few days later they arrested Bernardo Provenzano, and among the 'pizzini' they found one that referred to me.

The Heir

As we have seen, Vito Ciancimino's reckless adventures on earth concluded with the umpteenth mystery that shrouds the last moments of the Corleonese mayor, finally surprised and betrayed in the night by hypertension, a killer more treacherous than the ones he knew in his lifetime. There has been no investigation to try to piece together the night Don Vito passed away and it is therefore difficult to find any answer to the many questions about that hypertension, which at the time seemed to be under control. On the other hand, what can be said simply by following the chronology of events that happened after November 2002 is that, with his father dead, Massimo was asked to settle a series of accounts, which had not been presented before. It was he who – for better or worse – was to inherit the not inconsiderable burden of the paternal legacy, which certainly was comprised of economic resources, but also the unbearable weight of memories, which were so tangled they couldn't be shared with anyone. It was a burden that brought with it the role of suspect and convicted criminal to a man who was in some way the 'continuation' of his father's power, a power that couldn't help but bring trouble and unpleasant consequences as well.

MASSIMO: As long as my father was alive there was no prospect for me of any autonomy, no personal freedom or room for me to move on professionally. His presence in my life was total; seeing to his necessities – and helping out during his long prison sentence, then his illnesses – left no room for anything else. Even marriage had to wait. I'd known Carlotta for some years and I'd have liked to move forward and start a family. But this was only possible after my father's death, precisely because in the foreground there was only him and his problems.

He was released at the end of 1999 and he monopolized me practically immediately, exactly the same as it was in 1992 during 'the Deal'. Once he was home (as we've seen) he plunged into sorting through the enormous pile of documents that he was

intending to use as supporting evidence for the book he'd by
then decided to write in order to leave some record of all he'd
seen and lived through. And at the same time – as we've also
seen – he undertook a new battle to win back his total freedom
(by means of an amnesty) with the fundamental collaboration
of his old friend Lo Verde, his new friends in politics and Signor
Franco.

How could I ever begin to think of marriage in a situation
like that, where I was even running the risk of getting heavily
mixed up in his legal problems or indeed with more serious
and bloody consequences? It was for this reason I continued
to pass on Carlotta's devout requests that we should be married. When Baffo left us, he had a wonderful relationship with
the woman in my life and she with him, whom she found ironical and amusing. He used to make cutting jokes about me, as
when he wrote that he was troubled by the following conun-
drum: 'My human faculties stop me from understanding what
could possibly urge a beautiful, intelligent and well educated
young woman like Carlotta to live with someone like my son.
The fact gives me a measure of the divinity's inscrutable plans
about which I know nothing.' This was his way of giving me
some attention. Life had been like that from the moment he
chose me as his alter ego, without any consideration for the
risks I was running: 'In any case,' he said sarcastically, 'you're
not fit for anything else and would only end up in prison for
something much more mundane.'

But in the end it was obvious he trusted me, otherwise he
wouldn't have bestowed his will on me with his legal

possessions: 'I revoke all dispositions previously made and name my son Massimo Ciancimino and Luciana as heirs as long as they can jointly have access and control with regard to my property.' With these few lines my father handed over his papers and the memory of his scandalous life – a non-life in my view – but above all, to the surprise of my brothers, he decided to entrust me with what he held most dear in this life, which was not the love of a family nor any memories, but rather his infamous 'cash', his treasure, the cursed obscure object of his desire that still today strips away my credibility in the eyes of others and forces me continually to be on the defensive.

Carlotta and I were married in Bologna's Town Hall on 19 November 2003, the first anniversary of Baffo's death. And then in November 2004, a year after the marriage, his grandson was born, the grandson he would have so wanted to know, if for nothing more than to take comfort in the knowledge that he had left behind 'something good'. He had lost hope in another grandson to continue his line. But how much he would have welcomed him, especially when he learned that he'd be called Vito, Vito Ciancimino, the indestructible brand name. He joked about this possibility with us when he was alive: 'You're crazy . . . it's already a big deal if you've found someone who'll marry you and wants to have your son. But to find another person who's crazy enough to agree to calling him such an inconvenient name . . .' So he was no more when Vito arrived, Vito Andrea. And why did I give him such a name? Perhaps to go against him, even when he was dead, just as I'd always done when he was alive.

The Gas Company

But Don Vito's death didn't mean any break with his youngest son. The legacy of his 'cash' left an indelible mark. The former mayor had just been buried, Signor Franco had delivered Provenzano/Lo Verde's 'pizzino' of condolence, and already the magistracy was moving in on Massimo, his name on the register of those under investigation at the end of 2002 on suspicion of having links with the Mafia. However, it was an investigation that never took off, probably because Don Vito's death acted as Tippex to blank out all he had written and said on many occasions, especially in the light of the role he had assumed in the controversial business of the so-called 'Deal' with the Mafia.

This first investigation stayed in the shade until 2005, the year in which Massimo Ciancimino found himself involved in the investigation into the Gruppo Gas company that distributed domestic methane in Sicily. The investigation took shape from several 'pizzini' found on the Caccamo boss Antonio Giuffrè at the time of his arrest, which took place in Roccapalumba in 2002. But the history of this gas company goes back as far as 1983, when Vito Ciancimino launched himself into the business of methane gas distribution. The enterprise cruised along with wind in its sails, at least up to the beginning of 2000, when it became the prologue to what Massimo calls 'my long dark tunnel', not only because of the controversial court case that landed him with a conviction and a gaol sentence, but for the background of threats, hints and advice that highlighted serious anomalies in the investigation and also for intervention by the ineffable Signor Franco in the guise of *éminence grise* – as Massimo termed him to the prosecutors – who was able to steer the way the trial went.

MASSIMO: The company came into being in our house in Mondello in the summer of 1983 when, in the company of the faithful Enzo Zanghì – my father's cousin, secretary and fac-totum – Ezio Brancato, the engineer, and Prof. Gianni Lapis came to pay my father a visit. The former was employed in the Regional Agricultural Authority's office, while the latter was auditor for Sicilcassa's board of directors.

The idea of entering the energy business belonged to *Ingegnere* Brancato, who had broached the matter with Zanghì, who in turn floated the idea with my father. And so Siciliana Gas came into being and took control of a large slice of the island's methane supply.

As often happened, the business had to be shared with other politicians. Their names not being able to appear officially, these men were represented by friends who acted as their front men. In fact they fell into two groups: on one side there was Brancato's family which, besides my father's shares, also held the minor portions of Salvo Lima, the Hon. Calogero Pumilia, Fiore the constructor and Zanghì, while the other side comprised Prof. Lapis and the Campodonico, Mulè and Alia families. [These men have all been named in the proceedings in Palermo where Massimo Ciancimino is currently standing trial.]

The presence of influential personalities such as Vito Ciancimino and Salvo Lima ensured greater margins of success, but my father was the true architect of the enterprise. In fact it was he who, directly and by means of Lo Verde/-Provenzano, had to see to smoothing the way for the company, which was opposed by the local Mafia 'working for' another company. The agreement with Piddu Madonia, the Cosa Nostra boss of Caltanissetta, and initialled personally by Provenzano, was both difficult and indispensable. The conditions of the deal ensured that there was no direct contact between the Mafia and the company giving the sub-contracts. The bonuses for Cosa Nostra and management of the 'straightening up' (payment of kickbacks) were left in the hands of the local firms, the ones awarded the subcontracts. My father also succeeded in gaining another unwritten clause: conditions being equal, the subcontract would go to the firm he indicated. In all, this Siciliana Gas company proved to be a gold mine, and completely without the risk of investing any initial capital which, in the best Sicilian tradition, came from the public coffers. In fact, thanks to the good offices of Prof. Lapis, the company enjoyed huge advances on securities to the tune of 90 per cent of the region's total finances.

It's obvious that in attaining these conditions that excluded practically all competition, Cosa Nostra performed the lion's share of the work. The firms undertaking the subcontracting, in fact, invoiced an extra 3 per cent, which was allocated for the famous 'payoffs'. Not even my father had to invest any initial capital. His share in the business was established at about

15 per cent as a kind of recompense for his efforts at troubleshooting and resolving matters.

In brief, this was the story of Siciliana Gas. Massimo's problems came into being with the sale of the business, which was decided on by the heirs of *Ingegnere* Brancato (who in the meantime had died). Instead of choosing the path of amalgamation with other outside companies, the Brancato family preferred to sell.

MASSIMO: The sale of Siciliana Gas came at perhaps the least opportune moment, given that, because of a misunderstanding, it coincided with the paths of other investigations that had sprung up in the meantime from the 'pizzini' found on Giuffrè. They mentioned a 'Lapis business' and so they tapped the phones of Prof. Lapis, who had nothing to do with that business. Listening into the conversations – obviously this is my version of the events – generated such misunderstandings that they prompted the newspapers to write headlines such as 'Financial operations worth a billion in old lire' to be invested even in constructing a bridge across the Straits. Understandably, my surname was among the most appetizing: so the name Ciancimino – the son this time – continued to make headlines. I don't want to follow in the footsteps of the many who bleat about conspiracies. I'll simply say that a sale effected in the open light of day – Siciliana Gas was ceded to the Spanish company Gas Natural, a kind of Iberian ENI – turned into an investigation prompted by the suspicion that the Mafia had a hand in it. When it became clear that the Mafia had little to do with it, the Palermo magistrates decided that they needn't review their positions and so pounced on my name in order to keep up the media interest. In all this, legal considerations (such as for Brancato's heirs) vanished into thin air.

This is the way I see it and I can't refrain from saying that the sentence to which I've been condemned – albeit the libellous accusations of links with the Mafia and extortion have been struck off – practically sanctions the idea that one half of a company can come under suspicion while the other half remains unblemished.

The memory of when I entered that long dark tunnel is still alive in me.

On Trial

The trial for money laundering that sees Massimo today sentenced on appeal to three years and four months represents the final stage in an adventurous episode that reads like a novel. It is one of the most important moments, the final turning point that has changed his life, and directed him onto a path of no return. The narrative he tells of the sudden developments here bears witness to the change that occurred within him. A change that was almost inevitably brought about by the events that have dogged him these past three years and in which he has been able to see the deceptive nature of the myths his father followed, followed to the detriment of important things, such as love for one's children. He has been able to look into the real face of men like Lo Verde and Signor Franco and see in them the cynical features of power. And he relates his experience over the difficult decision to collaborate.

MASSIMO: On 6 June 2006, at 6.45 in the morning, the entry phone rang in my home in Palermo, which was 5 Via Torrearsa in the heart of the 'aristocratic' district around Via della Libertà. It was Carlotta who heard it and went to answer. 'Good morning, madam, our apologies for the time, but we're officers from the Carabinieri and the Guardia di Finanza [Excise Police] and we'd like a word with Signor Massimo Ciancimino. Is he at home?' I'll never forget that morning, even if I should live a thousand years, it'll still be hanging over me to the point of becoming a pathological syndrome: the sense of anxiety from the sound of the entry phone that tears you from a peaceful sleep. And I won't ever forget the sick feeling in seeing something come to pass that had been predicted for me not as prophecy, but as certain fact. It was Signor Franco who told me that they'd be arresting me. The discovery of some 'pizzini' (several of which spoke of me) in Provenzano's hideout made it easy to issue a custodial order, even if it was limited to house arrest. He'd sent the usual person to warn me in the shape of the 'captain', who was no such thing, but seemed to have become his alter ego. He told me to get rid of any documents and money I kept at home and I'd promptly done so. I'd even found a way of preparing Carlotta and our son for the event, having been used to my confinement at home.

Six months later in the middle of the Christmas festivities an unexpected upset happened. The Public Prosecutor's office had appealed against the decision of the judge who'd ruled for house arrest and they came to take me away to Ucciardone. I tried to keep a clear head and find strength in the reassuring words of Signor Franco, who continued to stick to his sense of optimism. But all this couldn't diminish the desperation I felt in the face of the coming solitude and the sense of alienation in the cell that would suddenly become my whole world. I took with me John Grisham's *The Innocent Man* but it was used more to write in than to read. I had no paper and used every blank space in the book to vent my feelings.

'. . . I've been taken away . . .' I wrote at noon on 14 December, 'from that which I hold most dear in the world, Carlotta and Vito Andrea . . . Four in the afternoon, entered Ucciardone prison after the usual depressing rituals: registration, search, medical. I've been assigned to maximum security section III, third floor, cell number two. I can't hold things back any longer and burst freely into tears . . . Everything is worse than can be imagined, no heating, no hot water, no sheets on the bed, only two blankets . . .'

And the following day I wrote, ' First morning waking up in prison . . . at 7.30 I get ready for the court hearing, again the search and the cold, the shame of handcuffs on the wrists . . . I think that prison makes you lose your identity, you're no longer a person, you're only a number . . .' I reached the courts as the Public Prosecutor (I think it was) was speaking about me: 'In contrast to his brothers, Massimo Ciancimino knew where his father was hiding the assets that came from an illicit source and was therefore an accomplice . . .'

I asked for permission to leave the courtroom and went to be sick.

I remained in prison little more than a week, but it seemed an age. I couldn't have survived without the thought of Vito Andrea and Carlotta.

A year had passed since the notification of investigation was served on me on 17 February 2005. And even then Signor Franco had been solicitous, keeping me informed about developments in the investigation as they happened but always by means of the same emissaries, asking me to be good and keep calm and saying that things will be 'sorted out'. I was advised not to tell the truth, not to speak about my father's involvement in the Gruppo Gas. And so I did, at least in the beginning.

I was seeing the pile of charges beginning to mount up, but I also saw – and this reassured me somewhat – that strange coincidences were regularly coming into play and ending up as obstacles to the invasions of the prosecuting magistrates. It was as if a guardian angel was keeping watch over things to block the progress of the investigations. This is how it had been in the period before my arrest in 2006. For example, let's take the search – or rather, the searches – on the day I received my first notice of investigation, which arrived simultaneously in Palermo and in Rome. It was February 2005 and Carlotta and I were in Paris to celebrate my birthday and our first Valentine's Day after Vito Andrea's birth. Franco's men had been keeping me up to date on developments, but as usual they'd added that we should all stay calm, that 'everything will die down', the important thing was to be at peace and keep silent.

What happened that day in effect reinforced the optimism of Signor Franco's emissaries. I was called from the Mondello house in Palermo by my associate Vittorio, the man who worked with me and looked after everything when I was away, the house, bills, plants, correspondence, everything. He told me that the Carabinieri were there with a warrant for a search to be carried out there and then. I asked to speak to whoever was in charge of the operation and was passed to an officer, Captain Angelo. On the phone he was extremely polite and assured me that there was no question of my being arrested and taken into custody; it was simply a matter of searching the house. He added that at the same time they also had to search the flat in Rome. I was certainly worried, but had no desire in the world to evade the course of justice. I asked him several times if I should leave Paris and come back to Palermo, but was told that there was no hurry and that I could present myself in the Public Prosecutor's office several days later.

I then spoke with Vittorio again, giving him all the necessary pointers to complying with the Carabinieri's requirements. I asked him to call my brother Roberto to have him be present as my legal representative at the search. I was then able to follow the course of developments by the use of my cell phone; again I repeated to the officer that he could ask anything at all of Vittorio. I told him that Vittorio had the keys to the safe, which – I assumed – he would certainly wish to have a look at. I repeated all this with the Carabinieri in Rome, starting by telling them about my correct address there, seeing that I no longer lived on the rise of San Sebastianello. By means of a lawyer friend, I made everything available to them that they might need.

But to my considerable surprise I later learned that the Carabinieri had no interest at all in either of the two safes in Rome and in Mondello. Vittorio told me he'd handed the keys over to the captain, but the officer had told him he wasn't interested. This was a shame for him, because he could have found many important documents that are only today in the hands of the prosecutors, starting with the famous 'papello' (which the investigators had been searching for without success for almost a decade), whose existence had always been denied by Mori and De Donno.

Anyway, the search carried on at length and went as far as the villa basement, which functioned as a storehouse for Chateau d'Ax, the sofa company for whom I was the representative. It was here that they came to seize several large boxes full of papers, among them the draft of the threatening letter that my father had written to send to Marcello Dell'Utri and Prime Minister Berlusconi. Naturally this discovery caused me some concern, because I would never ever want to find myself in the situation of having to explain that letter's significance. This is without counting the fact that among the papers taken there were even certain SIM cards of some importance. In particular there was one for my old cell phone (335252648) that contained Signor Franco's number on its contacts list, and I would not have been happy about responding to that either.

I was extremely worried, so immediately passed on news of the discovery to Franco. But he wasn't upset. He advised me to do nothing silly, just keep quiet and, above all, to say not a word about the business of the deal. I responded by saying that to me it seemed pure science fiction that all this could be kept a secret. And the letter to Berlusconi? And the SIM card with his number in it? 'Not to worry,' he replied, 'nothing will come out and the trial will evaporate.'

In fact things appeared to go in that direction given that, incredibly, they lost all trace both of the letter to Dell'Utri and Berlusconi and the SIM card, both of which went missing in the offices of the Carabinieri and were found again (with Franco's phone number) only later when – after I began to work with the authorities – I pointed out the anomaly to the deputy prosecutors Ingroia and Di Matteo. These coincidences, however, convinced me in some way that the assurances given by Franco and his men could be trusted. And besides, everything he claimed regularly turned out to be true.

So, undisturbed, I had all the time in the world to shift Riina's 'papello', the more compromising documents and also the money in the safe. As per instructions, I'd taken the 'package' abroad to a company in Hong Kong that held, among other things, an account and a safety deposit box in Liechtenstein. This was one of the main reasons why I was so delayed in handing over the material requested by the Public Prosecutor. But by a certain point, however, I had given all the information necessary for gaining access to the account.

Throughout all this I was persuaded to follow the voices

that were asking me not to tell the truth. Things happened that made me feel infinitely small and defenceless with respect to the power with which they managed to forecast and direct events. Again the omnipresent Franco had warned me that 'Something is about to happen from which it would be better if you were to keep a little distant.' It was April 2006, two months before my arrest, and I went on holiday to Sharm el-Sheikh in Egypt. I took Carlotta and Vito Andrea but, seeing as I expected the worst, I persuaded my lawyer to come with me. So there I was, at the beach with my trusted lawyer, waiting for what was to happen. And it did. On the 11th they arrested Bernardo Provenzano. Yet again Franco had been right. And in his anxiety to cover all traces of the deal, not knowing what they would find in the boss's hideout, he thought it wise to have me out of the way. And in fact something that involved me was found among Lo Verde's 'pizzini'.

Collaboration

Massimo Ciancimino has received a lot of criticism for what he's said about the safe that was ignored by the Carabinieri and about their behaviour, starting with the business of the deal with Mori and De Donno. Today the situation is slightly different: the prosecution's investigations seem to have come to a turning point with notifications of investigation given to several of the officers and NCOs who took part in the investigations over the Gruppo Gas trial. Captain Angelo is under investigation over the search, together with others, several of whom seem to have agreed to collaborate with the prosecution. And on the deal front, new documents have been discovered, notes written by Vito Ciancimino that denounce 'the false testimony of Mori and De Donno in the Florence trial [the hearing over the Rome, Milan and Florence bombings]'. The same officers (at the time of writing Mori is waiting for a verdict from the trial over the failure to capture Provenzano) are today on the register of those under investigation, together with the Mafiosi involved in the deal (Riina, Provenzano and Cinà) and other representatives of the authorities. Mori and De Donno were put on trial before Ciancimino's arrival and are still the subject of proceedings.

And so today Massimo Ciancimino's position is no longer what it was in 2006: despite having been charged and sentenced himself, he's also a witness for the prosecution in other trials (Calvi, Mori, but not Dell'Utri because the Appeal Court of Assizes has debarred him, pointing out the 'ever-changing' nature of his statements). And he'll appear as witness in others, when the first inquiry phases are complete in investigations initiated by his evidence. These are the results of his decision to collaborate with the judges, which came to a head after the traumatic arrest and his being found guilty in the first degree.

MASSIMO: Those who know me can understand very well how far I'm the opposite of what is usually defined as a Mafia type. I think the Mafia wouldn't ever let anyone like me become a member: I'm too superficial, incapable of taking myself seriously where they, on the other hand, give themselves out as big guys every time they're about to embark on anything, even if it ends up as absolutely ridiculous. When I went around with my father, I saw them strutting about in all their crude ignorance, ungainly but with the air of those who carry the fate of the world on their shoulders; all this exactly the opposite of the unconscious irony with which I nearly always manage to defuse any dangerous venture. In truth, it was the same with my father; although if he was very mindful not to upset anyone's sensibilities, he showed little respect for the Mafia's 'Goodfellas'. Witness to this was the way he received visitors on his bed in his pyjamas, using the informal second person with everyone yet almost demanding the formal third person and the title of *Ingegnere* in return. This was part of his character, always ready to help but only from a superior position, because in politics you had to hold the upper hand. He managed to be downright mocking, but again without overstepping the mark: his speciality being able to laugh at Riina for the way he dressed, while making him think he was admiring it and wanted to imitate it. The day he came to the house with the gold ingot – if you recall – he didn't give any sign of thanks and teased him with false admiration for his tie and his watch, which were both very costly eyesores.

So there it is, it's perhaps because of this that I didn't like that world. I was attracted by the ease with which the sons of bosses could spend money on expensive cars, boats and motorcycles, but the idea of sitting down to a meeting with those uptight poker faces, who never said all they were thinking, was enough for me to keep my distance. And it really was prison that underlined this feeling. Although I was in Ucciardone only a few days, it was long enough for me to know that the life of a Mafioso wasn't the one for me. In prison I was ready to confess to crimes I'd never even committed. I felt there was too much negativity in there for me, as well as the impossibility of moving around as I liked.

Cell number two in the Ucciardone was better for me than any psychoanalytic session. In there I was able to see what I really cared about, which was my son and my wife, because they represented everything that was missing from my own childhood. And I know that I want to be a very different husband and father from the one I had. And it's for the sake of Carlotta and Vito Andrea that I took the decision to change my tune.

It wasn't easy because I was coming under a lot of pressure from all sides. But I was torn, even though I'd formed the idea in the previous two years of digging things up in my father's memory, trying to create the narrative of a book he thought would be liberating. The self-deception was clear to me, and even to him, of how he had shut himself in a cage from which he'd never escaped. The same thing was happening to me: years and years of living dangerously in the shadow of a man always walking a tightrope, on the edge of a precipice and then – left on his own – the settling of accounts.

Everything became plain when, once again back under house arrest, I gathered how much Signor Franco's attitude towards me was changing. His men were always around, but I didn't feel as protected as I used to. It's true that the 'captain' once turned up in Via Torrearsa with a delivery of excellent fish and lobsters courtesy of Franco, but it's also true that on another occasion he turned up to advise me urgently to cool it about any hint to the Carabinieri of deals or the truth about the Gruppo Gas trial. That was one of the first times I really felt a tremor of fear.

But the real spur that told me where to stick the wise (and biased) advice of old friends was the reaction of Carlotta, who was by now tired of my caution in the face of everyone else: 'That's enough, Massimo, now you must think only about yourself and your family. I can't bear to see you in this state any longer. And why should you? In order to protect a bunch of crooks? Come on, Massimo, that's enough, now go and tell the truth, and whatever happens is going to happen.'

I took my time, and carried on ruminating. I was afraid of losing my protection, but I'm grateful to Carlotta for many reasons. I owe any courageous decision to my wife, to Carlotta. Our getting together was long and complicated and the start not a happy one, as she wouldn't even look at me. And why should she have been interested in me, given that at the time she was living with the scion of an important family, who was tall, handsome, elegant, owned a Porsche and was heir to a great coffee-manufacturing concern? So there she was, well placed, whereas for my brothers I was and still continue to be simply 'Shorty'. I was hanging around in Cortina's best spots and at the tables that counted. What happened there around the year 2000 was my only real act of 'laundering'. The single objective was to 'clean up' the name of Ciancimino, throwing it in the mix of Cortina's high life. As all the young men and women were over 1 metre 66 centimetres, think how hard it was for me, who was saddled with the name of Ciancimino as well. But I wasn't giving in: I remember when I first asked for the phone number of Sonia, who was one and a half times my height, she burst out laughing, looking down at me, and said, 'Have you taken a look at yourself?' We were together for three years.

But I had a thing about Carlotta. Sweet-natured, spoiled, good-humoured, happy and depressed. We became a couple in 2001 and it came as a real surprise, as did the attention she was able to show my father, taking long walks with him through Rome.

I'd spoken plainly to her, saying that I'd never have my freedom with such a demanding father. I didn't go into details, but she clearly understood the dangers inherent in his relations with people, above all Franco and Lo Verde. She was loving and understanding, which is why I'm so grateful to her.

She's never left me without her support, not even after the decision to collaborate openly with the magistrates, a choice which on the one hand put me in a better position to defend myself in my trial, but at the same time opened up a new page in our life. All of a sudden everything changed: what I had said to the Public Prosecutors in Palermo and Caltanissetta had immediate consequences. Halfway through May in 2009 I was assigned a bodyguard, and so Carlotta could no longer escape from the trouble in which I'd gone and landed myself. It was a difficult moment, because the worry over Vito Andrea began, knowing that he could no longer be as close to me as he'd once been. From that moment on, I couldn't take him to school any more.

But we've overcome that rocky moment and then, still more,

the shock of the evidence I gave. Who knows if Signor Franco and Lo Verde shared my final decision to reveal everything, right to the end? Certainly, someone must have been unhappy, judging from the messages I'm still getting today. The 'captain' came all the way to the Bologna entry phone to remind me that silence is good for the health.

And I've had to bear a lot of criticism. As happens in a world of inverted logic, the problem isn't about who makes use of the right to silence and keeps quiet, but who speaks and tells all. Of course, I've taken my time. But that time was necessary to conquer my fears and to gather and interpret the enormous amount of documentary material my father left. They've accused me of hiding the names of Signor Franco and his men and I reply by challenging anyone to face such underhand enemies without being able to count on any friendly advice.

Each time I thought of pushing myself a little towards it, I asked myself in a conditioned reflex: 'Who's going to help me? The Carabinieri, who didn't want to open the safe with the "papello" in it? Signor Franco, who tells me to keep quiet, or even his threatening messengers?' And all that happy bunch's little tricks would come back to haunt me: the passport for the newly born Vito Andrea, the 'pizzino' of condolence in the Capuchin cemetery, the word in my ear before Provenzano's arrest, those words over political support for 'the Deal', Provenzano's letter sent to my father in Rebibbia, the 'chance' meeting again in prison with the Salvo cousins, the lobsters in Via Torrearsa and many other actions to smooth the way.

There were people to fear, but in the end they're not anonymous faces. I recognized the photo of the 'captain' and also the other one. They've shown me an album full of anonymous faces, as in the practice set out for recognizing agents in the security services. I pointed out two 'numbers', two people whose identities are governed by secrecy. It remains for the magistrates to reveal the mystery. And for Signor Franco as well I've given useful particulars for his identification. I know very well that the world thinks I know his names and surname: I've given many pointers towards identifying him for the judges. I can say with certainty that his photo hasn't yet been shown me, but I can add another particular here: when he advised me to get out of Italy on the eve of Provenzano's capture, he did it in person. We met in Rome and he made the appointment in front of the American Embassy in the Holy See from which I saw him emerge.

But in the end it's for Baffo, my father, that I've chosen the path of collaboration. I remember in 1993 that he tried to cross the Rubicon and can't forget with what condescension his offer of collaboration came to be shelved. I'd even tried to make him speak with Falcone, but perhaps that was too early for such an event. One thing I can vouch for personally: that from the end of 1999 to his death my father was working to be able to leave a kind of manual that would help reconstruct the whole business of the Mafia and politics. If he'd remained alive and had been able to write his story, more than one magistrate would have been able to call on him for evidence. I've passed on what he would have wanted to write. It's as if he had entrusted me with the task of healing our old differences and reaching a new understanding.

It's true I often think of my father with anger, but also with the compassion that a child can't help but feel for whoever put it in this world. Certainly I can't forgive him for clipping my wings, such as the time when I opened the Brazil, a disco in Monte Pellegrino, and he did everything he could to have me close it. It was incredible: first he sent a bunch of Mafiosi to ask for protection money, and then he sent the Guardia di Finanza, who were implacable and deadly. Why did he behave like that? Simply because he'd figured out that running that club would have given me economic independence. And he didn't want this; he wanted to have me for his own purposes. And I also can't forget his severity, and his excessive attachment to cash. And the chain that he shackled me with, the storeroom in the dark where I served out my punishments, the sarcasm with which he brushed off any of my personal or career initiatives, running them down by praising the success of others. How much I'd like to tell him today my most successful witticism: 'When I went around with my father I'd often have to wait for him in the car together with the other young aspirants to success. I was his driver. And now Renato Schifani, President of the Senate, who drove the car for Peppino La Loggia, holds the second most important post in the state, and the President of Sicily, Totò Cuffaro, was the driver for Calogero Mannino. They made really good careers, didn't they, Papà, accused of having links with the Mafia?'

And I'd really like to be able to go back in time, to that morning when I was waiting in the barbershop of Signor Lo Piccolo. I'd pay a lot to be able to tell him, 'You can stick it, Papà. Stuff you and Signor Lo Verde. Don't you know what he is? If I see him once more in our house or if you make me meet him, I'm going to call the Carabinieri . . .' But then no, perhaps they wouldn't be quite right . . . The police? Signor Franco? But what do I know; it's all so murky . . . And today I feel afraid.

A Man Alone

But then I see him again, looking fragile as he did during his last two years, and I almost feel tenderness for him. I see a man alone, locked in under the weight of his memories, and his feelings of guilt, for the first time wishing to share the burden of his life. It seems a thousand years since the cheeky adventure of a strange encounter that took place in Rome, which he wrote down on a couple of sheets of paper. I found them during my daily researches in the bottomless St Patrick's Well of his papers that so many magistrates are now drawing on:

> One day last summer at four in the morning, I couldn't sleep and decided to take my usual daily stroll around Piazza di Spagna at that time.
>
> I was going home to Via Condotti, when two young men (twenty-five-year-olds, I later learned) came slowly towards me and, as I held their stares in a confident manner, one of them turned to me in a cocky manner and said:
>
> 'I'm sure we know each other, but how come?'
>
> Quick as a flash, I replied, 'In Rebibbia, I should think.' (This is the Roman prison where I was a 'guest' for about six months.)

The young men looked surprised and exclaimed in unison, 'That's not possible. We've only been in Regina Coeli' (for those who don't know, another Roman prison).

The ice, as we say, having been broken, the young men came closer, showing great courtesy and attention.

One of them (always the same one, the 'boss', I presumed), observed, 'But, given your personality [I don't know from what they derived this 'personality', except for the fact that I was dressed in jacket, shirt and tie, as per usual] and your age, you can only have been "inside" for "links with the Mafia".'

Struck by such perspicuity, I replied with a laugh:

'That's exactly right.'

At this point, looking them in the face, certain I'd become a 'somebody' for them, I asked with authority:

'But what do you do?'

'We're thieves,' they chorus.

Having established this familiarity, one (always the same one), went on:

'And yet I'm sure we know you. Who are you?'

I reflected for a few moments and thought, 'Here I go':

'My name's Vito Ciancimino,' I whispered.

I clearly had the feeling that I'd pronounced a magic word.

I still have the image of their faces embossed in my memory. They were taken by surprise, dumbfounded, and couldn't believe it. I remember that the 'boss' grabbed the other one and dragged him twenty or so metres away to the foot of the Spanish Steps and they had a confab for a few minutes. I could only see their gestures, which were expansive.

On returning, they said with great deference and humility:

'That's amazing. But please could you show us some proof of identity? A document or something?'

During the time they were muttering, I was amused and was distractedly running everything possible through my mind, all except a request like this.

I decided to play along and offered my identity card with a facetious air and said:

'You boys have more of a vocation as policemen than thieves.'

Having checked my identity, they bent down and took my hands with the obvious intention of kissing them; I removed them decisively away from any such effusions (which I can't abide) and in a humble manner they asked:

'But how come a personality like you's walking alone through Piazza di Spagna at 5.00 in the morning?'

With authority, I replied:

'Who says I'm alone?'

The young men looked about them and, seeing no one, they said disconsolately:

'We're idiots, we don't see anyone and yet there's dozens of young Mafiosi surrounding us.'

I'd obviously become a 'god' in their eyes, but I walked away.

I'd contributed and fed 'my legend'.

I was 'worse' (that's how I'd put it) than a journalist.

Chronology

1924

Vito Ciancimino is born in Corleone.

1956

May

The Christian Democrats win the elections for the Palermo city council that mark the ascendancy of the Giovanni Gioia camp (supporters of Amintore Fanfani, 1908–99, leading Christian Democrat, five times Prime Minister) and the rising stars of Salvo Lima and Vito Ciancimino.

1957

October

Mafia summit at Grand Hotel des Palmes: the Sicilian Cosa Nostra meets its American 'cousins'. The new international scale of the widespread drugs trade is decided.

1958

February

Cosa Nostra restructures: the 'Provincial Commission' is born, a sort of governing body for the fifty or so 'families' spread across the area.

May

Salvo Lima becomes mayor of Palermo, Ciancimino assessor for public services.

1959

November
New town planning scheme approved by the City of Palermo: Ciancimino
is assessor for public works.

1960

April
Signs of war: the clash inside Cosa Nostra is about to erupt. Deaths and
shooting on Palermo's streets.

1962

January
Lucky Luciano dies in Naples.

December
The First Mafia War explodes with the murder of drug pusher Calcedonio
di Pisa.

1963

February
Massimo, the penultimate of Vito Ciancimino's five children, is born on the
16th.

April
The car bomb attacks begin. At Cinisi (Palermo) the *capomafia* Cesare
Manzella is killed.

May
Mafia boss Angelo La Barbera is arrested in Milan.

June
Height of the Mafia war in Palermo: car bomb massacre at Ciaculli. Seven
public officials die, comprising Carabinieri, police and bomb-disposal
experts.

1964

May
Luciano Liggio arrested in Corleone.

1965

December

The trial of 114 Mafiosi, practically all from Palermo, ending at Catanzaro with a series of acquittals.

1969

June

The 64 accused in the Corleone Mafia war (1958–63) are acquitted in Bari, among them Totò Riina and Luciano Liggio. Totò Riina is then arrested again.

July

Riina is sentenced to internal exile and released from prison. He never reaches the place assigned, San Giovanni in Persiceto (Bologna), and goes into hiding.

November

Daring escape by Luciano Liggio from the Margherita Clinic in Rome while the Carabinieri are about to serve him a new arrest warrant.

December

Massacre in Via Lazio: a group from Corleone disguised as police officers assassinate the boss Michele Cavataio and three of his men.

1970

September

Journalist Mauro De Mauro of the daily newspaper *L'Ora* (1900–1992) disappears. The investigation is still ongoing in Palermo.

October

Vito Ciancimino is declared mayor of Palermo and appoints Giuseppe Trapani to the city council. He is in power for only twelve days due to public outcry and resigns in December.

December

Liggio is found guilty on appeal in Bari: a life sentence for the homicide of Michele Navarra and crimes in Corleone.

1971

May

The Public Prosecutor Pietro Scaglione is assassinated in Palermo with his driver Antonino Lorusso. He is the first magistrate to be killed by Cosa Nostra.

June

The Corleone clan kidnap Pino Vassallo, son of housing constructor Francesco (Ciccio), friend of Lima and Ciancimino.

1972

April

The Parliamentary Anti-Mafia Commission compiles files on 164 Mafia suspects, including many politicians. They are filed away as secret.

August

In Palermo, the kidnapping of Luciano Cassina, son of entrepreneur Arturo, director of the company with the concession for road maintenance. He pays a ransom of L1,300 million.

1973

March

In his confession to the police Leonardo Vitale describes the organization of Cosa Nostra. The names of Totò Riina and Vito Ciancimino appear for the first time as links between the Mafia and politics. The information is given no credibility.

May

General acquittal for the 75 men accused of the murder of Public Prosecutor Scaglione.

1974

May

Luciano Liggio is arrested by the Excise Police in Milan. He was living a quiet life in hiding as a wine merchant.

December

The first child of Totò Riina and Ninetta Bagarella is born while they live in hiding. In spite of this (as with the couple's other three children), the birth occurs in a highly respectable private clinic in Palermo, where the mother is registered under her own name.

1975

July

The Corleone clan kidnap tax collector Luigi Corleo, father-in-law of Nino Salvo. It is a smack in the face to Palermo's powerful group of Mafiosi. The hostage dies and his body is never found.

1977

August

Colonel Giuseppe Russo, commander of Palermo's detective squad, falls into a trap in Ficuzza (Corleone) together with the teacher Filippo Costa. The killers were Riina, Bagarella, Pino Greco and Giovanni Brusca. Three local shepherds are found guilty, but later proved innocent.

1978

May

Peppino Impastato, a young leftist militant, is killed in Cinisi (Palermo). His body was blown apart by a bomb, an act of deception to make the victim appear to have been a terrorist. The corpse of the statesman Aldo Moro, kidnapped by the Red Brigades 55 days earlier, is found in Via Caetani in Rome, a couple of steps from the headquarters of the Christian Democrat and Communist parties.

1979

January

The journalist Mario Francese is killed in Palermo by the Corleone clan.

March

Michele Reina, the Provincial Secretary of the Christian Democrats, is killed in Palermo. The period of attacks on politicians begins.

The journalist Mino Pecorelli is assassinated in Rome. Senator Giulio Andreotti is indicted for the crime in 1993, later acquitted in 1999.

July

Head of the Palermo Flying Squad, Giorgio Boris Giuliano, is assassinated in the Bar Lux. Investigations lead to the accusation against Leoluca Bagarella.

August
Declared bankrupt, Michele Sindona hides out in Palermo among Mafiosi and Freemasons, while supposed to be in the United States, where it is given out he is the prisoner of a left-wing terrorist group.

September
Death of chief examining magistrate Cesare Terranova and his police body-guard Lenin Mancuso. Terranova was a member of the Anti-Mafia Commission.

1980

January
The President of the Region, Christian Democrat Piersanti Mattarella, is assassinated in Palermo.

May
Murder of Carabinieri Captain Emanuele Basile in Monreale.

June
The Ustica disaster: an Itavia DC9 crashes, killing 81 people of whom only 38 are ever recovered. The hypothesis of one inquiry was that the aeroplane had been inadvertently hit during an operation by foreign secret services.

August
Palermo's Chief Public Prosecutor Gaetano Costa shot and killed on the street in Palermo. He alone had signed the warrants for the arrest of 60 Mafiosi and drug traffickers, after his deputies had refused.

1981

April
Mafia boss Stefano Bontade killed in Palermo. The offensive of the Corleone Mafia takes off against those of Palermo.

November
Death in Palermo of angiologist Prof. Sebastiano Bosio.

1982

March

Capture in Rome of Salvatore Contorno, a Mafioso of the losing (Palermo) faction. He becomes one of Giovanni Falcone's famous *pentiti* (turncoats or supergrasses).

April

Regional Secretary of the Italian Communist Party, Pio La Torre, is killed in Palermo with his driver, Rosario Di Salvo. Together with Christian Democrat Minister of the Interior Virginio Rognoni, the MP had presented a bill on the seizure of Mafiosi assets. General Dalla Chiesa appointed Prefect in Palermo immediately after.

June

The banker Roberto Calvi is found hanging under Blackfriars Bridge in London.

August

Forensic scientist Prof. Paolo Giaccone killed by bullets from a revolver. He had refused to alter a report on the fingerprints of a defendant belonging to the Corleonese clan.

September

A special Cosa Nostra commando unit kills Prefect Dalla Chiesa, his wife Emanuela Setti Carraro and his driver Domenico Russo.

The relatives of the *pentito* Tommaso Buscetta start to be killed: his two eldest children disappear, then his brother and nephew, his father-in-law and two more nephews, his brother-in-law and even the witness of his marriage.

November

Police officer Calogero Zucchetto is killed in a Palermo bar. He was about to be married. He was one of the leading investigators in the squad run by Superintendent Ninni Cassarà.

1983

January

Murder in Valderice (Trapani) of Deputy Prosecutor Giacomo Ciacco Montalto.

June

Carabinieri Captain Mario D'Aleo is massacred together with Corporal Bonmarito and military serviceman Marici. The officer had taken over Emanuele Basile's command.

July

A car bomb explosion in Via Pipitone Federico in Palermo kills chief examining magistrate Rocco Chinnici. Two Carabinieri in his bodyguard are also killed, Marshal Mario Trapassi and Corporal Salvatore Bartolotta, as well as the concierge of the apartment block where the Prosecutor lived.

October

Tommaso Buscetta is arrested in São Paulo, Brazil. He becomes a collaborator for Giovanni Falcone in the investigations leading to the Cosa Nostra Maxi-Trial.

1984

January

Writer and journalist Giuseppe Fava killed in Catania.

April

Capture in Madrid of Mafia boss Gaetano Badalamenti, who was extradited to the United States.

September

Falcone's blitz on the Mafia is unleashed: 366 warrants for arrest and the Maxi-Trial is born.

October

The Cortile Macello killings. Clash inside the Mafia: eight corpses found on slaughterhouse floor.

Vito Ciancimino is sent in exile to the outskirts of Patti (Messina) for being a 'social danger'.

November

Vito Ciancimino is arrested in Palermo on the orders of Giovanni Falcone. From this moment on, Massimo Ciancimino's life is changed, being constantly obliged to attend to his father. Nine days later on the 12th, Nino and Ignazio Salvo are arrested.

Member of the Sicilian Regional Assembly and ex-Regional Secretary of the Christian Democrats, Rosario Nicoletti, commits suicide by leaping to his death.

December
The *pentito* Leonardo Vitale, at first declared insane, is assassinated in Palermo when Riina begins his campaign against the collaborators with justice.

Bomb explodes on the Naples–Milan Express Train 904: 16 dead. Pippo Calò, Cosa Nostra's 'Cashier', and a Camorra group are later found guilty. The motive is never explained.

1985

February
Businessman Roberto Parisi, director of Icem (company with the concession for Palermo's street lighting) and President of Palermo's football team, is killed along with his driver Giuseppe Mangano.

April
Massacre of Pizzolungo (Trapani): a bomb meant for the judge Carlo Palermo blows up Barbera Asta and her two twin brothers, Salvatore and Giuseppe.

May
Pippo Calò, Cosa Nostra's 'Cashier', is arrested in Rome.

July
Head of the Flying Squad snatch group, Beppe Montana, is assassinated in Porticello (Palermo).

August
Deputy Director of the Palermo Flying Squad Antonino Cassarà is butchered in an ambush below his apartment. The police officer who, although he was on holiday, was his bodyguard, was also killed.

November
Vito Ciancimino is sent on internal exile to Rotello in Molise.

1986

January
Tax collector Nino Salvo dies in a clinic in Bellinzona, Switzerland.

February
The Maxi-Trial against Cosa Nostra opens in the specially built Palermo courtroom-bunker: 476 defendants behind bars.

1987

December
Initial sentences handed out in the Maxi-Trial: 19 life sentences and 2,265 years in prison.

1988

January
The Mafia kills the ex-Christian Democrat mayor of Palermo, Giuseppe Insalaco.

Police officer Natale Mondo assassinated: he had survived the ambush on Ninni Cassarà.

September
Magistrate Alberto Giacomelli killed in Trapani.

President of the Court of Appeal Antonio Saetta and his disabled son are murdered along the Canicattì–Palermo road.

In Trapani, the journalist Mauro Rostagno killed by rifle shots. He also worked in the Saman community for the rehabilitation of drug addicts.

1989

May
Murder of Regional administrator Giovanni Bonsignore.

June
An explosive device (75 sticks of dynamite) is found on the rocky beach at Addaura (Palermo) where Judge Falcone was on vacation.

1990

March
Disappearance in Palermo of Emanuele Piazza, ex-policeman who became a collaborator with the civil secret service.

June
Vito Ciancimino is arrested then released after less than a month.

September
Murder in an ambush on the Canicattì–Agrigento road of the 'Boy Judge' Rosario Livatino.

1991

February
Report by Carabinieri officers of ROS on 'Mafia and Contracts'. Officers Mario Mori and Giuseppe De Donno name 45 people. The inquiry ends with only five judicial proceedings.

August
While on vacation in Calabria, Deputy Prosecutor Antonino Scopelliti in the Court of Cassation is killed. He was preparing to support the sentences handed out in the final hearing of the Maxi-Trial.

The businessman Libero Grassi is assassinated in Palermo. He had appeared on television to expose a protection racket.

1992

January
The Court of Cassation (Supreme Court or Court of Final Appeal) upholds the outcome of the Maxi-Trial.

March
MEP Salvo Lima assassinated in Mondello.

April
Carabinieri Marshal Giuliano Guazzelli killed in Agrigento.

May
Giovanni Falcone, his wife Francesca Morvillo – also a magistrate – and three bodyguards, Antonino Montinaro, Rocco Di Cillo and Vito Schifani, perish in a terrifying attack on the Punta Raisi–Palermo motorway.

June
Start of negotiations about the 'Deal' between the state and the Mafia: according to what he has told the magistrates, Massimo Ciancimino 'happened to be met' by Captain De Donno on an aeroplane flight.

July
Mafioso Gaspare Mutolo confesses.

Car bomb in Via D'Amelio takes the lives of Palermo's Deputy Prosecutor, Paolo Borsellino, and five of his bodyguard: Agostino Catalano, Eddie Walter Cosina, Vincenzo Li Muli, Emanuela Loi and Claudio Traina.

Inspector Giovanni Lizzio is assassinated in Catania.

September
Tax collector Ignazio Salvo, sentenced for his links with the Mafia, is murdered in an ambush in Santa Flavia (Palermo).

December
New unexpected arrest of Vito Ciancimino while he acts as go-between for the Carabinieri and Totò Riina. He is sent to Rebibbia prison (Rome).

The deputy director of the Italian civil intelligence service (SISDE), Bruno Contrada, is arrested for colluding with the Mafia.

1993

January
In Barcellona Pozzo di Gotto (Messina) journalist Beppe Alfano is assassinated.

On the run for thirty years, Totò Riina is arrested in Palermo. The manner of his capture has never been revealed.

February
Arrest of neurologist Antonino Cinà, Riina's intermediary in the negotiations conducted by Vito Ciancimino.

March
Giulio Andreotti is accused of 'external links with the Mafia'.

May
Car bomb attempt in Via Fauro, Rome, against journalist Maurizio Costanzo and his wife Maria De Filippi, but both unhurt. Another car bomb in Via dei Georgofili, Florence, kills five: Caterina Nencioni, Nadia Nencioni, Dario Capolicchio, Angela Fiume and Fabrizio Nencioni. Forty-eight are injured.

July
Five die after a car bomb explodes in Via Palestra, Milan: municipal policeman

Alessandro Ferrari, firemen Carlo La Catena, Sergio Pasotto and Stefano Picerno and Driss Moussafir, a Moroccan national.

A double car bomb attempt in Rome, fortunately without victims: at the Vicariate offices in the Basilica of St John Lateran and the church of San Giorgio in Velabro.

September

Don Pino Puglisi, parish priest of Brancaccio, Palermo, is killed. The area's Mafia bosses are unhappy about his work with young people.

November

Luciano Liggio dies in prison in Sassari.

Kidnapping of Giuseppe, the 12-year-old son of *pentito* Santino Di Matteo, key witness in the Capaci Massacre. The Mafia's intention is to induce him to retract what he has said. The boy is later strangled on the orders of Brusca and Bagarella and his body dissolved in acid.

1994

January

Giuseppe and Filippo Graviano arrested in Milan.

1995

September

The trial of Giulio Andreotti begins in Palermo.

1996

June

In Catania the Mafioso Luigi Ilardo is killed on the eve of his entry into the witness protection programme for *pentiti*.

1997

November

Arrest of the Carmelite monk Don Mario Frittitta, accused of having celebrated mass in the hideout of fugitive Pietro Aglieri.

Businessman Benny D'Agostino is sent to prison. According to the judges he was managing Mafia funds.

1998

July

Riina, Provenzano, Aglieri and Ganci are sentenced to life imprisonment for the murder of Salvo Lima.

October

Assassination of trade unionist Domenico Geraci in Caccamo (Palermo).

1999

July

Assassination of Filippo Basile, administrator on the Regional Board of Agriculture.

Giancarlo Caselli starts as head of DAP (Administrative Department for Prisons). Pietro Grassi is to head the Palermo Public Prosecutor's Office.

September

Andreotti, Vitalone, Calò, La Barbera and Carminati acquitted of the murder of journalist Pecorelli.

Vito Ciancimino is released from prison and placed under house arrest in his Rome apartment.

October

Giulio Andreotti is acquitted of the charge of having external links with the Mafia. Having just taken over from Giancarlo Caselli, Pietro Grassi hears the defeat in court.

November

Don Mario Frittitta acquitted on appeal.

2000

January

Salvatore Riina and Giuseppe Graviano sentenced to life for the 1993 massacres in Rome, Florence and Milan.

April

Tommaso Buscetta dies in the United States.

June

Court of Cassation magistrate Corrado Carnevale is acquitted of the accusation of external links with the Mafia.

2001

January
The case of the disappearance of journalist Mauro De Mauro is reopened.

2002

February
The sum of roughly €15 million is seized from Mafia boss Tommaso Cannella.

April
Gaetano Badalamenti is sentenced to life imprisonment for the murder of Peppino Impastato.

May
The inquiry into the unknown instigators of the massacres of Capaci and Via D'Amelio is shelved. Under investigation were Dell'Utri and Berlusconi.

Bernardo Provenzano receives life for the murder of journalist Mario Francese.

August
Assets worth €250 million are confiscated from businessman Antonino Buscemi, who is later sentenced to life for murder.

November
Goods worth €150 million are seized from housing constructor Francesco Zummo, ex-business associate of Vito Ciancimino. Vito Ciancimino dies in his apartment in Piazza di Spagna, Rome. The cause of death is never ascertained.

2003

May
Colonel Mario Mori is called to give evidence in the Public Prosecutor's Office in Palermo over the failure to discover Riina's hideout.

2004

June
Arrest of Mafia boss Nardo Greco, aider and abettor of Provenzano.

October
The Court of Cassation upholds Giulio Andreotti's appeal against the charges upon which he had previously been convicted.

December
Senator Marcello Dell'Utri is sentenced in the first instance in Palermo to nine years for having links with the Mafia. He has denied the charge and his appeal is ongoing.

2005

February
Massimo Ciancimino, Prof. Gianni Lapis and another four businessmen and tradesmen are investigated for money laundering.

General Mario Mori and Lieutenant Colonel Sergio De Caprio ('Capitano Ultimo') are indicted in Palermo for failing to find Riina's hideout in Via Bernini.

2006

April
Arrest in Corleone of Bernardo Provenzano, on the run since 1963, in a farmhouse in Montagna dei Cavalli.

June
Massimo Ciancimino and the lawyer Giorgio Ghiron arrested, accused of money laundering.

July
Arrested for belonging to the Mafia, consultant radiologist of Palermo's Municipal Hospital Giovanni Mercadante, regional member for Forza Italia.

2007

March
Massimo Ciancimino, Giorgio Ghiron and Gianni Lapis each sentenced to five years.

September
The ANAS (national state roads department) surveyor, adviser and 'postman' for Provenzano, Pino Lipari is arrested for the fourth time in Palermo.

2008

January

Resignation of Sicily's Governor, Totò Cuffaro. He had been sentenced to five years for aggravated aiding and abetting of individual Mafiosi. A photograph showing him eating pastry horns celebrating a lighter sentence than he had feared leads to his resignation.

February

A scandal erupts over Borsellino's missing red diary. Carabinieri Colonel Arcangioli is investigated, later acquitted.

Michele Greco, the first head of the Cosa Nostra Commission, dies in a hospital in Rome.

Massimo Ciancimino confirms the existence of the notorious 'papello' and the 'Deal' between the state and the Mafia. It is the beginning of his collaboration with the judiciary.

September

Palermo: the trial of General Mori and Colonel Mauro Obinu begins, both accused of aiding and abetting Provenzano's years as a fugitive.

October

The Mafioso Gaspare Spatuzza collaborates with National Public Prosecutor Pietro Grassi and offers an alternative version of the Via D'Amelio Massacre.

December

During a VIP list trial, physician Antonino Cinà admits to having met Provenzano.

2009

May

The Committee for Public Order and Safety assigns a bodyguard to Massimo Ciancimino.

July

The Brancaccio (Palermo) Mafia boss, Gaspare Spatuzza, agrees to collaborate and offers another version of the Via D'Amelia Massacre, already shelved by a ruling from the Court of Cassation. The *pentito* opens another shocking chapter in the story of the 1993 Mafia massacres.

November

Arrest in a villa in Camporeale (Palermo) of the Mafia boss Mimmo Raccuglia, the last great fugitive of the Palermo Mafia. The Flying Squad finds him with arms, 'pizzini' (Mafia 'postcards') and a great deal of money.

December

Capture in Milan of the old guard Mafia chief Gaetano Fidanzati by the chief of the Flying Squad Alessandro Giuliano, son of Boris, the Deputy Chief Commissioner of Police killed by the Corleonesi in Palermo in 1979. In the same operation, a couple of steps from the Palermo court house, they capture the young Gianni Nicchi, who has already launched on an unstoppable Mafia career.

The year ends with the appeal court ruling on Massimo Ciancimino. The court reduces his sentence to three years and four months for money laundering. In the first instance he was sentenced to five years and six months.

Index